3-D HUMAN MODELING AND ANIMATION

2nd Edition

Illustrations and Text

by

Peter Ratner

WILEY

John Wiley & Sons, Inc.

Copyright © 2003 by John Wiley & Sons, Inc. All rights reserved.

Published by John Wiley & Sons, Inc., Hoboken, New Jersey
Published simultaneously in Canada

Limit of Liability/Disclaimer of Warranty: While the publisher and author have used their best efforts in preparing this book, they make no representations or warranties with respect to the accuracy or completeness of the contents of this book and specifically disclaim any implied warranties of merchantability or fitness for a particular purpose. No warranty may be created or extended by sales representatives or written sales materials. The advice and strategies contained herein may not be suitable for your situation. You should consult with a professional where appropriate. Neither the publisher nor author shall be liable for any loss of profit or any other commercial damages, including but not limited to special, incidental, consequential, or other damages.

For general information on our other products and services or for technical support, please contact our Customer Care Department within the United States at (800) 762-2974, outside the United States at (317) 572-3993 or fax (317) 572-4002.

Wiley also publishes its books in a variety of electronic formats. Some content that appears in print may not be available in electronic books. For more information about Wiley products, visit our web site at www.wiley.com.

Library of Congress Cataloging-in-Publication Data:
Ratner, Peter.
    3-D human modeling and animation / illustrations and text by Peter Ratner.—2nd ed.
      p.   cm.
    Includes bibliographical references and index.
    ISBN 0-471-21548-1 (pbk. : alk. paper)
    1. Computer animation. 2. Comptuer simulation. 3. Human figure in art.
    4. Three-dimensional display systems. I. Title: Three D human modeling and animation.
    II. Title.

TR897.7 .R38 2003
006.6'96—dc21
                                            2002027229

Printed in the United States of America

10 9 8 7 6 5 4 3 2

To Sharon, Ori, and the ECK

CONTENTS

PREFACE

Since most of us are used to seeing other humans more often than anything else, it becomes quite a challenge to create digital ones realistically. At the time of this writing no one has been able to make computer graphics humans that have been mistaken for real ones in movies and photos when viewed at close range. Until technology evolves to the point that this becomes possible, creating an artistic representation of a human is still a worthwhile goal.

Throughout history artists have depicted human subjects in a great variety of styles. No matter how skillful the artist, the materials determined the final appearance of the human subjects. Take a look at the incredible sculptures of Bernini—perhaps the greatest marble sculptor. One can marvel at the awesome detail, expression, and faithful representation of the human form. As remarkable as his sculptures are, they can never be mistaken for real humans. This does not lessen their value but makes them even more unique since it elevates them beyond the mundane everyday experience.

Art has more often been about man's quest to find order in the visible and invisible world. Imagination was the instrument for expressing the ideal. A specific style often emerged that artists and the public found so satisfying that it often lasted for centuries. What started out as a unique form of expression became an autocratic system, which was later overthrown by a handful of adventurous artists. Thus, they gave birth to a new style of art.

Today, in computer graphics, a number of artists cherish the belief that the more realistic they can make their characters, the greater their worth. Animations that depict the realistic movement of hair or the presence of lifelike textures elicit reactions of awe. Artists are encouraged to rush headlong toward the goal of greater realism.

Interesting as it may seem to make a flawless replica of humans with digital media, one can easily fail to observe that the closer a character becomes to an everyday human, the more ordinary it will appear. This may work fine for practical commercial uses such as digital stunt performers, crowd scenes, or game characters, but it falls short as an expression of the artistic ideal.

Synthetic humans most often lack personality. Computer characters that try to mimic human movement through unedited motion capture techniques generally look like puppets or store mannequins that have come to life. Subtleties of human behavior are often lost when a computer artist slavishly tries to emulate them. As contradictory as it sounds, when animators exaggerate the movements and expressions of their characters, they appear more lifelike and realistic. This fact was discovered years ago by Disney animators when the art of animation was still in its infancy.

This book can be used as a guide for learning how to model and animate a variety of characters. It does not encourage any particular style of expression but is intended to direct the aspiring 3-D artist by teaching fundamentals of modeling and animation. The lessons start with simple modeling, which then evolve into intermediate techniques for creating characters. Before embarking on the challenging task of modeling humans, a brief overview of human anatomy is presented in order to teach the basic principles of proportion and structure. The sections on modeling humans are broken up according to various body parts. After completing the human model, texturing and lighting, as well as setting up the digital person for animation, are discussed. The remainder of the book focuses on animating humans.

Educators who wish to use this book as a classroom text will find calendars with assigned lessons at the back of the book. Each calendar and its assignments refer to specific chapter sections that are meant for three different course levels: beginning, intermediate, and advanced.

I would like to express my gratitude to the people who have contributed to this book. A number of artists from around the world have contributed images to the color insert and the gallery section of the CD-ROM. Many of my students have provided models and animations for the CD-ROM. Mark Hannon generously permitted the use of some nude model photos from his Figure 2 Productions CD. I am also grateful to Margaret Cummins, my editor at John Wiley & Sons, for allowing me to use photos from John Cody's *Atlas of Foreshortening: The Human Figure in Deep Perspective, Second Edition.* Another individual whose help was greatly appreciated is David Markowitz, who provided the renderings and settings of the various hair attributes at the end of Chapter 8. My greatest thanks go to my wife, who has stood by and supported me in this large endeavor.

Peter Ratner
Professor of 3-D Computer Animation
James Madison University

ABOUT THE CD-ROM

Thank you for purchasing *3-D Human Modeling and Animation,* Second Edition. The CD-ROM contains 2-D and 3-D templates for modeling humans. These are cited in various parts of the book to help you work through the human modeling exercises. In addition, you will also find human models created by my students. Most of these are from beginning-level students who used the information from this book to create their own versions of digital humans. All the models are provided in some of the most popular 3-D formats—dxf, lwo, obj, and Maya. Currently, there are over 30 different 3-D software packages, most of which will recognize one or more of these formats.

If you decide to use the 3-D templates, then you will have a choice between high-resolution and medium-resolution template models. The medium-resolution templates are the preferred choice for most modeling tasks, including models that will be rendered as subdivision surface objects. The high-resolution templates will yield too many polygons for a subdivision model. They should be used only if you do not have subdivision surfaces capabilities in your software. The high-resolution template models have approximately twice the polygon count of the medium-resolution models.

Besides the 3-D human model templates, there are also templates for modeling the various simple objects in Chapters 1 and 2. Since most of the book is printed in black and white, color renderings of specific illustrations have been provided on the CD-ROM in .jpg format. Most image browsers should be able to open these. The Chapter 10 folder contains human textures that you can use when surfacing your model. It also has color images of the lighting setup, an important resource since colored lights are utilized.

The Chapter 11 and Chapter 12 folders contain example animations illustrating various principles. These are in QuickTime format. If you do not have QuickTime installed on your hard drive, then you can download it from the Apple website at www.apple.com. To play the movies in real time, you should copy them from the CD-ROM to your hard drive. The Chapter 11 folder of the CD-ROM contains 2-D and 3-D templates to help you create walking and running animations. Besides my own animations, you will also find some student movies, showing their solutions to specific animation challenges. Unfortunately, due to space constraints, only a limited amount of student work could be shown on the CD-ROM.

Color images depicting digital humans by various artists are in the gallery folder of the CD-ROM. These are extra images that could not be printed on the color pages insert due to space constraints.

For those who plan to use this book as a classroom text, there are lesson plans for beginning- through advanced-level animation in the "Lesson Plans" folder of the CD-ROM. The lessons are in calendar format and can be opened in Microsoft Word. Each lesson is for one course that meets for one semester, twice a week, and for two and a half hours per class session. Since Microsoft Word files are provided on the CD-ROM, the lessons can be altered to fit your own teaching style.

Since this book is non-software-specific, it should not become dated as quickly as software-oriented books. The principles of modeling, lighting, texturing, and animation outlined here will work with most medium- and high-level 3-D software programs. Most of the techniques have been used successfully by 3-D artists for years and should continue to be viable for many more. New software tools are perpetually being developed to make the process easier, but the methods for achieving specific goals remain constant.

Houdini™ is a registered trademark of Side Effects.

Inspire 3D™ and Lightwave 3D™ are registered trademarks of NewTek, Inc.

Maya™ is a registered trademark of Alias/Wavefront.

Photoshop™ is a registered trademark of Adobe, Inc.

QuickTime™ is a registered trademark of Apple Computers, Inc.

Softimage™ is a registered trademark of Avid.

3D Studio Max™ is a registered trademark of Discreet.

COLOR INSERT

Beginning Modeling Techniques 1

Just like a child, one has to learn to crawl before one can walk. The same holds true with 3-D modeling. Unless you have had previous experience modeling all kinds of objects, you might want to follow these exercises to create some basic models.

This chapter will take you through the steps for creating very simple objects. The basic principles of modeling utilized here will apply later on when you start making more complicated models such as the human form.

Currently, the two most popular modeling techniques are *patch modeling* and *subdivision modeling*. Patch modeling can be accomplished by creating points, polygons, splines, or nonuniform rational b-splines (NURBS). In its most elementary sense, patch modeling means creating an object in sections. Each adjoining part shares points with its neighbor. One can compare it to a crazy quilt made up of many patches. The simple objects modeled in this chapter are made up of only a few patches, while the more complicated ones in subsequent chapters have many patches.

Some artists prefer to start with the smallest unit possible: the point, or vertex. After placing a series of these vertices, one can connect them as a spline or create polygons from them.

Polygons can be created a few at a time. When they are laid next to each other, the shared points are welded or merged. Despite their straight edges, polygons are quite versatile. They can be made in many ways, as well as manipulated by cutting, bending, stretching, twisting, flipping, and so on. One method of patch modeling with polygons is to use extrusion techniques such as beveling to create adjoining polygons connected to the original one. Since polygons lend themselves perfectly to subdivision modeling, they will be discussed in more detail later in this chapter.

Splines are flexible line segments defined by edit points or vertices. Sometimes splines are referred to as curves. A series of connected splines make a wire mesh. Adjoining wire meshes are, in effect, patches. Thus spline modeling lends itself nicely to the patch modeling method.

NURBS are flexible lines of a higher mathematical order than splines. *Control vertices* (CVs) define the shape of NURBS. These CVs lie outside the actual line, creating a cagelike environment for manipulating the spline. A wire mesh can be made up of NURBS. Quite a few modelers who use NURBS create their objects by patch modeling. When two NURBS planes share adjoining edges, the shared points are stitched to prevent gaps.

MODELING SIMPLE OBJECTS WITH SPLINES/NURBS

The following objects will be modeled using splines or NURBS. Most midlevel and high-end 3-D software implements one or the other and sometimes both. In certain cases splines will be created from points, while other times the lines are simply drawn with a tool. Three-dimensional templates of all the objects in various stages are available on the CD-ROM in the Chapter 1 folder.

MODELING A KNIFE

One of the easiest things to model is a knife. It is made up of only a few parts and these are usually lacking in complexity. Figure 1-1 shows what the knife will look like when it is completed. A color image of the knife can be found in the Chapter 1 folder of the CD-ROM. Figure 1-2 illustrates the spline cage that will be modeled from splines or NURBS.

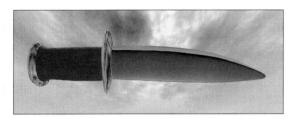

Fig. 1-1 A view of the knife that will be modeled.

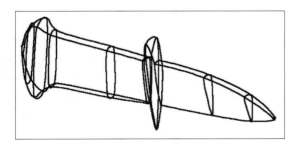

Fig. 1-2 A spline cage view of the knife.

Step 1.

If you decide to use the 3-D templates from the CD-ROM, then open the one named "step1." Place it in a background layer. Now, while you work in a foreground layer, notice there are three splines. These will make the outline of the knife blade. Working in the front view, either draw a spline or make a series of points outlining the top of the knife blade. Figure 1-3 shows the first spline. Try to use a minimum amount of points. This will simplify the modeling process.

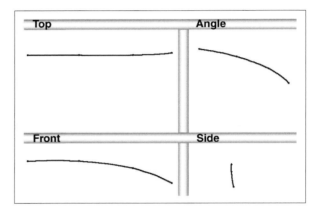

Fig. 1-3 Step 1. The first knife spline.

Use the top or side views to move points away from the 0 x axis so that the blade will have some thickness. Use the template if you have to. Once you have the first spline, mirror-duplicate it in the side view on the 0 z axis, so that you now have two splines for the top of the knife blade (Figure 1-4).

The bottom knife blade spline can also be made by mirroring one of the top splines. Select one of the top splines and in the front view, mirror it on the y axis. Now move points on the bottom blade spline so they line up with those of the template.

Select the entire bottom blade spline and use a set value operation to move it and all its points on the 0 z axis. Your three knife blade splines might now look like Figure 1-5.

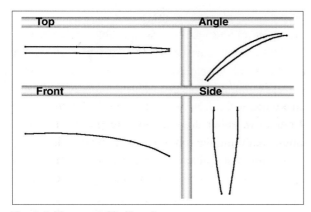

Fig. 1-4 The second knife spline.

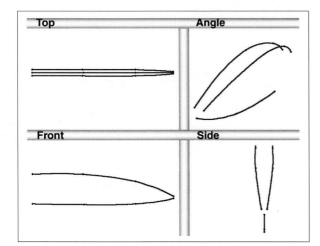

Fig. 1-5 All three knife blade splines.

Step 2.

After creating the three knife blade splines it is time to connect them. Depending on your software, this can be accomplished by either lofting or selecting vertices in order and connecting them with a closed curve. If you are lofting, then select the three curves in order and loft. If you are connecting points, select the three points at the widest part of the knife blade (Figure 1-6).

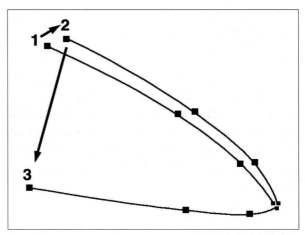

Fig. 1-6 Step 2. Connecting the first three knife blade points.

Continue connecting the corresponding sets of three knife blade vertices, including those at the tip. Figure 1-7 shows all the points on the knife blade splines connected.

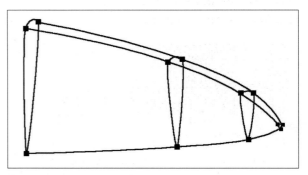

Fig. 1-7 The finished knife blade spline cage after connecting all the vertices.

Step 3.

The knife blade is, in effect, our first spline patch. The hilt will be the adjoining knife patch that shares points at the widest part of the knife blade. Select the shared closed curve at the widest part of the knife blade (Figure 1-8). Copy it and paste it into another layer. In this new layer, copy the closed curve again and paste it. In

3

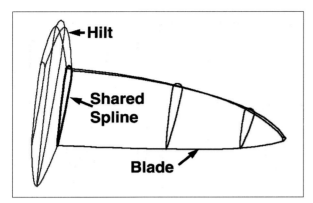

Fig. 1-8 The shared closed curve located at the beginning of the hilt and the end of the blade.

your front view, move it to the left of the first curve. Scale it up somewhat so it is almost twice as tall and a little wider than the first closed curve. Copy the first curve, paste it, and move it to the left of the largest curve. You should now have three closed curves similar to the ones in Figure 1-9.

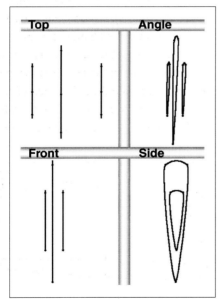

Fig. 1-9 Step 3. The three closed curves for the hilt.

Step 4.

The three closed curves can now either be lofted or have their points connected with open splines. A good rule of thumb to remember with splines is that when you are building spline cages that are totally enclosed, you usually connect with the opposite spline type from that of the original ones. For example, if you start with closed splines, you then connect them with open ones. This also works in reverse, such as in this case when you are connecting the closed curves of the hilt. You connect them with open curves. This rule does not apply when you model half objects that later are to be mirrored. These normally have all open curves.

Figure 1-10 depicts the three closed-hilt curves after lofting or connecting corresponding curves with open splines.

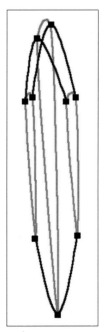

Fig. 1-10 Step 4. The black lines indicate the open curves connecting the closed ones.

Step 5.

Start the knife handle by selecting the closed curve at the end of the hilt (Figure 1-11). Copy and paste it into another layer. Duplicate the closed curve and in the front view move it slightly to the left of the first spline. Insert an extra vertex at the bottom of the second curve (Figure 1-12). Move the two bottom points so that they are equally distant from the 0 z axis. Copy and paste this curve with the four vertices. Move it to the left in the front view. Continue copying, pasting, and moving closed curves until you have the framework for the knife handle. Scale some of the curves so that they now look somewhat like the ones in Figure 1-13. Of course, you may decide to shape the curves a different way for another kind of knife.

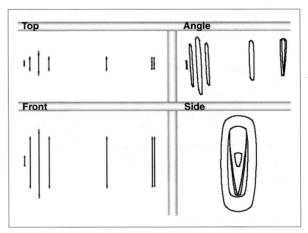

Fig. 1-13 All the closed curves for the knife handle.

Step 6.

You can now select the curves in order and loft them or select corresponding points in order and connect them with open curves. Since the first handle curve has only three vertices compared to the other ones with four, you will have to connect the two bottom ones on the second curve to the single point on the first curve. Figure 1-14 shows the connected handle curves.

Depending on your software, you now have two choices. If your modeling package uses polygons, then surface the spline cage with them. For example, Lightwave 3D™ has an AutoPatcher plug-in that adds polygons on top of the spline cage. Each section of the spline

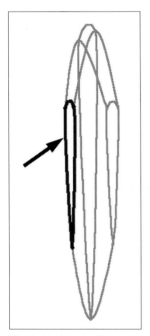

Fig. 1-11 Step 5. The same spline that ends the hilt begins the handle.

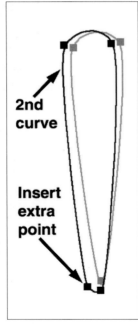

Fig. 1-12 An extra vertex is added to the bottom of the second handle curve.

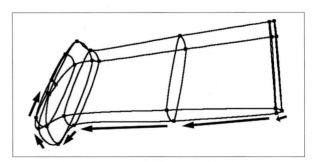

Fig. 1-14 Step 6. Connecting the handle curves.

cage has to have either three or four points around it; otherwise, you will get holes in the polygon mesh. Once the spline cage has been patched with polygons, the two are separated using the Polygon Statistics command.

If you are using a spline- or NURBS-based package then you should already be able to see the surface of the mesh in shaded view. In either case, you have the choice of bringing the blade, hilt, and handle into the same layer. You can then merge the duplicate points that are shared or stitch them together.

Some people prefer to assign textures to the separate parts before bringing them together. It is easier to do this than having to select individual areas after they have been merged. Whether you decide to keep the parts separate or not, select them, name the various surfaces, and assign colors to them.

The two holes at the tip of the blade and end of the handle have to be closed by either welding points or bringing them close together. This completes the patch modeling lesson for creating a knife.

TROUBLESHOOTING

Sometimes holes appear on a polygon mesh even though it seems that there are only three or four vertices around each shape. This could be because duplicate curves are sitting on top and occupying the same space as the original ones, resulting in more than four points per shape. Use a Merge Points command followed by a Unify Polygon command to delete the extra points and polygons. If this does not work, then check to make sure you do not have extra points close to but not quite on top of each other. Once you find those, weld them together.

Another situation that results in holes is when a vertex that is supposed to connect two splines is on only one of them. The second curve only appears to be connected to the point. You can test the spline cage

by moving the splines to see if they all stay connected to their cross sections. If any are not connected, then add a point to the curve that is missing one and weld it to its corresponding curve.

Splines that cross each other but are not connected by a common vertex will also create holes. Be sure to add a point to connect the two.

In some rare instances, someone will make two-point polygons that look like lines but are not true splines. You can tell the difference between a spline and a polygon by the nature of the line. Polygons have straight lines between vertices, while splines have curved ones. If for some reason your spline cage has straight lines, then go to your polygon statistics box, select the ones that say "faces" or "polygons," and delete them. The polygon statistics box should list only curves.

Sections on the spline cage that appear to have more than four vertices around them will have to be split up. You can do this by selecting opposite points and making an open curve to connect them.

After separating the polygons from the spline cage, you will most likely find that the polygon statistics box is also handy for finding polygons that have more than four sides and less than three. These may cause problems later on if you try to change your polygon mesh into a subdivision object. In your polygon statistics box, simply select the one- and two-point polygons and delete them. If you see polygons listed with more than four sides, select these and split them into three- and four-sided ones.

MODELING A SPOON

Continuing the lesson on modeling simple objects with splines or NURBS, a spoon will be created next. This object is so simple that only one spline cage will suffice. It will not be necessary to make it utilizing separate patches.

A rendered image of the spoon appears in Figure 1-15. A color image of the spoon can be found in the Chapter 1 folder of the CD-ROM. Figure 1-16 shows the spline cage of the spoon.

Fig. 1-15 A rendered view of the spoon.

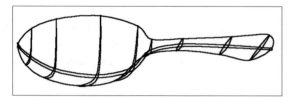

Fig. 1-16 The spoon spline cage.

Step 1.

Start modeling the spoon by drawing the outline with a spline in the top view or making a series of points and then connecting them with an open curve (Figure 1-17). In the front view move some of the points to shape it like the one in Figure 1-17.

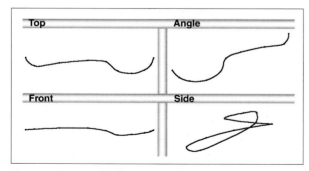

Fig. 1-17 Step 1. The first spoon spline.

Step 2.

Use a mirror tool in the top view to make a duplicate of the spline on the 0 z axis. Figure 1-18 shows the two splines.

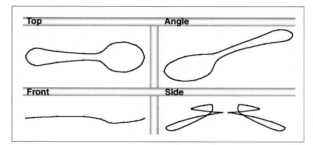

Fig. 1-18 Step 2. The second mirrored spoon spline.

Step 3.

To make the third open curve, select one of the spoon splines, copy it, and paste it. Use a set value to move all the points on the third curve to 0 on the z axis. In the front view, move the third curve down a little and drag the points for the cup part of the spoon even farther down. Figure 1-19 illustrates the third open curve.

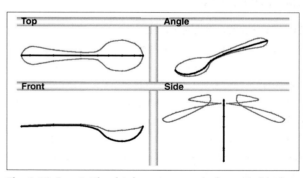

Fig. 1-19 Step 3. The third spoon curve is shown in black.

Step 4.

In order to give the spoon some thickness a fourth curve will have to be made. This will be a duplicate of the third spline that is moved down slightly in the front-view window (Figure 1-20).

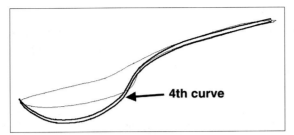

Fig. 1-20 Step 4. The third and fourth spoon curves are illustrated as thick black lines.

Step 5.

To complete the spoon spline cage you can either select the curves in order and loft them or select corresponding points to make closed curves. Figure 1-21 depicts the order in which points are selected to make one of the closed connecting curves.

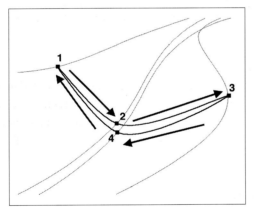

Fig. 1-21 Step 5. One of the spoon cross sections. Points are selected in order to make the closed curve.

All the cross sections can be viewed in Figure 1-22. As you can see so far, the spline/NURBS patch method is an outstanding way of modeling objects. Artists who draw and paint often prefer this method since it is similar to sketching the outline of a form.

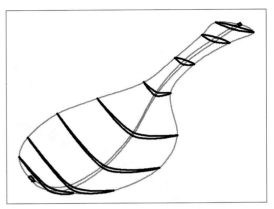

Fig. 1-22 All the closed curves that connect the four open spoon splines.

People who have a disposition to sculpt will most likely prefer the subdivision modeling method discussed later. This is because subdivision modeling does not outline objects as much as the spline/ NURBS method. Instead, one creates large blocks of shapes, segments them, and then shapes them by pulling and pushing points.

MODELING A SPATULA

Proceeding with our utensils, a simple spatula will be sculpted next. The two patches will be the scoop section and the handle. Figure 1-23 illustrates the completed spatula.

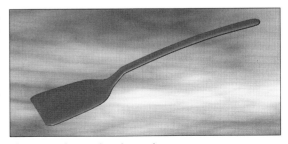

Fig. 1-23 The rendered spatula.

Figure 1-24 shows the spline cage that makes up the spatula. You should notice that, as before, open curves are combined with closed ones to make the mesh.

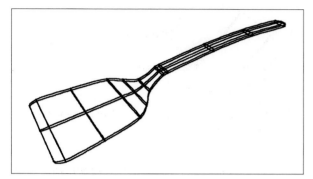

Fig. 1-24 The spatula spline cage.

Step 1.

In the top-view window, draw the outline for one side of the scoop section (Figure 1-25). As in previous steps you can either draw the spline or create points and connect them with an open curve.

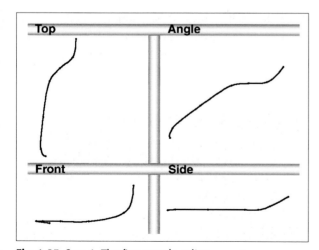

Fig. 1-25 Step 1. The first spatula spline.

Step 2.

Use a mirror tool to duplicate the first spline in the top view on the 0 x axis. The splines should now look like the ones in Figure 1-26.

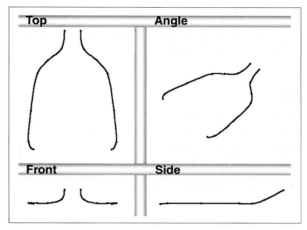

Fig. 1-26 Step 2. The second mirrored spatula spline.

Step 3.

Select one of the curves, copy it, and paste it. Use a set value on the duplicate curve to move all the points on the 0 x axis. There should be three splines, one on each end and one in the middle, as seen in the top view of Figure 1-27.

Step 4.

Select all three curves, copy them, and paste them. Move them down slightly in the side or front view so that they resemble the illustration in Figure 1-28.

Step 5.

Connect the open curves by either lofting or selecting corresponding points in order to join them with closed curves. Figure 1-29 shows the closed connecting splines of the spatula scoop.

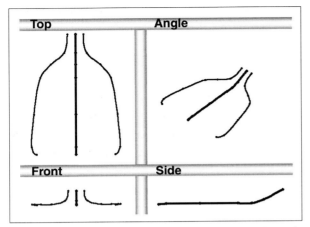

Fig. 1-27 Step 3. A third curve (thicker black line) is made with a set value of 0 on the x axis.

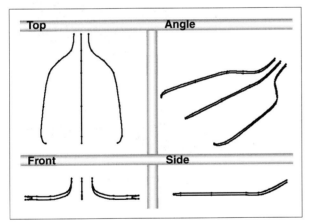

Fig. 1-28 Step 4. Copying, pasting, and moving the three duplicate splines down completes the six open curves of the spatula scoop.

Be sure to bring the points together at the front edge of the spatula; otherwise, you will have a hole there. The spatula will also look better with a sharp edge there.

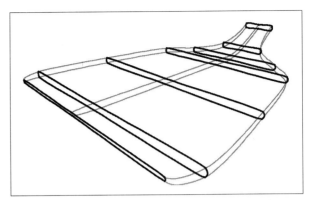

Fig. 1-29 Step 5. Closed curves connect the open splines to finish the spline cage for the scoop part of the spatula.

Step 6.

The handle part of the spatula is next. Select the last closed curve on the narrow part of the spatula scoop (Figure 1-30). Copy and paste it into another layer.

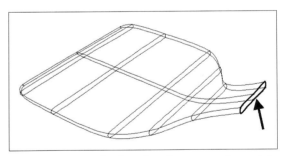

Fig. 1-30 Step 6. The last closed curve on the spatula scoop will be used to begin the handle.

Step 7.

Copy, paste, and move this closed curve to start the handle. Keep making duplicates and moving them so that they are distributed along the length of the handle (Figure 1-31). Scale certain curves to define the shape of the handle. The last one should be quite a bit smaller than the others since it will close up the handle.

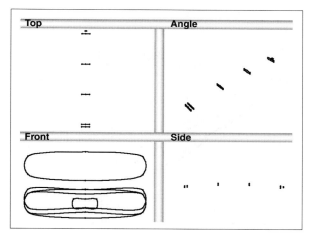

Fig. 1-31 Step 7. Copies of the first handle closed curve are distributed accordingly.

Step 8.

Connect the closed curves with open ones. Figure 1-32 shows the handle splines after they have been joined.

You can now surface the scoop and handle spline cages with polygons or, if the final product will be strictly a spline/NURBS object, merge the two parts. Since they share the same curve, as seen in Step 6, they should make a seamless patch model. Be sure to

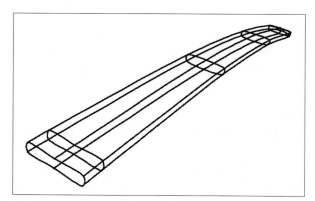

Fig. 1-32 Step 8. The spatula handle after connecting the closed curves with open ones.

close up the points at the end of the handle to avoid having a hole there.

Modeling a Frying Pan

After making a spatula, you might want to make a frying pan to go with it. This lesson will use similar methods to make the frying pan handle and lathing for the pan part. Figure 1-33 shows the rendered frying pan. The wire mesh can be viewed in Figure 1-34.

Fig. 1-33 The rendered frying pan.

Fig. 1-34 The frying pan seen in wireframe mode.

Step 1.

In the side view, create an open curve that follows the contours of the outside and inside of the frying pan (Figure 1-35). Since this spline will be lathed, you only need to make half a width size of the pan.

Lathe the spline 360 degrees on the y axis. If you want a smoother-looking pan, use a higher setting for the number of sides. You should now have the pan part like the one seen in Figure 1-36.

11

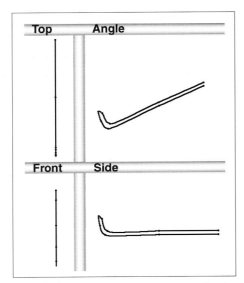

Fig. 1-35 Step 1. The first open curve for the frying pan.

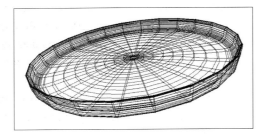

Fig. 1-36 The pan after lathing the first curve.

Step 2.

Now you will begin the handle. With the pan part placed in a background layer, draw a spline in the top view outlining the shape of the handle (Figure 1-37). Make sure the beginning of the spline starts a little inside the pan. Shape the curve somewhat in the front window.

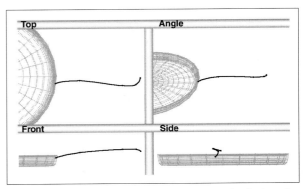

Fig. 1-37 Step 2. Creating the first open curve for the handle.

Step 3.

Use a mirror tool to duplicate the curve in the top-view window. Figure 1-38 shows the second pan handle curve.

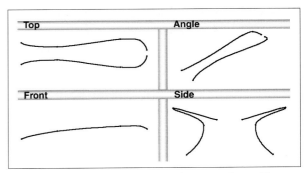

Fig. 1-38 Step 3. The first handle curve is duplicated by mirroring it in the top view.

Step 4.

Select one of the handle splines, duplicate it, and paste it. Use a set value to move all its points to the 0 z axis. In the front view, move all the points except the one at the far right above the other two curves (Figure 1-39).

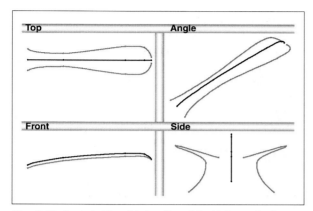

Fig. 1-39 Step 4. The third spline (black) is made from a duplicate whose points are moved to the 0 z axis.

Step 5.

In the top-view window, select the first spline and its mirror copy. Copy the two curves and paste them. In the front view, move the two duplicates down on the y axis. Pay attention to the depth of your frying pan since this is how much you want to move the two bottom handle splines. Figure 1-40 illustrates the five open handle curves.

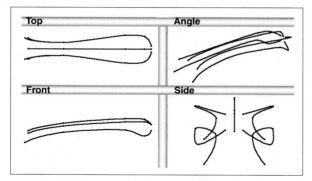

Fig. 1-40 Step 5. Two top splines are duplicated and moved down on the y axis to make a total of five open curves.

Step 6.

You can now connect the five handle splines by either lofting or selecting corresponding points in a clockwise or counterclockwise order and creating closed curves. Figure 1-41 shows the connecting closed curves as black lines.

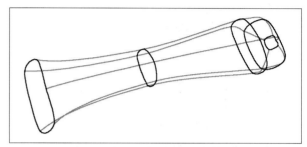

Fig. 1-41 Step 6. Either the five open curves are lofted or corresponding points are selected and connected to make closed curves.

Check the wide end of the handle to make sure the closed curve is sitting somewhat within the wall of the round pan. If you are working with polygons then surface the spline cage and separate the polygon mesh from the curves.

Close up the end of the handle to get rid of the hole. Place both the handle and the pan in one layer, and you are done.

MODELING A PALETTE KNIFE

For those of you who are not familiar with the process of painting, a palette knife is an instrument used to mix oil or acrylic paint on a palette. Some artists use the palette knife in place of a brush to create bad paintings.

Figure 1-42 depicts a rendered version of the palette knife. The color image can be viewed in the

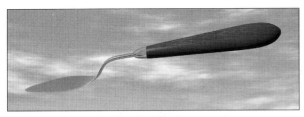

Fig. 1-42 The rendered palette knife.

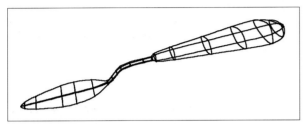

Fig. 1-43 A wireframe view of the palette knife.

Chapter 1 folder of the CD-ROM. The wireframe model can be seen in Figure 1-43.

Step 1.

In the top-view window draw a spline similar to the one in Figure 1-44. Some of you may decide to make the spline by creating points and connecting them with an open curve. Use the front view to bend the spline (Figure 1-44).

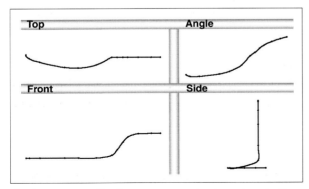

Fig. 1-44 Step 1. The first open curve for the palette knife.

Step 2.

Select the first palette knife curve and mirror-duplicate it in the top view. The two splines should look like the ones in Figure 1-45.

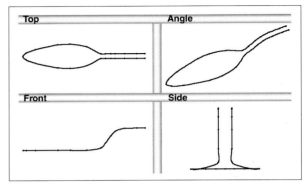

Fig. 1-45 Step 2. The second curve is made by mirroring the first in the top view.

Step 3.

Copy and paste one of the curves. Use a set value to move all its points to the 0 z axis (Figure 1-46). In the front view, move the vertices on the stem part above the two previous splines.

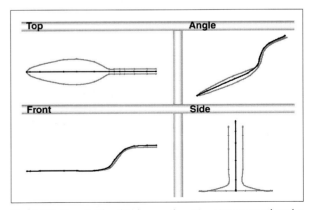

Fig. 1-46 Step 3. The third curve has its points moved to the 0 z axis with a Set Value command.

Step 4.

Make a duplicate curve from the third one and move the points on the stem part down a little (Figure 1-47). All four curves should now resemble the ones in Figure 1-48.

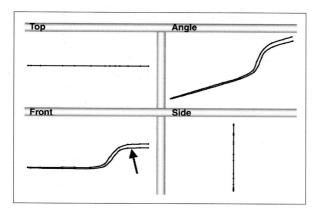

Fig. 1-47 Step 4. The fourth curve is made by duplicating the third one and moving some of the points down.

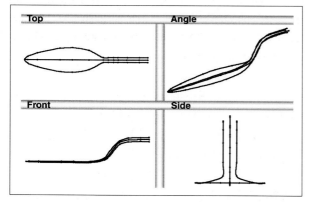

Fig. 1-48 The first four curves that define the blade portion of the palette knife.

Step 5.

Connect the four open curves with closed ones by either selecting matching points or lofting the splines (Figure 1-49).

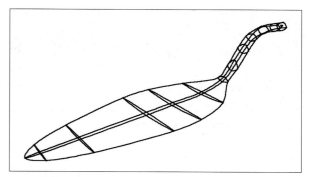

Fig. 1-49 Step 5. The four open curves are connected with closed ones.

Step 6.

In another layer, start making the handle of the palette knife. In the top view, draw a spline outlining the shape of the handle (Figure 1-50). Check the layer with the blade portion to make sure the handle spline overlaps it somewhat.

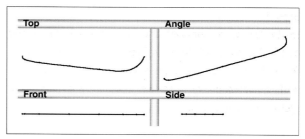

Fig. 1-50 Step 6. The first open curve for the handle of the palette knife.

Step 7.

Select the first handle curve and make a mirror duplicate of it in the top view. Figure 1-51 shows the two curves.

Step 8.

Select both handle curves, copy them, and paste them. Rotate the two duplicate curves 90 degrees on the x

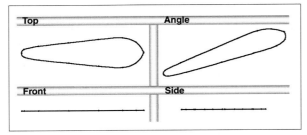

Fig. 1-51 Step 7. A mirror duplicate of the first curve makes the second one.

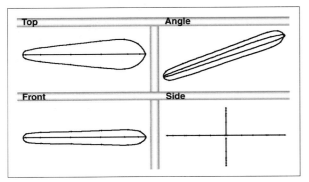

Fig. 1-52 Step 8. Two duplicates of the handle curves are rotated 90 degrees. Their points are brought closer together to improve their shapes.

axis. In the front view, drag points down from the top spline and drag points up from the bottom spline to give the handle a better shape (Figure 1-52).

Step 9.

It is time now to connect the four palette knife handle curves. Figure 1-53 shows the closed connecting curves (black) against the four open curves (gray).

The final step is to surface the spline cage with polygons or, if you are working with a spline/NURBS modeler, bring the two sections together into one layer. Close the ends of the palette knife by welding their points or bringing them closer together.

This concludes the lesson on creating simple mod-

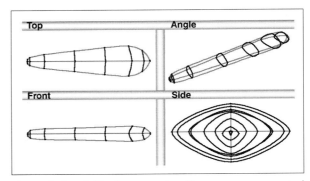

Fig. 1-53 Step 9. The four open handle curves are connected with closed ones.

els with splines/NURBS. You should now have a better understanding of how to model by outlining the contours of objects. The experience you have gained here will act as a foundation for the more complex 3-D sculpting discussed in later chapters.

MODELING SIMPLE OBJECTS WITH SUBDIVISION SURFACES

Sometimes this method of modeling is referred to as *box modeling*. This is because many times one starts with a box shape, which gradually becomes more complex. Obviously, in order to implement subdivision modeling one has to use software that supports it.

This system requires modeling a low-polygon control mesh and then applying a smoothing algorithm to subdivide the polygons. Even though the polygon count appears to be low, the Subdivide command makes the object appear smooth.

The quality of the model can usually be set by the amount of patch division that is applied to the subdivided object. Higher values result in smoother surfaces since the polygons are divided into smaller and greater amounts. Your graphics card, processor capabilities, and random-access memory (RAM) are the final determining factors for the amount of patch division that will be used.

Normally, when an object is in subdivision mode, a cage will surround the polygon mesh. Points on the cage are moved in order to affect the object within it. During the modeling stage, one usually switches back and forth between the low-polygon version and the smooth subdivision surface. In low-polygon mode, it is often easier to pick out specific points for editing. It is also the preferred state for beveling polygons in or out as well as slicing them into smaller ones. When the model is in the smooth-subdivision state, it is easier to see what the final result will look like.

Once the object becomes more complex, you may want to find and select points with the model in low-polygon mode, then switch to subdivision mode to shape the object by moving the selected vertices.

As you toggle back and forth between the smooth and rough versions, you will most likely find that most of your time is spent pushing and pulling points. This is why artists who have an inclination toward sculpture prefer the subdivision method to spline/ NURBS modeling. If you have a tendency to draw by outlining your subjects, then you may favor the spline/NURBS modeling method.

The following tutorial will have you model simple subdivision objects. You should have the capability to split polygons, extrude/intrude, bevel, weld points, and toggle back and forth between low-polygon and subdivision modes. Extrusion/intrusion takes the selected polygon faces and moves them out or in. Beveling is similar, but the diameter of the extruded/ intruded face is scaled as part of the operation.

MODELING A HAMMER

This exercise shows how to build a hammer from a box. Beveling will be used as well as slicing of poly-

gons. Even though values are given for the amount to bevel, the measurement could vary among different software packages. Figure 1-54 shows the rendered hammer. The wire mesh can be viewed in Figure 1-55.

Fig. 1-54 The rendered hammer.

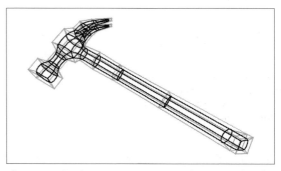

Fig. 1-55 The hammer seen in wireframe mode. The gray lines indicate the subdivision cage around the model.

Step 1.

Make a box with the following settings (Figure 1-56):

    Low X –50 cm
    Low Y: –50 cm
    Low Z: –30 cm
    High X: 50 cm
    High Y: 50 cm
    High Z: 30 cm

Segments X: 1
Segments Y: 1
Segments Z: 1

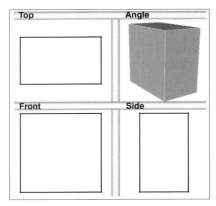

Fig. 1-56 Step 1. Creating a simple box for the hammer. Most subdivision modeling starts with a box.

Step 2.

Bevel the back polygon in with the following settings (Figure 1-57):

Shift: 15 cm
Inset: 25.5 cm
Edges: Inner

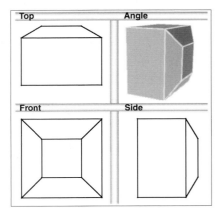

Fig. 1-57 Step 2. Beveling back the first section.

Step 3.

Bevel the back polygon back straight with the following settings (Figure 1-58):

Shift: 65 cm
Inset: 0
Edges: Inner

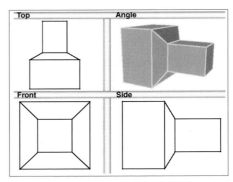

Fig. 1-58 Step 3. The third section is beveled back.

Step 4.

Bevel the back polygon out with the following settings (Figure 1-59):

Shift: 15 cm
Inset: −25.5 cm
Edges: Inner

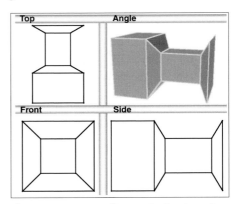

Fig. 1-59 Step 4. Beveling out the fourth section.

Step 5.

Bevel the back polygon straight with the following settings (Figure 1-60):

    Shift: 85 cm
    Inset: 0
    Edges: Inner

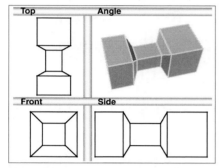

Fig. 1-60 Step 5. The rear polygon is beveled straight back.

Step 6.

Bevel the bottom back polygon down and in with the following settings (Figure 1-61):

    Shift: 19.5 cm
    Inset: 17 cm
    Edges: Inner

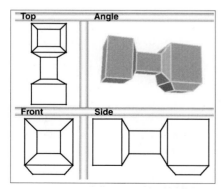

Fig. 1-61 Step 6. Beveling the bottom polygon down and in.

Step 7.

Bevel the back polygon in with the following settings (Figure 1-62):

    Shift: 15 cm
    Inset: 25.5 cm
    Edges: Inner

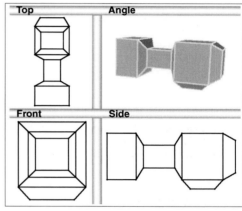

Fig. 1-62 Step 7. The rear polygon is beveled in.

Step 8.

Use the knife tool on the back polygon to split it vertically down the center (Figure 1-63). Split the resulting five-sided top and bottom adjoining polygons into three-sided ones.

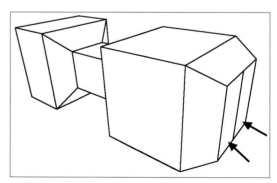

Fig. 1-63 Step 8. The arrows point to the rear polygon that is split vertically.

Step 9.

Bevel the back two polygons in with the following settings and scale and move them down so they are narrower on the y axis (Figure 1-64).

Shift: 1.7 m
Inset: 10 cm
Edges: Inner

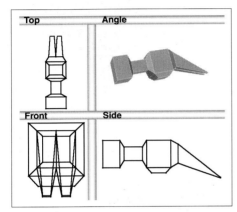

Fig. 1-64 Step 9. The rear polygons are beveled back and in. The two newly beveled rear polygons are scaled and moved down on the y axis.

Step 10.

Use the knife tool to split the back fork part of the hammer vertically twice (Figure 1-65).

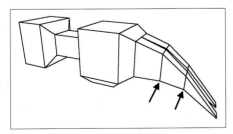

Fig. 1-65 Step 10. The arrows point to the split in the back fork part. This will make it possible to bend the hammer's fork.

Step 11.

Bevel the bottom middle polygon straight down with the following settings (Figure 1-66):

Shift: 8 m
Inset: 0

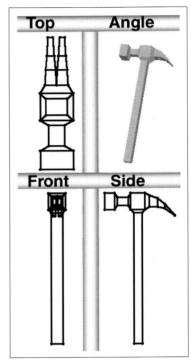

Fig. 1-66 Step 11. The handle is made by beveling the bottom polygon straight down.

Step 12.

Use the knife tool to split the handle polygons horizontally on the x axis. Select points or polygons on the handle and use the stretch tool to increase or decrease their size for shaping the handle (Figure 1-67). Turn on subdivision surfaces and continue refining the hammer.

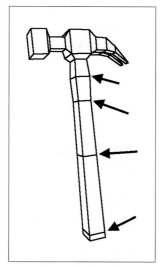

Fig. 1-67 Step 12. Splitting the handle polygons horizontally makes it possible to alter its width at key points.

Fig. 1-68 The rendered armchair.

Modeling an Armchair

Subdivision or box modeling of a chair will be a little more complicated than modeling the hammer. In this tutorial you will have to weld points and delete polygons that are located inside the model. When you have hidden polygons on the inside of an object, they can pull on the mesh, creating undesirable gaps, holes, and creases. Figure 1-68 shows the rendered armchair. The wire mesh can be viewed in Figure 1-69.

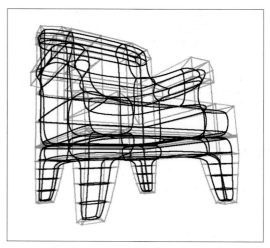

Fig. 1-69 The wireframe armchair with the subdivision cage in gray.

Step 1.

Make a box with the following settings:

Low X: –60 cm
Low Y: –15 cm
Low Z: –60 cm
High X: 60 cm

High Y: 15 cm
High Z: 60 cm
Segments X: 1
Segments Y: 1
Segments Z: 1

Step 2.

Select the top polygon of the square and bevel it up and in with these settings (Figure 1-70):

Shift: 1 cm
Inset: 2 cm
Edges: Inner

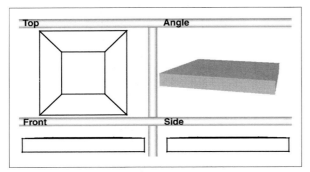

Fig. 1-70 Step 2. Beveling the top polygon in and up slightly.

Step 3.

Select the top polygon and bevel it up and out with these settings:

Shift: 1 cm
Inset: -2 cm
Edges: Inner

Step 4.

Select the top polygon and bevel it straight up with these settings (Figure 1-71):

Shift: 24 cm
Inset: 0
Edges: Inner

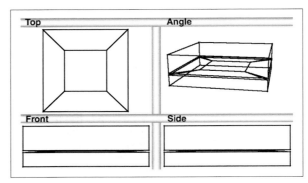

Fig. 1-71 Step 4. Beveling the polygon straight up.

Step 5.

Subdivide the polygons in the front and side views with a knife tool so that they now look like Figure 1-72.

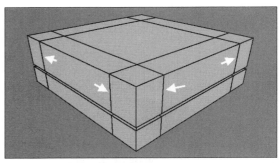

Fig. 1-72 Step 5. Splitting the object with a knife tool (white arrows). The top shows the four newly created squares in the corners.

Step 6.

In the top view, select all the back and side polygons and merge them into one (Figure 1-73). Merging polygons will ensure that when you bevel the polygon you will not have gaps between beveled objects. After beveling, the merged polygon is usually split into four-sided polygons.

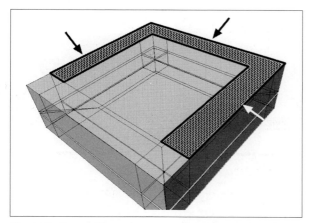

Fig. 1-73 Step 6. The polygons on the top are merged (patterned area).

Step 7.

Bevel up the merged horseshoe-shaped polygon with the following settings (Figure 1-74):

Shift: 44 cm
Inset: 0
Edges: Inner

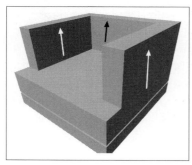

Fig. 1-74 Step 7. The merged top polygon is beveled straight up to make the sides and back.

Step 8.

Select the top horseshoe-shaped polygon and split it into three polygons: one for the back and two for the

sides (Figure 1-75). This is the splitting process that occurs after merging and beveling up a polygon. Hiding all the polygons except for the one that will be split makes the process easier.

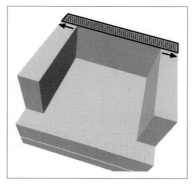

Fig. 1-75 Step 8. Select the points at the top and split them across (arrows). You will now have a top back polygon that can be beveled up for the back.

Step 9.

Bevel up only the top back polygon to make the backrest. Use these settings (Figure 1-76):

Shift: 40 cm
Inset: 0
Edges: Inner

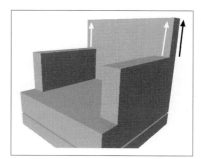

Fig. 1-76 Step 9. The back rest is beveled straight up.

Step 10.

After beveling up the top backrest polygon, split it up so that each section has only four-sided polygons. Select the four corner polygons on the bottom of the chair and bevel them down with the following settings (Figure 1-77):

Shift: 36 cm
Inset: 6 cm
Edges: Inner

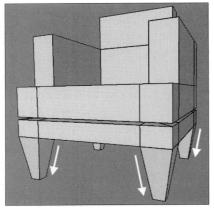

Fig. 1-77 Step 10. The four corner polygons along the bottom are beveled down to make the legs.

To finalize the chair, you may decide to continue splitting polygons so as to bevel them out in specific parts. For example, the sides of the armrests could be beveled out to give them a rounder shape. The back of the chair could also be split near the top and beveled out a little (Figure 1-78). Remember that if you plan to bevel a number of polygons up, out, or down at the

Fig. 1-78 Finalizing the chair by beveling out the sides of the armrest and back and splitting the legs for a better shape.

same time, you should merge them first. After beveling you can split the polygon again into four-sided ones.

Work in both low-polygon and subdivision modes to shape the chair. When you are done, select and name the various surfaces for texturing.

Now that you have a basic understanding of both spline/NURBS and subdivision modeling, the next step is to begin modeling some simple characters. The same methods will be used, but there will be more steps and, of course, more curves and polygons that will have to be dealt with.

If you have followed all the previous exercises, then you should be ready to work at an intermediate level. The next lesson has you modeling two cartoon characters that are neither simple nor complex. The first lesson shows how to model a cartoon cow using subdivison modeling. The second lesson makes use of patch modeling methods to create a cartoon chicken.

It is advantageous to have modeling skills in at least both areas. Too many 3-D artists limit themselves by choosing one or the other and often disparage all methods besides the one they choose. Specific modeling and animation techniques often become fads. When this happens, some artists judge them to be superior to all other solutions. This bias is similar to that of the "art fascists" who claim that anything done on the computer is inferior to art made with traditional materials.

The question often asked is, "Which method is superior—spline/NURBS patch or subdivision modeling?" The answer most likely can be found somewhere in between. If your software has spline or NURBS as well as polygon modeling tools and supports subdivision surfaces, then you have the flexibility to combine both. You can use curves to outline the shapes of models by following the contours of drawings or photos. When it becomes difficult to visualize the template as a three-dimensional object, then switch to box modeling and create a quick primitive of your model. Refine the object by tracing its shape with splines or NURBS. Build each section as a separate spline/NURBS patch. Convert the spline patches to polygons and add extra detail in places and/or merge polygons to simplify other areas. Turn on subdivision mode to see a smooth version of the model. Pull and push points to fine-tune the object.

The most important thing to remember about 3-D modeling is *not* to limit oneself. Experiment with different methods and tools. The mind is an excellent tool, but unfortunately it loves habits. Its tendency is to run in grooves, especially when it finds something it enjoys. Like a broken record player, it will keep playing the same song over and over again unless it is jogged out of its routine. You can see this with some people who have strong likes and dislikes. They are often very narrow-minded and have difficulty thinking out of the box.

CREATING A CARTOON COW WITH SUBDIVISION MODELING

A cow similar to the one shown in Figure 2-1 will now be modeled. Figure 2-2 shows the same cow in subdivision mesh mode. Before starting, you may want to use templates. The Chapter 2 folder on the CD-ROM contains both 2-D and 3-D templates of the cow. Figures 2-3 and 2-4 illustrate the 2-D templates available.

Fig. 2-1 A rendered view of the subdivision cartoon cow.

Fig. 2-3 The sketched side-view template.

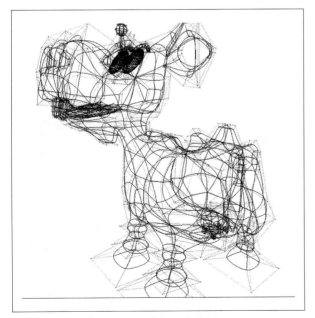

Fig. 2-2 A wireframe view of the subdivision cartoon cow.

Fig. 2-4 The sketched front-view template.

Once you start modeling your own characters, it is recommended that you draw your own template sketches.

THE COW HEAD

Step 1.

Make a box with the following settings (Figure 2-5):

Low X: –15 cm
Low Y: 16 cm
Low Z: 40 cm
High X: 15 cm
High Y: 33 cm
High Z: 55 cm

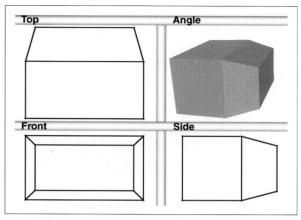

Fig. 2-6 Step 2. Beveling the polygon back and in.

Step 3.

Bevel the back polygon back and in again with the following settings (Figure 2-7):

Shift: 11 cm
Inset: 2.5 cm

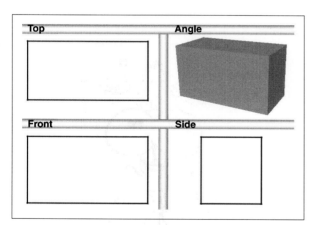

Fig. 2-5 Step 1. A box to make the cow head.

Step 2.

Bevel the back polygon back and in with the following settings (Figure 2-6):

Shift: 9 cm
Inset: 2.5 cm

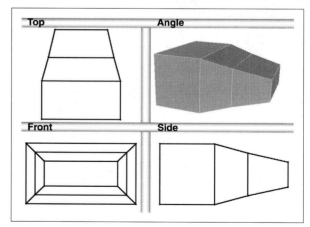

Fig. 2-7 Step 3. The polygon is beveled back once again.

Step 4.

Select the bottom polygon of the middle section and bevel it down (Figure 2-8).

> Shift: 15 cm
> Inset: 2 cm

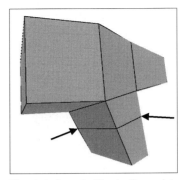

Fig. 2-9 Step 5. The knife tool is used to slice across the neck.

Step 6.

Select the top front neck polygon and bevel it forward for the chin (Figure 2-10).

> Shift: 9 cm
> Inset: 1.5 cm

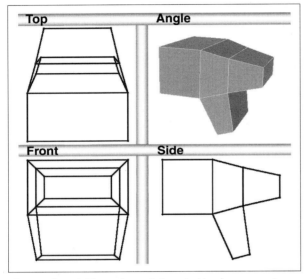

Fig. 2-8 Step 4. The polygon is beveled back once again.

Step 5.

Reposition the bottom polygon to the right location for the bottom of the neck. Use the knife tool to split the neck polygon in half (Figure 2-9).

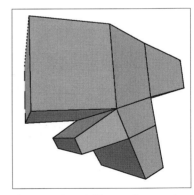

Fig. 2-10 Step 6. The top front neck polygon is beveled forward.

Step 7.

Move points to refine the shape of the head. Work in both low-polygon and subdivision modes (Figure 2-11).

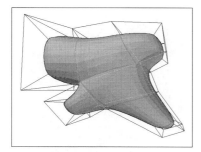

Fig. 2-11 Step 7. Refining the shape of the head in subdivision mode.

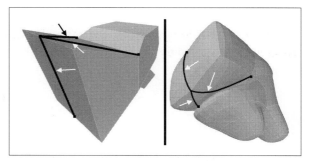

Fig. 2-13 Step 9. The front of the nose polygon is split in half. Notice that the arrows point to the polygons that are split so they will not have five points around them. The right image shows the head in subdivision mode.

Step 8.

Select the bottom chin polygon and bevel it down (Figure 2-12).

    Shift: 3 cm
    Inset: 2 cm

Refine the shape of the chin. Use the knife tool to slice across the chin for extra points to pull and push.

Step 10.

Bevel the nose forward and in (Figure 2-14).

    Shift: 7.5 cm
    Inset: 2 cm

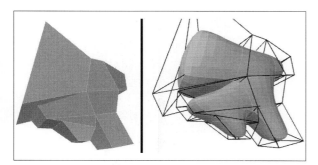

Fig. 2-12 Step 8. The chin is beveled down and shaped in subdivision mode.

Step 9.

Split the front nose polygon down the middle. Make sure the top and bottom adjoining polygons don't have more than four points by splitting them into three-sided ones (Figure 2-13).

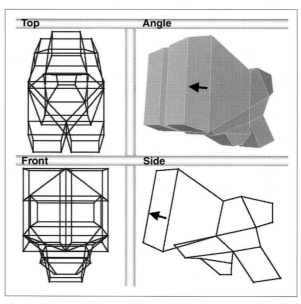

Fig. 2-14 Step 10. The two front nose polygons are beveled forward and in.

Step 11.

Refine the shape of the nose. Select the top polygon of the head (right behind the nose) and bevel it up (Figure 2-15).

    Shift: 10 cm
    Inset: 2.5 cm

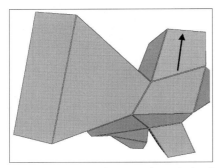

Fig. 2-15 Step 11. The top polygon behind the nose is beveled up for the head.

Step 12.

Refine the shape of the head in subdivision mode. Select the two polygons on both sides of the head and bevel them out (Figure 2-16).

    Shift: 3 cm
    Inset: 2 cm

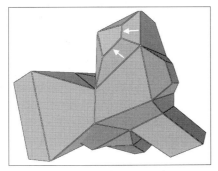

Fig. 2-16 Step 12. The two polygons on both sides of the head are beveled outward (arrows).

Step 13.

Bevel the two polygons from the side of the head again to form the ears (Figure 2-17).

    Shift: 9 cm
    Inset: −2 cm

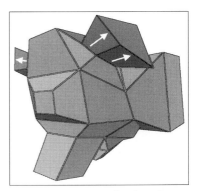

Fig. 2-17 Step 13. Both side polygons are beveled again to make the ears (arrows).

Step 14.

Bevel the two selected ear polygons again to make the tip of the ear (Figure 2-18).

    Shift: 5 cm
    Inset: 2 cm

In subdivision mode, refine the shape of the ear.

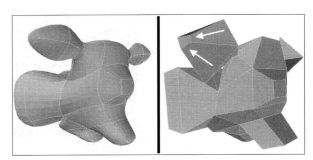

Fig. 2-18 Step 14. One more bevel on the ear completes the form.

Step 15.

Select the ear polygons and rotate them forward so the wide parts of the ears are facing forward. Continue refining the head. Select the two polygons on the side of the head above the ears and bevel them out for the horns (Figure 2-19).

> Shift: 2 cm
> Inset: −7 mm

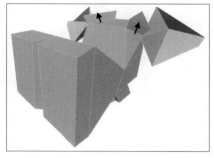

Fig. 2-19 Step 15. Both arrows indicate the bevel direction of the top two head polygons that will start the horns.

Step 16.

Continue beveling out the horn polygons to make the tips (Figure 2-20).

> Shift: 10 cm
> Inset: 2 cm

Refine the shape of the horns.

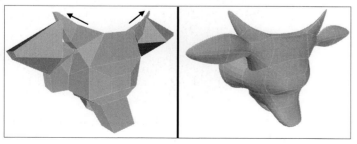

Step 17.

Split the side of the nose polygons vertically with the knife tool and refine the shape of the nose. Scale the front of the nose down to taper it more (Figure 2-21).

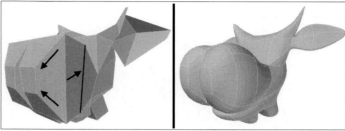

Fig. 2-21 Step 17. The black arrows indicate where the side of the nose is split and the two front polygons are made smaller. Notice the right subdivision view now shows the nose with a more rounded look.

Step 18.

Select the polygons at the end of the nose and bevel them back and in for the nostrils (Figure 2-22).

> Shift: −1.2 cm
> Inset: 1.5 cm

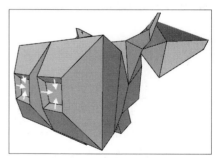

Fig. 2-22 Step 18. Nostrils are made by beveling in the front nose polygons (arrows).

Fig. 2-20 Step 16. One more bevel for the horns makes the tips (arrows).

Step 19.

Bevel the nostrils back and in some more (Figure 2-23).

    Shift: −2.5 cm
    Inset: 1.8 cm

Shape the nostrils.

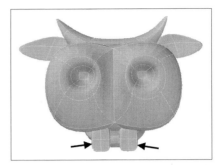

Fig. 2-24 Step 20. The two front teeth (arrows).

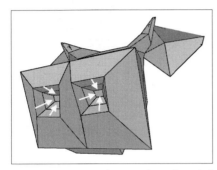

Fig. 2-23 Step 19. The nostrils are beveled back and in one more time.

Step 20.

Add some teeth by modeling them. A quick way is to make a box with the following dimensions (Figure 2-24):

    Low X: −6 cm
    Low Y: 16 cm
    Low Z: 40 cm
    High X: −3.5 cm
    High Y: 22 cm
    High Z: 41 cm
    Segment X: 2
    Segment Y: 2
    Segment Z: 2
    High Y: 33 cm

Scale down the thickness of the teeth at the bottom. Move the box for the teeth and mirror it.

Step 21.

Add eyeballs and pupils by flattening spheres. You might also want to make eyelids from a half sphere. You can improve the cow by making eyebrows, a tongue, and maybe even a ring for the nose. Try to make the forms on the head as round as possible. Unfortunately, box modeling can result in boxy models if the polygons are left too large and sections are not tapered. Figure 2-25 shows the completed cow head.

Fig. 2-25 Step 21. The complete cow head with folderol.

THE COW BODY

Step 22.

Select the bottom neck polygon and bevel it down (Figure 2-26).

   Shift: 31 cm
   Inset: –5.5 cm

Position and rotate the beveled polygon so it ends at the shoulders. Adjust the width of the polygon.

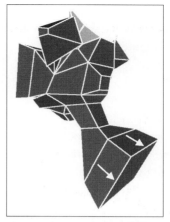

Fig. 2-27 Step 23. The bottom polygon is beveled down again (arrows).

Step 24.

Bevel the selected end polygon again toward the stomach but ending just after the forelegs (Figure 2-28).

   Shift: 7.3 cm
   Inset: –4 mm

Adjust the position by moving and rotating the polygon.

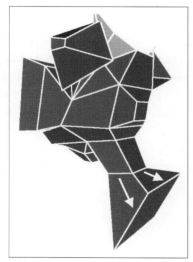

Fig. 2-26 Step 22. Beveling the bottom neck polygon down (arrows).

Step 23.

Bevel the selected polygon again toward the stomach area but ending before the forelegs (Figure 2-27).

   Shift: 11.8 cm
   Inset: –2 cm

Adjust the location and width of the selected polygon.

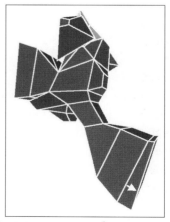

Fig. 2-28 Step 24. Beveling the bottom polygon again (arrow).

Step 25.

Bevel the selected polygon back toward the middle of the stomach (Figure 2-29).

> Shift: 12 cm
> Inset: −2 cm

Adjust the position of the polygon so it ends in the middle of the stomach. Work in subdivision mode to adjust the half torso according to your template.

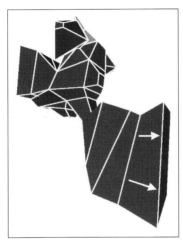

Fig. 2-29 Step 25. The polygon is beveled toward the middle of the stomach (arrows).

Step 26.

In low-polygon mode, select the last polygon that you beveled and bevel it back some more to end at the beginning of the back legs (Figure 2-30).

> Shift: 9 cm
> Inset: −1 cm

Work in subdivison mode to adjust the shape of the torso.

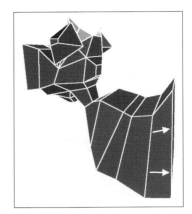

Fig. 2-30 Step 26. Another bevel of the back polygon (arrows).

Step 27.

In low-polygon mode, bevel the last polygon back some more to end just after the back legs (Figure 2-31).

> Shift: 8 cm
> Inset: 7.5 cm

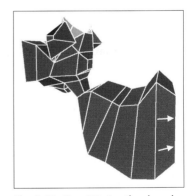

Fig. 2-31 Step 27. Another bevel of the back polygon (arrows).

Step 28.

Select all the polygons on the torso and the bottom polygon of the neck. Use the knife tool to split all these polygons right down the middle from the butt to the neck (Figure 2-32). The back polygon will have five sides to it, so you will need to split it up. Check your polygon statistics to make sure you don't have any other polygons with more than four sides or less than three sides.

Fig. 2-32 Step 28. Arrows point to the line in the middle of the torso made by splitting polygons.

Step 29.

Select the two top polygons at the shoulders and bevel them up a little.

    Shift: 3.2 cm
    Inset: 1.35 cm

In subdivision mode, adjust the shape of the shoulders. Select the two top polygons at the butt and bevel them up a little.

    Shift: 6 cm
    Inset: 3.5 cm

In subdivision mode, shape the top of the butt (Figure 2-33).

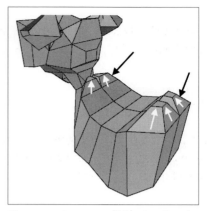

Fig. 2-33 Step 29. Polygons for the shoulders and the top of the butt are beveled up and in (arrows).

Step 30.

Select the two back polygons of the butt and bevel them back a little (Figure 2-34).

    Shift: 6 cm
    Inset: 6 cm

Shape the butt in subdivision mode.

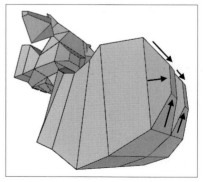

Fig. 2-34 Step 30. Arrows point toward the direction in which the two back polygons are beveled for the butt cheeks.

Step 31.

Select the two polygons at the bottom for the forelegs and bevel them down to the knee (Figure 2-35).

Shift: 10 cm
Inset: 3.5 cm

Make the bottom polygons at the knees smaller and spread them apart somewhat. Work in low-polygon as well as subdivision mode.

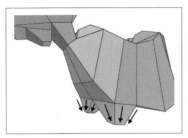

Fig. 2-35 Step 31. Two bottom polygons are beveled down to make the front upper legs.

Step 32.

Bevel the two polygons at the knee down and out a little to make the middle of the knee area (Figure 2-36).

Shift: 3.5 cm
Inset: −3 cm

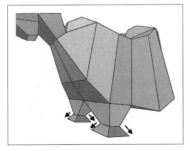

Fig. 2-36 Step 32. The front leg polygons are beveled down and out for the knees.

Step 33.

Bevel the knee polygons down and in a little to make the rest of the knee (Figure 2-37).

Shift: 4 cm
Inset: 3 cm

In subdivision mode, refine the shape of the knees.

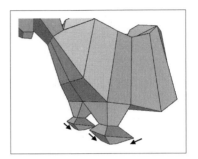

Fig. 2-37 Step 33. Knee polygons are beveled down and in.

Step 34.

Select the bottom knee polygons and bevel them down and out (Figure 2-38).

Shift: 10.5 cm
Inset: 5 cm

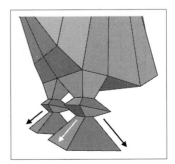

Fig. 2-38 Step 34. The lower legs are made by beveling the bottom polygons down and out.

Step 35.

Begin modeling the hooves by selecting the bottom foot polygons and beveling them in a little (Figure 2-39).

Shift: –1.3 cm
Inset: 2.5 cm

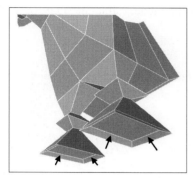

Fig. 2-39 Step 35. Starting the hooves by beveling the polygons up and in.

Step 36.

Bevel out the hoof polygons (Figure 2-40).

Shift: 14 cm
Inset: –9 cm

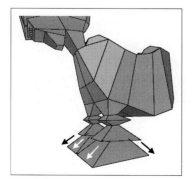

Fig. 2-40 Step 36. Completing the hooves by beveling the polygons down and out.

Step 37.

Work mostly in subdivision mode to shape the front legs. You may also decide to make them shorter and rotate them back a little so the bottoms of the hooves are flat on the ground (Figure 2-41).

Fig. 2-41 Step 37. Shaping the front legs in subdivision mode.

Step 38.

Repeat Steps 31 through 37 to make the back legs. The shape of the back legs will differ from the shape of the front legs (Figure 2-42).

Fig. 2-42 Step 38. The back legs are modeled in a similar manner as the front ones.

Step 39.

Split and merge polygons at the butt so that you have a smaller polygon for beveling out the tail. Make sure no polygons have more than four sides (Figure 2-43).

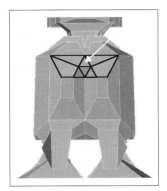

Fig. 2-43 Step 39. Splitting and merging polygons at the back of the butt so that the tail can be beveled out (arrow).

Step 40.

Select the small polygon at the top of the butt and bevel it back a little (Figure 2-44).

    Shift: 7 cm
    Inset: 4 mm

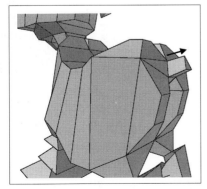

Fig. 2-44 Step 40. The first bevel for the tail (arrow).

Step 41.

Bevel the tail polygon back again.

    Shift: 28 cm
    Inset: 0

Bevel the tail polygon once again.

    Shift: 15 cm
    Inset: −3 cm

Bevel the tail polygon for the last time to make the tip of the tail (Figure 2-45).

    Shift: 17 cm
    Inset: 4 cm

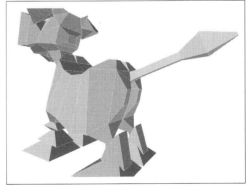

Fig. 2-45 Step 41. Beveling out the rest of the tail.

Step 42.

Use the knife tool to split the tail into more sections to make it easier to bend. Bend the tail. Work in subdivision mode to shape and scale the tail (Figure 2-46).

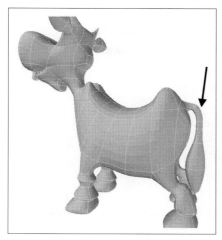

Fig. 2-46 Step 42. The tail is split into smaller polygons and bent down.

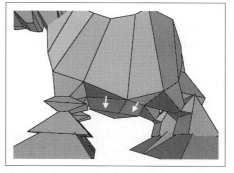

Fig. 2-48 Step 44. The diamond-shape-polygon is beveled down for the udder.

Step 43.

Select the bottom polygons on the stomach and merge them into one. Split polygons so that you have only three- and four-sided ones (Figure 2-47).

Step 44.

Bevel the bottom stomach polygon down a little to start making the udder (Figure 2-48).

> Shift: 6 cm
> Inset: 2 cm

Step 45.

Work in subdivision mode to scale and shape the beginning of the udder. Bevel the polygon for the udder again.

> Shift: 7 cm
> Inset: 4 cm

Shape the udder in subdivision mode and move it back toward the back legs (Figure 2-49).

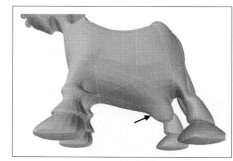

Fig. 2-49 Step 45. Beveling, shaping, and moving the udder back.

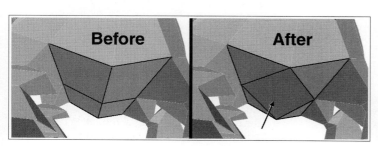

Fig. 2-47 Step 43. The bottom stomach polygons are split up and merged to make a diamond shape for beveling the udder.

Step 46.

To make the teats, select the four polygons on the sides of the udder and bevel them out and in a little.

Shift: 3 cm
Inset: 3 cm

Give the shape of the polygons for the teats a more square appearance by moving points closer (Figure 2-50).

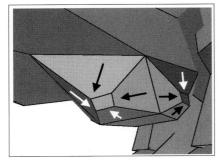

Fig. 2-50 Step 46. Four polygons on the side of the udder are beveled out and shaped.

Step 47.

Bevel the four teat polygons out (Figure 2-51).

Shift: 7 cm
Inset: 0

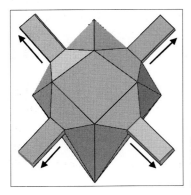

Fig. 2-51 Step 47. A bottom view showing the teats beveled straight out.

Step 48.

Use the knife tool to divide the teat polygons so that it is easier to bend them down. Bend the teats down and work in both low-polygon and subdivision modes to shape them (Figure 2-52).

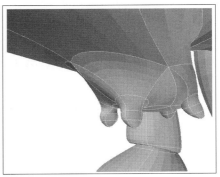

Fig. 2-52 Step 48. The teats are split up into smaller sections and bent down.

Step 49.

Continue refining the model by splitting polygons and moving points. To keep it from looking boxy, divide and shape the larger polygons.

You might also want to split the model down the middle so that you only have to work on half of it. Once you are done, you can mirror-duplicate the half

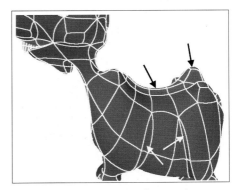

Fig. 2-53 Step 49. Finalizing the cow. Adding a spine and middle hump, defining the upper part of the legs, and splitting large polygons.

and merge the points down the middle. Be sure to model a middle hump between the two back humps. The upper parts of the front and back legs should have a more well-defined look. A spine is also an important addition (Figure 2-53).

Assign surface names to the different parts, and you are done.

CREATING A CARTOON CHICKEN WITH PATCH SPLINE/NURBS MODELING

A cartoon chicken similar to the one in Figure 2-54 will be modeled using the patch spline/NURBS method. The Chapter 2 folder on the CD-ROM contains 2-D templates like the ones in Figures 2-55 and 2-56 as well as a 3-D template..

Combining subdivision and patch modeling is an effective method for making a quick 3-D template and a spline/NURBS object. Subdivision or box modeling is used to make a 3-D template from 2-D ones. Splines

Fig. 2-55 The side-view sketch of the chicken available on the CD-ROM as a 2-D template.

Fig. 2-56 The front-view sketch.

are then placed over the box model to make a more refined model.

The 2-D templates work well as a guide, and the box modeling method is easy to use for creating a quick 3-D object. Since box modeling often lacks detail and can look somewhat chunky, patch modeling using the 3-D box template can make a more rounded and detailed model.

If you have been following the directions so far, you should now be somewhat familiar with subdivision modeling. For the first part of this exercise we will begin with 2-D templates, create a quick box model, and then use this as our 3-D template for patch modeling.

Fig. 2-54 A rendered view of the patch-modeled chicken.

MAKING THE 3-D TEMPLATE WITH BOX MODELING

Step 1.

Make a box and shape it somewhat like the one in Figure 2-57. This will be used to make the upper beak. Select the polygon in the side view that runs vertically and is the smaller of the two. Bevel it out and in like the one in Figure 2-58.

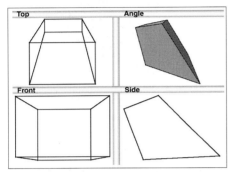

Fig. 2-57 Step 1. A box is made for the top part of the beak.

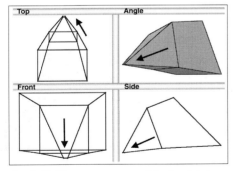

Fig. 2-58 The narrow part of the beak is beveled out and in.

Step 2.

Select the bottom polygon at the base of the beak and bevel it down and in (Figure 2-59). In the left side view, select the left bottom polygon of the lower beak and bevel it out and in several times so that it now looks like Figure 2-60.

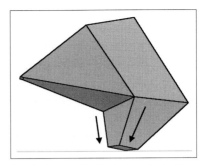

Fig. 2-59 Step 2. Beginning the bottom beak by beveling down.

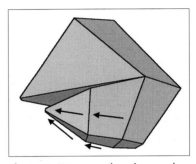

Fig. 2-60 Two more bevels complete the bottom portion of the beak.

Step 3.

Start the head by selecting the polygon at the base of the upper beak and beveling it back a couple of times (Figure 2-61).

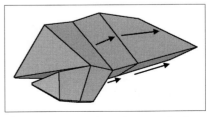

Fig. 2-61 Step 3. The polygon at the base of the upper beak is beveled back two times.

Step 4.

Select the two polygons at the top of the head and bevel them up and in. Weld the two points at the top between the two newly created polygons. The top of the head should be one unit. Delete the inside polygon. Whenever you have inner polygons that will not be seen on the outer surface, eliminate them. In subdivision mode, these interior polygons can often pull on the surface ones, causing unsightly holes or imperfections on the external parts of the model (Figure 2-62).

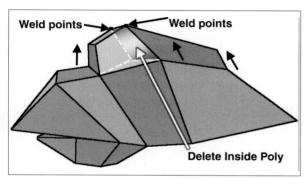

Fig. 2-62 Step 4. Polygons at the top of the head are beveled up. Two sets of points at the top are welded and the inside polygon is eliminated.

Step 5.

The crest or comb on top of the head can be started by beveling up the two top polygons (Figure 2-63).

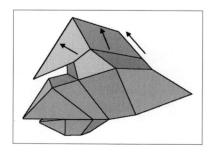

Fig. 2-63 Step 5. Beginning the cockscomb by beveling up.

Step 6.

Now it is time to divide the comb. Separate some of the sections. Be sure to keep the polygons to three- and four-sided ones (Figure 2-64).

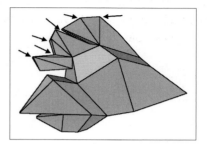

Fig. 2-64 Step 6. The comb is divided and parts are separated.

Step 7.

Bevel the bottom head polygons down to make the neck. Delete the inside polygons after welding neighboring points (Figure 2-65).

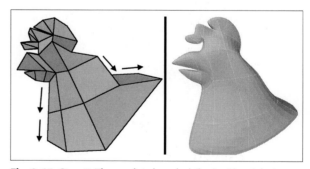

Fig. 2-65 Step 7. The neck is beveled down. The right image shows the chicken at this stage in subdivision mode.

Step 8.

Select the polygon at the bottom of the lower beak and bevel it down to make the bowtie. Split it into two separate polygons (Figure 2-66).

43

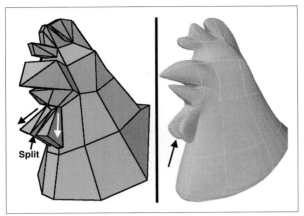

Fig. 2-66 Step 8. The polygon at the bottom of the lower beak is beveled down to make the bowtie. Splitting and separating it into two sections completes the tie.

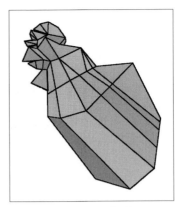

Fig. 2-68 Points on the bottom of the body are welded, inside polygons are deleted, and the body is split up for extra detail.

Step 9.

The three polygons at the bottom are now beveled down to start the body (Figure 2-67). Note that they are separate sections whose points will have to be welded at the ends to make the whole body. As usual, the inner polygons are deleted. The body is then divided into extra polygons to make more detailed sections (Figure 2-68).

Step 10.

Model the body and the neckline so that it partially covers the body (Figure 2-69).

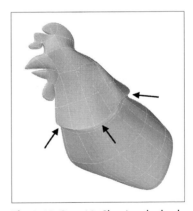

Fig. 2-69 Step 10. Shaping the body and neckline.

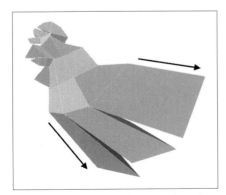

Fig. 2-67 Step 9. Beveling the three bottom polygons to make the body.

Step 11.

Start the tail feathers by beveling out the end polygons on the body. Refine the shapes of the feathers and body (Figure 2-70).

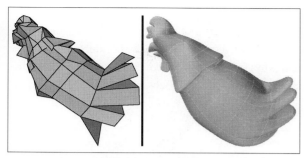

Fig. 2-70 Step 11. Polygons are beveled out and shaped to make the first section of the tail feathers.

Step 12.

Bevel out the tail feathers some more and taper the ends (Figure 2-71).

Fig. 2-71 Step 12. The tail feathers are beveled out more and their shape is improved.

Step 13.

Begin the legs by beveling down the two bottom polygons on the underside of the body (Figure 2-72).

Fig. 2-72 Step 13. The tops of the legs are beveled down and in.

Step 14.

Select the bottom polygons of the legs and bevel them up and in a little. Bevel the same polygons down for the long parts of the legs (Figure 2-73).

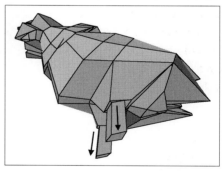

Fig. 2-73 Step 14. Polygons for the legs are beveled up and in a little and then beveled down.

Step 15.

Divide the legs horizontally and then vertically. Weld points to get rid of any polygons that have more than four sides. The bottom front parts of the two legs should have three polygons for each leg. The backs of the legs should have only one polygon on each. Select the the front three polygons on each leg and bevel them out to make the front toes. Bevel out the back two polygons on the feet to make the two back toes. Delete all the inner polygons in the legs and feet (Figure 2-74).

Step 17.

Select the polygons at the front of the toes and bevel them in and then out to make the nails. Divide the nail polygons and bend them down a little. Follow the same steps to make the back nails. (Figure 2-76).

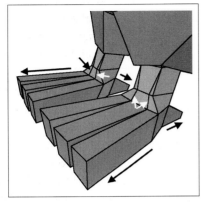

Fig. 2-74 Step 15. The tops of the legs are beveled down and in.

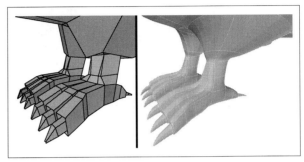

Fig. 2-76 Step 17. The polygons for the nails are first beveled back and in a little and then beveled out. Dividing the nail polygons makes it possible to bend them somewhat.

Step 16.

All eight toes should be divided and bent like those in Figure 2-75.

Step 18.

The wing is made by choosing the polygons on the side of the body and beveling them out. Weld the points of the wing to make them into one piece and eliminate the inside polygons (Figure 2-77).

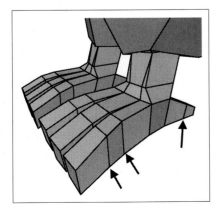

Fig. 2-75 Step 16. Dividing the toes and bending them.

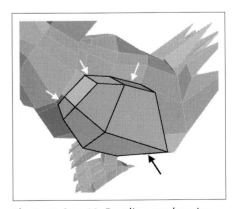

Fig. 2-77 Step 18. Beveling out the wing.

Step 19.

Refine the shape of the wing by dividing it into smaller polygons. Move the end points in and out to make sharper wing tips. Add an eye, and you have the 3-D template for patch modeling (Figure 2-78).

Fig. 2-78 Step 19. The wing is divided and points are moved to make the tips of the feathers.

PATCH MODELING THE CHICKEN

The subdivision-modeled chicken can now be used as a template to make a more detailed spline/NURBS chicken. Whenever you have to patch model, a 3-D template can be very useful. Unlike box modeling, which has you sculpting with full 3-D objects, patch modeling often has sections that are narrower, making it hard to visualize the entire object in three-dimensional space.

Those of you who are working in a program that supports spline and polygon modeling might want to autopatch or surface each spline cage section one at a time as you make them. Before patching the spline cage make sure each section has only three or four points around it. If your polygon mesh has holes in it, then refer to the troubleshooting section in Chapter 1 at the end of the knife tutorial.

Some of you may find it easier to create new patches in separate layers. Patches with adjoining points can be built by copying the points to another layer and then creating the neighboring patch in this new layer. Once all the patches have been made, they can be copied and pasted into one layer and their adjoining points merged either on the polygon or on the spline mesh.

Some software packages require that you stitch adjoining points to avoid gaps and tears in the mesh when it is deformed during animation. Whether you are working with polygons, splines, or NURBS, the final object will have to be made seamless. You can do this by either merging or stitching all the points that share space with each other.

The Chapter 2 folder on the CD-ROM contains 3-D chicken templates showing each step. In this exercise you will only have to model half the chicken. Mirror-duplicating it at the end will complete it. To avoid holes along the middle seam, make sure all the points along the center section are at 0 value on the x axis.

Step 1.

Using the Step 1 template or the box-modeled one, draw four splines or make points and connect them to make splines. Every spline should have the same number of vertices, which should be about four. Link the four splines together by either lofting or selecting their points in order and connecting them (Figure 2-79).

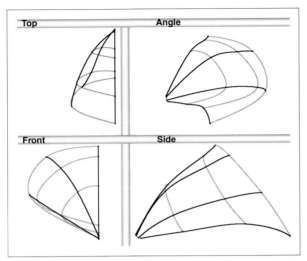

Fig. 2-79 Step 1. The dark splines are made first for the upper beak. The gray lines are the connecting splines.

Step 2.

The lower beak is started by using two points from the upper beak spline (Figure 2-80). After making four splines, connect them for the lower beak.

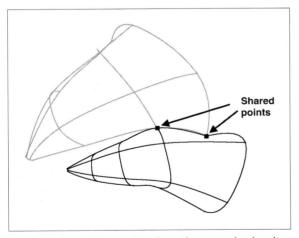

Fig. 2-80 Step 2. Two points from the upper beak spline are used to start the lower beak. The four new splines are connected to make the lower beak.

Step 3.

Using Figure 2-81 and the Step 3 template as your guides, create the head of the bird. Notice the points on the beak that are shared with the head. If your software does not allow you to create new splines from existing points on the beak, then you will have to either weld or stitch adjoining sections.

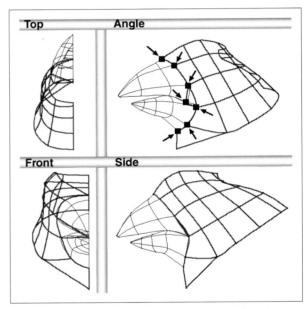

Fig. 2-81 Step 3. The head is started by using shared points from the upper and lower beak (arrows in angled view). Using neighboring points to make new patches will ensure that there are no breaks or gaps between meshes.

Step 4.

The next patch is the cockscomb, the fleshy red crest found on the heads of gallinaceous birds. Using the points or spline on top of the head, begin making the cross sections for this part (Figure 2-82). Connect the cross sections to complete the comb.

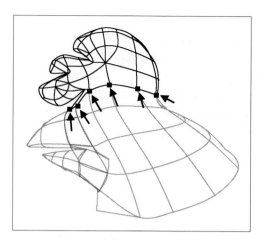

Fig. 2-82 Step 4. The cockscomb is started by using existing points on top of the head.

Step 5.

Figure 2-83 shows how the neck is modeled using the bottom head spline and its points. This same spline begins the top of the neck. The bottom portion of the neck is tucked under.

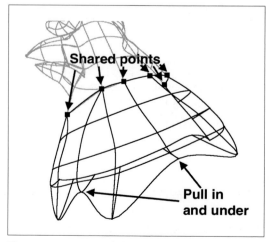

Fig. 2-83 Step 5. Modeling the neck from the bottom head points or spline.

Step 6.

Now it is time to make the bowtie under the lower beak. Since this part is made up of two independent forms, it will be modeled as an enclosed object with closed curves. When the final chicken is mirror-duplicated, you will have two separate parts of the bowtie that are split along the center.

Select the four points at the end and bottom of the lower beak and make a closed curve out of them (Figure 2-84). Duplicate and move the three copies below the first one. Scale them to make the framework and then connect the curves. The top of the bowtie shares points with part of the lower beak.

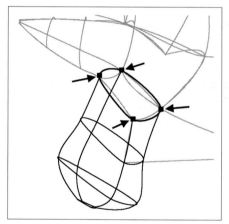

Fig. 2-84 Step 6. The bowtie that hangs from the lower beak is made from a series of closed curves.

Step 7.

This next part breaks the rule of patch modeling by making a section that is not connected to the neck. Since this part of the body is inserted underneath the neck section there is no need to connect it. The spline cage is built so that there is a hole in the side for the wing (Figure 2-85).

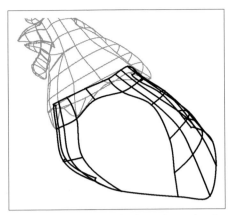

Fig. 2-85 Step 7. The body tucks under the neck. Notice the hole on the side for the wing.

Step 8.

The previously modeled body has a hole in the side, which will now be used to start the wing. Select the points along the perimeter of this opening and make a closed curve (Figure 2-86). Continue making splines that connect across the closed curve. For the wing tips be sure to model some of the curves so that they form a kind of zigzag pattern.

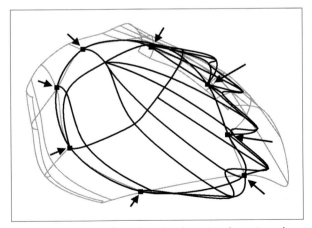

Fig. 2-86 Step 8. Making the wing by using the points along the perimeter of the body's open area.

Step 9.

Select points along the bottom of the body and make an open curve from them (Figure 2-87). Create new splines from this curve that form the upper part of the leg. The bottom of this patch has a closed curve that will be used to make the enclosed form of the leg.

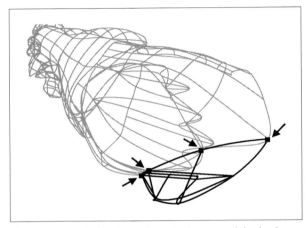

Fig. 2-87 Step 9. Vertices along the bottom of the body are used to start the upper leg.

Step 10.

Steps 10 through 14 will have you model the tail feathers. Points along the back of the body are selected to start each tail section. For the first section, you can select the first set of four points on the back of the body and copy them to another layer (Figure 2-88). Create another vertex and make an open curve to start the tail feather. Duplicate this open curve four times and move each one to make the framework for the tail feather. Each spline should gradually get smaller. Connect the five splines with open curves.

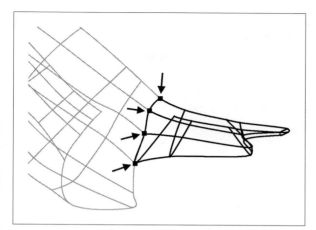

Fig. 2-88 Step 10. The first tail feather is made by using four points along the back of the body. After adding a fifth vertex, the points are connected to make the first open curve.

Step 11.

For the second tail feather, use three existing points along the body and the first tail feather (Figure 2-89). You will also have to make a new point to complete the first curve. Use the same procedure as in Step 10 to complete the second tail feather. This time, you will need only three cross sections of splines instead of five.

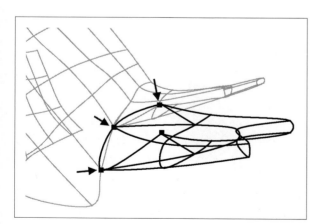

Fig. 2-89 Step 11. The second tail feather uses three shared points and a newly made fourth one. The arrows indicate the shared vertices.

Steps 12–14.

Figure 2-90 shows the rest of the tail feathers. Model these the same way that you did the previous two. You should now have five segments in total.

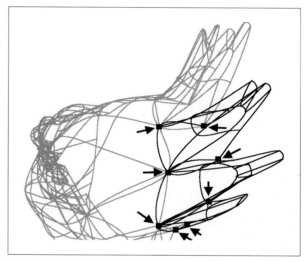

Fig. 2-90 Steps 12–14. Three more tail feather sections are modeled using shared points.

Step 15.

The first part of the leg is made from the four points along the bottom of the previously modeled upper leg (Figure 2-91). Copies of the first closed curve are placed along the length of the leg. Open curves connect these oval splines. Note that the bottom front of the leg has three shapes in front and one in the back. These will be used to make the foot.

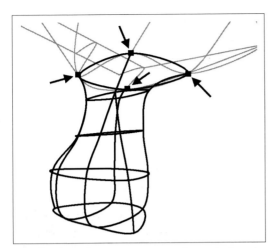

Fig. 2-91 Step 15. Closed curves make up the leg. The original points are taken from the upper part of the leg.

Step 16.

Select four of the vertices along the front bottom part of the leg and make a closed curve out of these (Figure 2-92). Copy and paste four curves from the first one. After scaling and shaping these closed curves, connect them with open curves.

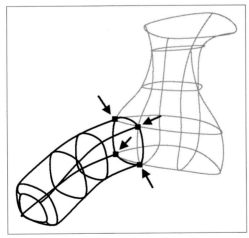

Fig. 2-92 Step 16. The first toe uses existing points along the front of the leg. A closed curve is made from these four vertices.

Steps 17 and 18.

Make the other two front toes the same way as outlined in Step 16. As before, points are shared with the leg (Figure 2-93).

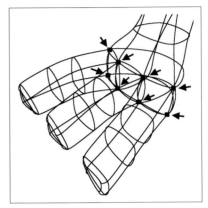

Fig. 2-93 Steps 17 and 18. Completing the three front toes. The arrows indicate the shared points.

Step 19.

Model the back toe using points along the back portion of the leg (Figure 2-94). The closed curves are duplicated and connected with open ones.

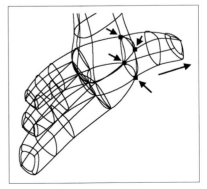

Fig. 2-94 Step 19. The back toe is modeled the same way as the front ones, using preexisting points on the leg.

If you are patching the spline cages with polygons be sure to eliminate the inside polygons where the leg meets the upper leg, and where the toes meet the leg. This will prevent pinching and other unsightly blemishes that often appear when the model is changed into a subdivision object.

Step 20.

The toenails are started with points along the front of the toes (Figure 2-95). After making the closed curves, connect them with open ones. The tips of the toenails are closed by either welding points or bringing them close together.

This completes the patch-modeled chicken (Figure 2-96). After merging all the points, you can mirror-duplicate either the polygon chicken or the spline/NURBS one.

Fig. 2-96 One half of the spline cage chicken.

If you are working with polygons, be sure to eliminate any inner polygons before changing the model to subdivision mode. Also check for polygons that have less than three and more than four points and remove them.

Add other details such as an eye. Assign surface names to the various parts of the chicken, and you are done.

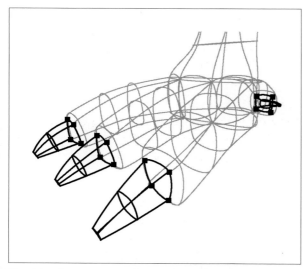

Fig. 2-95 Step 20. Toenails use points along the ends of the toes and are modeled similarly, with closed curves.

Anatomy of the Human Figure 3

Leonardo da Vinci said, "The supreme misfortune is when theory outstrips performance." Although this book strives to be a practical guide, there are certain assumptions about the human anatomy that ought to be discussed in a more analytical manner. Although this chapter examines anatomy, it does not pretend to be a full study of it. Entire books have been written about this subject. These should serve as more appropriate guides for the serious art student desiring an in-depth study of anatomy.

Art students should realize that drawing, sculpting, and 3-D modeling of the human figure require a knowledge of the human anatomy. Lacking this information about the underlying structure, it becomes too easy for someone to create forms that look ambiguous and incorrect. Often one can see this in depictions of humans by novice artists. Arms and legs look like sausages without any definition, proportions are wrong, and the model will look like it was strung together from separate pieces that have no relationship to each other.

Some people wonder why artists so often depict the human body in the nude. The answer is very simple. Clothing hides the solid form of the figure. One needs to start with a clear concept of the basic human frame rather than spend time worrying about folds

and details in the clothes. The same holds true with animation. In the beginning it is more useful for students to see how the body moves rather than obscuring the actions of muscles and bones with drapery. Animating clothing in itself presents new problems that should be addressed later.

PROPORTION

Throughout history, artists have tried to depict the human figure in ideal proportions. Generally, the average height of a man or a woman can be measured as seven heads tall. When seen on a two-dimensional surface, the seven-heads-tall figure does not satisfy the concept of the ideal. Compare the same female in Figures 3-1 and 3-2. The model in Figure 3-2 that is eight heads tall appears more elegant and statuesque.

If your goal is to create and animate the ideal male and female, then consider modeling them eight heads tall. If you are using 2-D or 3-D templates, stretch their proportions first and then use them as your guides. Then again, if you are planning to create caricatures, try making the heads extra large and the entire body only five or six heads tall. Superheroes are often portrayed as very tall with tiny heads.

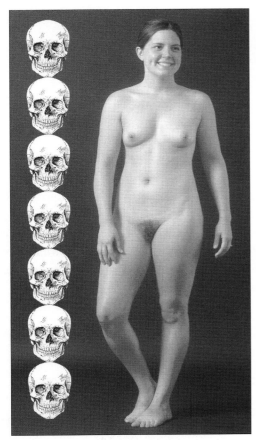

Fig. 3-1 Normally the figure can be measured as seven heads tall.

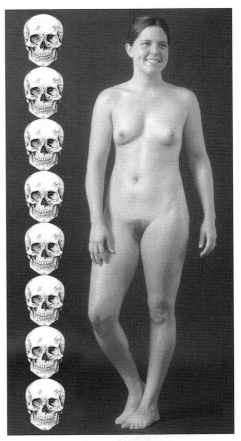

Fig. 3-2 The eight-heads-tall figure appears more stately.

Sometimes an artist will deliberately create a model according to the manner in which it will be viewed. Michelangelo's *David* is a perfect example of this. Since the size of the statue was modeled to be very big and meant to be viewed looking up at it, Michelangelo had the foresight to model the head extralarge, knowing that viewed in perspective it would look normal.

Figure 3-3 illustrates the average shoulder width of the female and the height of the torso. The female appears to have a shoulder width of two and two-thirds heads. The male has a shoulder width of three heads (Figure 3-4). Measured from the top of the head to the crotch, both male and female are approximately four heads tall.

Although at first it helps to know the general proportions according to certain measurements, it is better to rely on your own eyes and judgment as to what looks right and what does not. With experience, one learns to gauge proportion according to one's own good sense

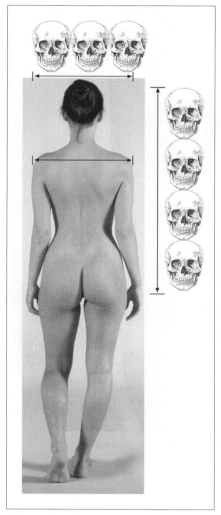

Fig. 3-3 The shoulder width and torso height of the female.

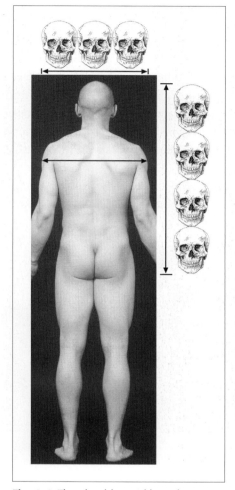

Fig. 3-4 The shoulder width and torso height of the male.

rather than spending time measuring the figure with a ruler.

When first starting out, scientific knowledge of human proportions and anatomy is helpful but it can become an impediment when adhered to slavishly.

Strive to make convincing models by mastering structure, and then eventually develop a personal style. When artists depart from conventional ways of representing the figure, their work often becomes more individual and interesting.

THE SKELETON

The skeleton serves as the frame upon which the muscles, tendons, fat, and skin are stretched. The body takes its form from the skeleton. It is the skeleton that gives our bodies proportion. One can compare the skeleton to the framework of a house. It protects and supports what is inside (vital organs) while serving as a foundation for outer parts such as the muscles, fat, and skin.

The underlying skeletal structure also affects the outer contours of the figure. This requires extra attention to detail since the bones are sometimes less pro-

nounced in some areas. Figures 3-5 and 3-6 illustrate some of the parts of the figure in which the bones are noticeable.

It would be difficult to create models with convincing forms without first studying the skeleton. The figure would have little shape without it. Michelangelo shows us an example of this in his painting *The Last Judgment,* in which he shows his own flayed skin held up by St. Bartholomew (Figure 3-7). It is a wonderful example of the body devoid of a skeleton.

The artistic study of the skeleton is much simpler than a medical one. Students who fail to notice or

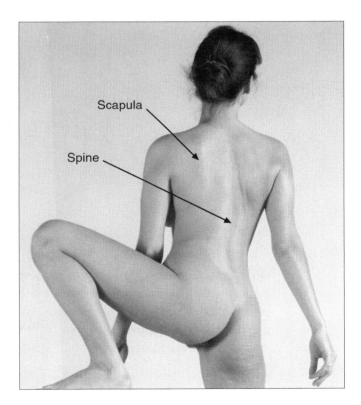

Scapula

Spine

Fig. 3-5 Some of the visible bones.

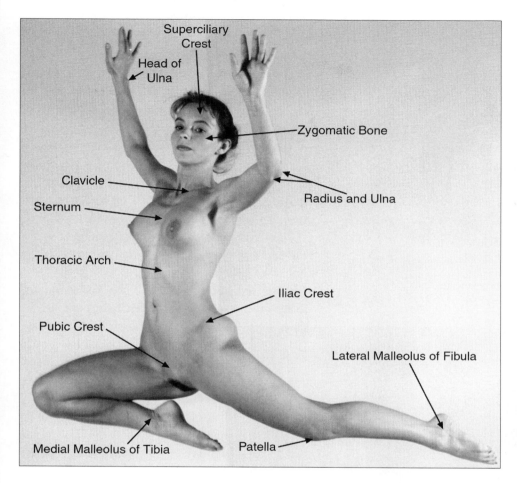

Superciliary Crest

Head of Ulna

Zygomatic Bone

Clavicle

Radius and Ulna

Sternum

Thoracic Arch

Iliac Crest

Pubic Crest

Lateral Malleolus of Fibula

Medial Malleolus of Tibia

Patella

Fig. 3-6 Some areas in the front and side of the body where bones are visible.

ignore the skeleton limit themselves to a mere depiction of bulges and depressions when modeling the human form. Without knowing the underlying construction, purpose, proportion, and importance of the skeleton, beginning 3-D modelers will often treat it as just another puzzling factor that appears to change the contours of the figure.

The experienced 3-D modeler recognizes the value of depicting the underlying architecture. There is a realization that the components of the body can be established by the recognition of the large parts of the skeleton. The seasoned animator realizes that all movement originates from the skeleton, which both supports and propels the muscles.

Figure 3-8 depicts various views of the skeleton. Its major sections consist of the skull, spinal column, rib cage, shoulder, pelvis, arm, and leg.

Fig. 3-7 Detail of St. Bartholomew and the flayed skin from Michelangelo's *The Last Judgment.*

THE SKULL

Twenty-two bones make up the skull. Figure 3-9 illustrates several views of the skull marked with some of the more prominent bones. The standard method for relative measurements of the body is with skull heights.

The only mobile bone on the skull is the jawbone (mandibula). The rest of the skull bones are rigidly held together by immovable joints. The skull can be divided into two sections: the cranium, which encloses the brain, and the bones of the face.

The frontal bone is located at the anterior of the cranium. It forms the brows as well as the protective curve over the eyes.

Other prominent bones that are visible on the fleshed-out human are the superciliary bone, or the brow ridge; the canine fossa, a concavity below the eye socket; the lower ridge of the nasal bone; the zygomatic bone, or cheekbone; and the mandibula, or jawbone.

Students of 3-D modeling might find it useful to study the skull. Since the layers of muscle and fat are stretched relatively thinly over the skull, its bone structure is more prominent than that of any other part of the body (Figure 3-10).

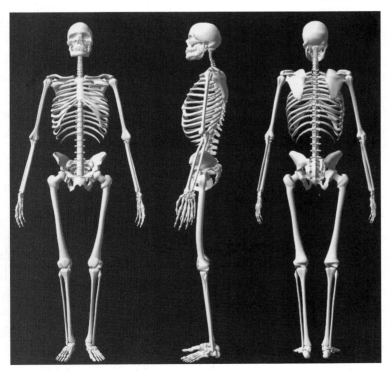

Fig. 3-8 Skeleton views.

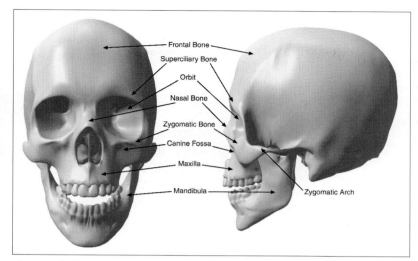

Fig. 3-9 Skull views.

Frontal Bone
Superciliary Bone
Orbit
Nasal Bone
Zygomatic Bone
Canine Fossa
Maxilla
Mandibula
Zygomatic Arch

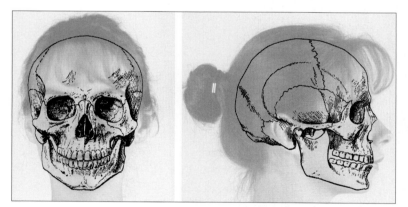

Fig. 3-10 The skull has a great influence on the shape of the head.

THE SKELETON OF THE TORSO

The upper- and lower-torso skeleton can be split into four sections: spine, rib cage, shoulder girdle, and pelvic girdle (Figure 3-11). All four parts are grouped around the spine. The spine is composed of 33 ver-

tebrae. The lowest 9 are fused together to form the sacrum and the coccyx. The remaining 24 vertebrae are highly flexible (Figures 3-12 and 3-13). They are separated by a fibrous pad of elastic cartilage that cushions and makes movement possible between them. Animators who rig or set up a skeleton should take this into consideration and thus create a series of connected bones with qualities similar to those of a real spine.

It is interesting to note the reasons for the manner in which the spine curves. The coccyx and sacrum arch toward the back, allowing room for the internal organs within the pelvic girdle. Above that the spine curves toward and under the ribs, which it supports. Behind the ribs the spine bends toward the back to support the chest. The neck vertebrae turn toward the front and under the skull. They support the skull almost perfectly at its center of gravity so that there is very little effort required to hold up the head. The shape of the spine regulates the major directions of the trunk.

The barrel-shaped rib cage is smaller at the top. Twelve pairs of ribs and a sternum (breastbone) protect the lungs and heart. Of interest to animators is the fact that the rib cage is supple enough to expand and contract with respiration. Modelers should note that the cartilage in the front, where the seventh, eighth, ninth, and tenth ribs join, can often be seen on the surface as an arch underneath the chest muscles (Figure

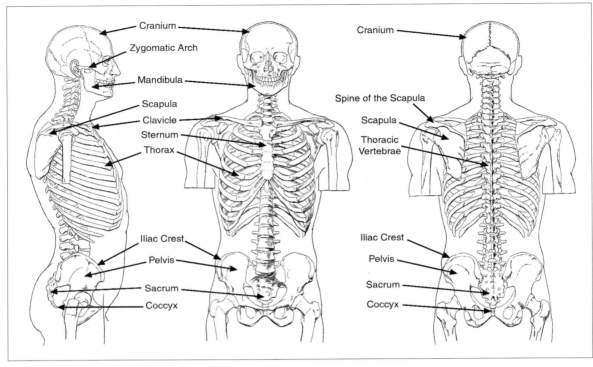

Fig. 3-11 The skeleton of the upper body.

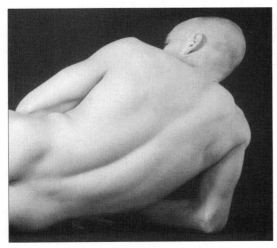

Fig. 3-12 The movable vertebrae of the spine allow considerable degrees of bending and twisting.

3-14). This upside-down V-shaped form is called the thoracic arch. The sternum is formed from three firmly joined bones. It is also visible on the surface as a furrow separating the chest muscles (Figure 3-14). The sternum rises and falls with the expansion and contraction of the chest.

The shoulder girdle has the clavicle (collarbone) and scapulae (shoulder blades). Seen from the top, it has a bowlike shape. From the front, the clavicle appears to have an S-curve (Figure 3-15). The clavicle is capable of extensive movement. This adds to the mobility of the arms.

Each scapula is a triangular-shaped plate (Figure 3-15). It is only indirectly joined to the body by its connection to the clavicle. The form of the scapula is

Fig. 3-13 Groups of powerful muscles around the spinal column make it possible to bend, twist, and turn.

in line with the shape of the rib cage against which it slides freely. Besides gliding in any direction, it can be lifted from the rib cage to appear very prominently under the skin. This becomes obvious when the arm is raised above the shoulders. The scapula then moves out to the side of the rib cage.

Lacking the mobility of the shoulder girdle, the

pelvic girdle has strength and hardness. Its construction is meant to transfer the weight of the body to the load-bearing legs.

The pelvis is the part of the body from which most of the important actions originate. A great amount of energy is transmitted from this region to the upper parts of the body. This is an important consideration

Fig. 3-14 The thoracic arch of the rib cage frequently becomes a visible part of the figure.

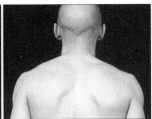

Fig. 3-15 The shoulder girdle comprises the clavicle (front) and scapulae (back).

when animating the human figure. Actions will look more convincing if one can show movement originating from the activity of the hips. When setting up a skeleton for animation, the parent bone should start at the pelvis.

Two symmetrical hipbones surround the sacrum. An irregularly curved edge named the iliac crest (Figures 3-11 and 3-16) is often seen distinctly on the skin surface. The hipbones appear as winglike structures, especially on thin figures.

The proportions of the male and the female pelvis vary somewhat. The female pelvis is wider and shorter, while the male pelvis is more massive, taller, and more angular (Figure 3-17). In the side view the female pelvis also tilts forward to a greater degree.

Fig. 3-16 The iliac crest of the pelvis forms a highly visible bony projection.

Fig. 3-17 The male pelvis is thicker and more angular than the female pelvis.

THE BONES OF THE ARM

The most maneuverable bones of the body are found in the arm. Their range of gesture and instrumentality are further enhanced by the fluid maneuverability of the shoulder girdle and the dexterity of the fingers and thumb. Since the arm bones do not have to support the body like those in the legs, their forms are more slender.

Figure 3-18 illustrates the bones of the arm. The upper arm bone, called the humerus, has a ball-like

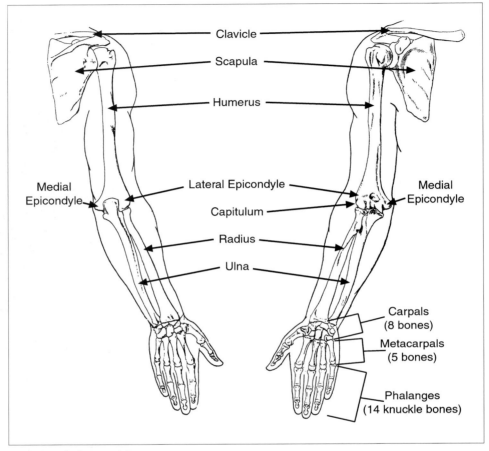

Fig. 3-18 The bones of the arm.

form at the top that fits into the shallow cavity of the scapula. Since this socket lacks depth and the joining ligaments are loose, the arm has the greatest mobility compared to all the other limbs.

The two bones in the lower arm are the radius and the ulna. A hinge joint connects the ulna with the humerus. The radius rotates around the ulna (Figure 3-19). This is accomplished by the bending and stretching of the lower arm muscles. The action of the two bones is evident when rotating the lower arm from a palm-up to a palm-down position. The position in which the radius and ulna are parallel is called supination. Pronation occurs when the radius crosses the ulna (Figure 3-20).

Surface characteristics of the arm bones can be seen at the shoulder, where the head of the humerus makes an inner bulge in the deltoid muscle. At the elbow, three bumps can be seen when the arm is bent.

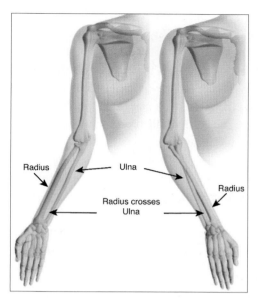

Fig. 3-19 When the palm of the hand is turned face up, the radius and ulna are parallel. When the palm is turned face down, the radius crosses over the ulna.

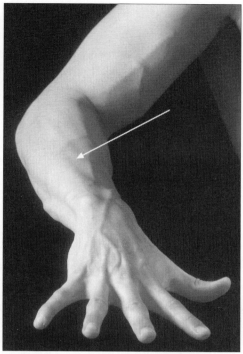

Fig. 3-20 Surface characteristics of the lower arm during pronation (turning of the radius).

This blocky group of bones is located at the end of the humerus and the beginning of the ulna. The rounded head of the ulna can be seen at the wrist.

Three groups divide the bones of the hand. They are the carpals, the metacarpals, and the phalanges. The eight carpal bones are arranged at the wrist in two crosswise rows. Their placement makes it easy to bend the hand up and down. Side-to-side movement is more limited.

The five metacarpals of the hand are joined to the four lower carpal bones. The four metacarpals leading to the fingers are quite rigid. In contrast, the metacarpal of the thumb has a joint that allows a great range of movement. When animating the hand, one can take advantage of this maneuverability to position the thumb in practically any direction. The heads of the metacarpals are quite visible when the hand forms a fist. Extending the fingers and thumb makes them disappear.

The phalanges are the 14 bones within the thumb and fingers. They gradually become smaller and taper to flat forms, to which the nails are joined.

When modeling the hand it is important to know its bone structure. Without this knowledge one cannot model an accurate hand. A common error is to model the hand too small. Extended, the hand covers four-fifths of the face. One can usually judge an amateur representation of the human figure by the manner in which the hands are depicted.

THE BONES OF THE LEG

The leg bones are somewhat similar to the ones in the arm. There is one upper leg bone called the femur and two lower leg bones called the tibia and the fibula (Figure 3-21). Just as in the shoulder, there is a ball-and-socket joint at the hip and, similar to the elbow area, there is a hinge joint at the knee. The hinge joint at the ankle corresponds to the one at the wrist.

However, the bones in the leg are heavier and stronger and have less freedom of movement than those in the arm. This is because the leg bones were developed for mobility and weight bearing.

The femur, or thighbone, fits into the pelvis with a ball-and-socket joint that allows restricted motion in every direction. The prominent bulge at the femur, called the greater trochanter (Figure 3-21), marks the widest area of the male hips. In the female, the widest part is lower due to a deposit of fat.

The hinge joint at the knee is similar to the elbow except it allows only backward movement, while the elbow joint allows only forward motion. Viewed from the front and side, the knee is in line with the hip socket. Its shape is somewhat triangular and its lower edge is level with the knee joint.

Figure 3-22 illustrates the bones inside the leg and how they establish its position and alignment. Bones have their greatest width at the joints and it is there that they become visible on the surface.

The tibia in the lower leg is a thick and massive bone that supports the weight of the femur. Its broad head can be seen on the surface and its shaft forms the ridge of the shinbone. The shin is a familiar reference point on the lower leg and is one of the few places where a bone lies directly underneath the skin.

The fibula is slender since it does not carry weight

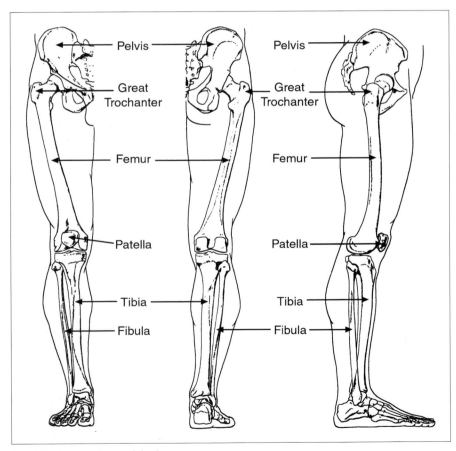

Fig. 3-21 The skeleton of the leg.

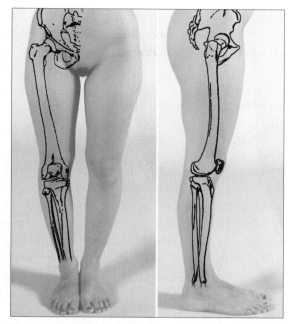

Fig. 3-22 The curve and location of the femur, tibia, and fibula affect the shape of the legs.

but serves as an attachment for the muscles. The head of the fibula shows on the outer surface just below the knee. At its end it projects outward to shape the outer ankle. The inside ankle is positioned higher than the outside ankle (Figure 3-23).

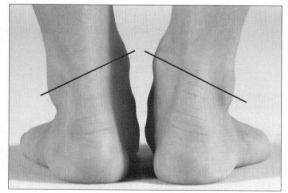

Fig. 3-23 The inside ankle is higher than the outside one.

The shape of the foot is defined almost entirely by its skeleton (Figure 3-24). The muscles and ligaments covering the foot have very little influence on its form. The inside of the foot has an arch, while the outside lies flat. The main longitudinal arch from the heel to the ball of the foot and the secondary transverse arch across the instep support the weight of the body (Figure 3-25).

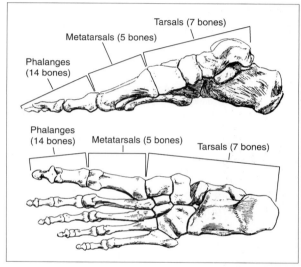

Tarsals (7 bones)
Metatarsals (5 bones)
Phalanges (14 bones)

Phalanges (14 bones)
Metatarsals (5 bones)
Tarsals (7 bones)

Fig. 3-24 The foot bones.

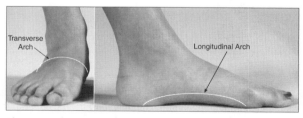

Transverse Arch

Longitudinal Arch

Fig. 3-25 The two arches of the feet.

Three groups of bones divide the foot (Figure 3-24). The tarsals are a group of seven bones that form the heel and part of the instep. The five metatarsals constitute the instep. Fourteen segmented phalanges make up the toes.

The heel of the tarsals is the largest bone in the foot and receives the force of the body weight at the rear of the longitudinal arch. The other five small tarsal bones fit together at the top of the arch. There is room for motion between the tarsals and the metatarsals, which creates a springy rather than a rigid structure. As a result of this, the shocks of walking, jumping, and running are distributed throughout the foot construction.

Corresponding to the metacarpals of the hand are the five metatarsals of the foot. Their undersides are curved, completing the longitudinal arch at their ends. Strong ligaments hold the metatarsals together (Figure 3-26).

The fourteen phalanges number two for the big toe and three each for the remainder of the toes. In length they are shorter than the phalanges of the fingers. The lesser toes are also thinner. The ends of the toes are flattened forms to which the nails are attached.

THE MUSCLES

The surface forms of the body are shaped mostly by the various muscle groups. When a person is active, the superficial contours change during muscle contraction (thickening), expansion, and twisting.

Muscles are made of short, parallel fibers that attach to the bones or other tissues with tendons. These are tough, nonelastic fibers found at the ends of long muscles and at the margins of broad ones.

Muscles pull the bones during contraction. They also keep the skeleton fixed and unmoving. Of interest to animators is the fact that no single muscle ever acts alone. When a muscle contracts, other opposing ones become active to regulate the action of the one that is contracting. By their opposing arrangement, muscles make it possible to perform intricate actions and enable body parts to return to their former rest states.

The female has the same muscles as the male. The difference is that the female's muscles are smaller and usually less developed. Females' muscles are also covered with a thicker fatty layer, which tends to hide their contours. Studying the muscles is much more complicated than learning about the skeleton.

THE MUSCLES OF THE HEAD

Unlike other parts of the body, the muscles of the head are comparatively thin. It is the bones of the skull that most influence the shape of the head.

Those interested in facial animation should take

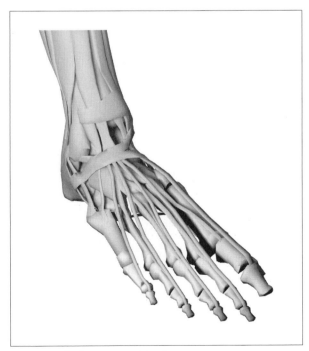

Fig. 3-26 The ligaments of the foot.

some time to study these muscles and the manner in which they affect facial expressions. Chapter 9, which discusses facial animation, identifies the most important muscles responsible for speech and other expressions. A study of these is more important to the animator than to the modeler. When modeling a face, it is of greater value to study the structure of the skull.

Figure 3-27 names the most distinctive muscles of the head. The largest of these, the temporalis and the masseter, act upon the lower jaw by pulling up on it. Muscles in the neck pull down on the mandible (jaw).

A few muscles of the face have the distinction of not being attached to bone. Either these originate in or insert into ligaments or skin or they connect to other muscles. Other muscles develop from bone but terminate in skin, fascia (connective tissue), cartilage (gristly elastic tissue), or fibers from other muscles.

THE MUSCLES OF THE NECK

The neck can be separated into two separate sets of muscles. One group regulates the movement of the mandible, while the other acts upon the skull.

The three muscles of the neck responsible for affecting the base of the tongue and lowering of the jaw are the digastricus, the omohyoid, and the sternohyoid (Figure 3-28).

The splenius, levator scapulae, scalenus, trapezius, and sternomastoid exert influence upon the skull and

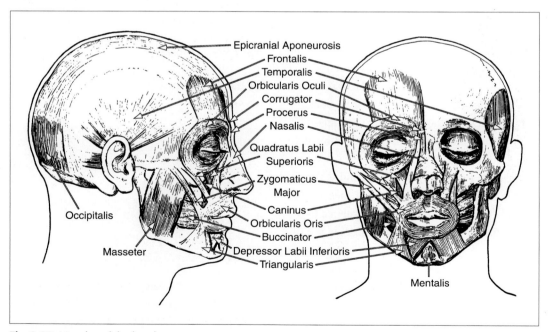

Epicranial Aponeurosis
Frontalis
Temporalis
Orbicularis Oculi
Corrugator
Procerus
Nasalis
Quadratus Labii Superioris
Zygomaticus Major
Caninus
Orbicularis Oris
Buccinator
Depressor Labii Inferioris
Triangularis
Occipitalis
Masseter
Mentalis

Fig. 3-27 Muscles of the head.

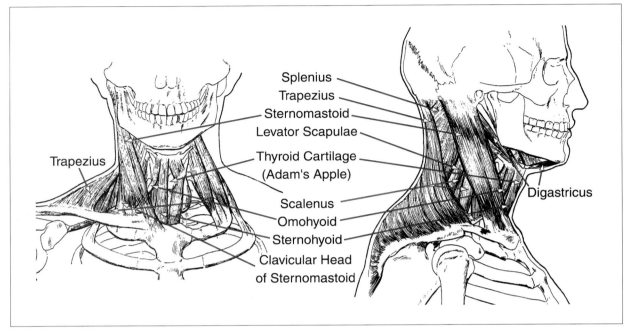

Fig. 3-28 Muscles of the neck.

neck vertebrae (Figure 3-28). The main function of the splenius is to tilt the head back and assist in angling it sideways. The levator scapulae also aids in inclining the skull to the side. The principal muscle responsible for inclining the head to the side is the scalenus. This deep muscle inserts into the first rib, enabling it to exert a strong pull on the skull.

Unlike the splenius, levator scapulae, and scalenus, which do not normally show on the surface except when the head is turned a considerable distance to the side, the trapezius and sternomastoid muscles are often conspicuous on the surface of the neck (Figure 3-29). Viewed from the front and the back, the trapezius appears as a flat inclining plane. The sternomastoid muscle is prominently visible when the head is turned to the side. In concert the trapezius and sternomastoid tilt the skull backward and rotate the head. Individ-

ually they help lean the skull to the side. The two sternomastoid muscles are attached by cords at the pit of the neck, which form a V shape that is almost always visible.

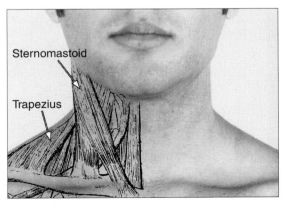

Fig. 3-29 The two most prominent muscles of the neck.

THE MUSCLES OF THE TORSO

The torso's structural feature is a result of its erect posture. Unlike in other mammals, the shoulders do not need to support the head and chest, and therefore are separated at a distance to increase the usefulness of the arms. The chest cavity is distinguished by its width rather than its depth.

Two groups of muscles act upon the upper and lower trunk. The top group affects the shoulders and upper arms, while the lower set of muscles stretching from the rib cage to the pelvis manipulates the motions at the waist. Figure 3-30 illustrates the superficial muscles of the torso.

The trapezius muscle forms a diamond shape that extends from the base of the skull to the middle of the back. The top section of the trapezius is an upright base at the back of the neck. The middle part is a thick, slanting ridge that sits on top of the shoulders. The lower segment is relatively thin and conforms to the shape of the rib cage and edges of the shoulder blades. Running down the middle of the trapezius muscle is a spear-shaped flat tendinous area. This is the region where the spinous processes of the vertebrae become visible on the surface (Figure 3-31). The trapezius bends the head back, raises and pulls back the shoulders, and rotates the shoulder blades.

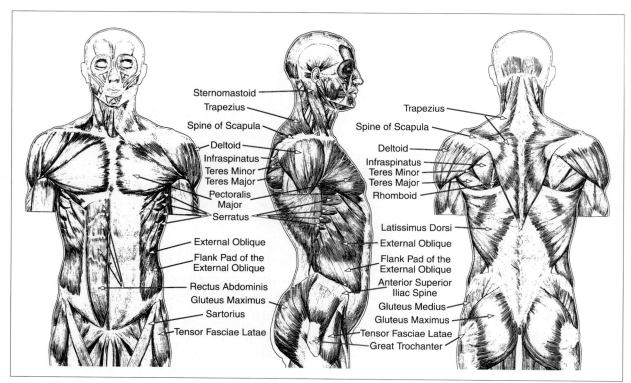

Fig. 3-30 The muscles of the torso.

Fig. 3-31 The spinous processes of the vertebrae become visible in the middle of the trapezius muscle.

A number of saw-shaped strips make up the serratus muscle. It is a large and deep muscle that pulls the shoulder blade forward and raises its lower corner. This function contributes greatly to various arm movements. Each of the four fleshy points on both sides of the torso are more noticeable when the arm is raised.

The pectoralis major is a triangle-shaped muscle of the breast that is attached to the collarbone and breastbone. Its thickest fibers converge under the armpit and attach to the upper arm bone. Its main activity is to bring the arm forward. The contours of the muscle are often visible in the male but not in the female, where they are completely obscured by the breast (Figure 3-32).

Another triangle-shaped muscle that appears at the back and extends to the side is the latissimus dorsi. Similar to the pectoralis, its fibers twist just before

Fig. 3-32 The breasts point slightly away from each other, with the nipples appearing on the outside of center.

inserting into the front of the arm bone. The latissimus dorsi pulls the arm backward. In concert with the pectoral and teres major, it draws the arm down and in toward the body.

Four groups of muscles—the deltoid, the infraspinatus, the teres major, and the teres minor—originate from the shoulder girdle and attach to the humerus (Figure 3-33). They assist one another in pulling the arm.

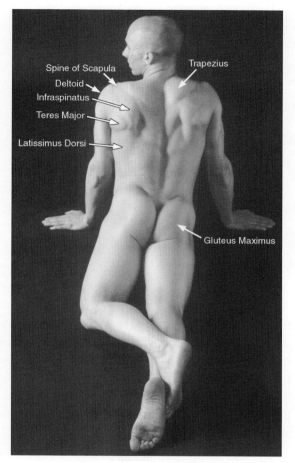

Spine of Scapula
Deltoid
Infraspinatus
Teres Major
Latissimus Dorsi
Trapezius
Gluteus Maximus

Fig. 3-33 Some of the more superficial muscles seen on the back of the upper and lower torso.

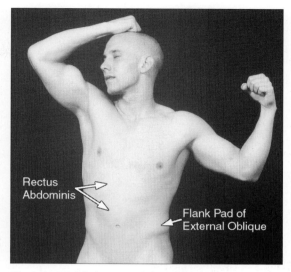

Rectus Abdominis
Flank Pad of External Oblique

Fig. 3-34 Visible lower muscles of the front torso.

most featured muscles in Greek and Roman sculptures. The rectus abdominis is covered by a thin tendinous sheath. The rectus muscle is thickest around the navel. In well-developed bodies it is characterized by two rows of four fleshy pads, each row separated by horizontal tendons. Vertical furrows of tendons create borders between each of the four muscle groups. The rectus abdominis bends the body forward at the waist. Between the gluteus medius and the gluteous maximus is the dimple of the thigh (Figure 3-35). These two gluteal muscles will be discussed later, along with the muscles of the leg.

The lower set of muscles includes the external oblique and the rectus abdominis. The external oblique becomes most noticeable at the root of the thigh. This is called the flank pad (Figure 3-34). It was one of the

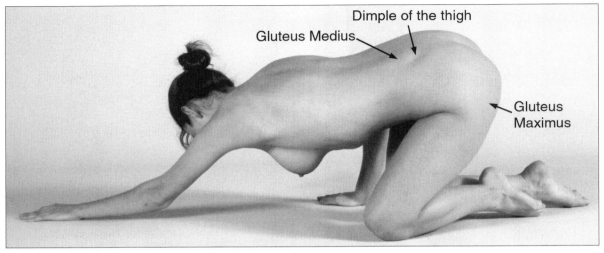

Fig. 3-35 Between the gluteal muscles is the conspicuous dimple of the thigh.

THE MUSCLES OF THE ARM

The muscles of the arm can be divided into two groups. The upper set controls the elbow hinge joint, while the lower set manipulates the wrist hinge joint. When you visualize the arm hanging at the side of the torso, the upper arm muscle groups are located on the front and back of the arm. These act as flexors and extensors to pull the lower arm up. The muscle groups in the lower arm are located side by side to maneuver the hinge joint of the wrist at a right angle to the elbow process. Figure 3-36 illustrates some of the familiar muscle groups of the arm.

The deltoid is considered both a shoulder and an arm muscle. This heavy, triangular-shaped muscle helps bring the arm forward and back.

Two well-known muscle groups are found on the upper arm: the triceps and the biceps. The triceps derive their name from their long lateral, and medial heads. They are located on the back of the humerus (upper arm bone) and extend its full length to the elbow. In a relaxed state they appear as one muscle on the surface, but when tensed they become more distinct. The biceps are long muscles that taper at each end. Their name comes from the two heads that arise from two separate points on the shoulder blade. The biceps flex the arm at the elbow for efforts such as climbing. The triceps are extensors that oppose the actions of the biceps.

Another muscle found between the biceps and the triceps is the brachialis. Working in concert with the biceps, it acts as a flexor of the forearm. This muscle is rarely seen on the surface.

The lower arm muscles can be divided into the flexor and the extensor groups. These control the actions of the wrist and hand. They also twist the forearm and operate the movements of the fingers. As flexors, they pull the fingers together to make a fist. When acting as extensors, they stretch out the fingers. Two muscles, the supinator longus and the pronator teres, draw the radius over the ulna in a circular motion. Although there are 13 muscles in the forearm, the supinator longus and the flexor

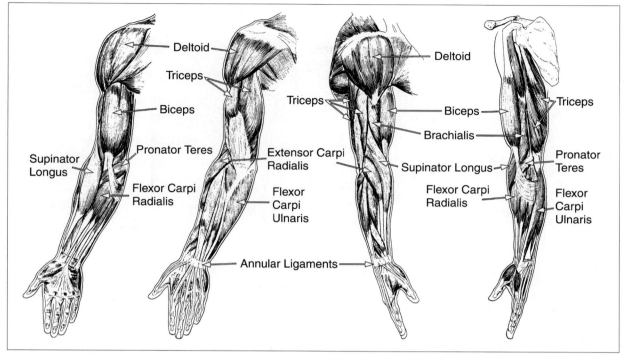

Fig. 3-36 Muscles of the arm.

carpi radialis make it appear to have only three muscles.

THE MUSCLES OF THE LEG

The pelvis is the supporting base of the upper body weight. It also serves as a fixed foundation for the movements of the legs. This carries over to an inverse kinematics setup in which the parent (pelvis) and right and left hipbones are unaffected by IK so as to act as stabilizing forces for the IK-driven legs.

Figure 3-37 illustrates some of the main muscles of the leg. The gluteus medius and gluteus maximus begin the contours of the leg. The gluteus maximus is the largest and strongest muscle of the body. It acts as

an extensor muscle, drawing the leg back for activities such as walking, running, and jumping. It also aids in holding the body upright. On the surface the buttock has a rectangular shape. This is not due to the shape of the muscle but rather to a deep overlay of fatty tissue.

Three sets of muscles on the thigh, or upper leg, control its movements and position. The front group, composed of the rectus femoris, the vastus lateralis, the vastus medialis, and the sartorius, straightens the leg at the knee. The rectus femoris, vastus lateralis, and vastus medialis appear on the surface when the leg is tensed. The lower part of the vastus medialis is often noticeable as a tear-shaped muscle above the knee. These three muscles act as extensors of the lower leg at the knee. The rectus femoris is the pri-

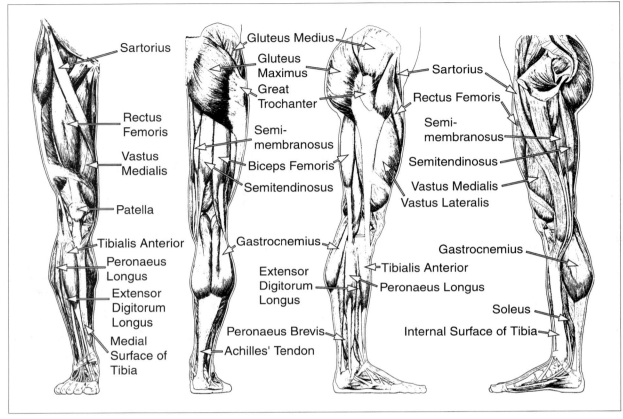

Fig. 3-37 The leg muscles.

mary flexor of the thigh at the hip joint. The sartorius is a long, thin band that runs diagonally across the front of the leg to end below the knee, where it inserts into the tibia. It does not have much of an effect on the surface forms of the leg. Its function is to help flex the thigh at the hip and the lower leg at the knee.

Sometimes referred to as the hamstring muscles, the biceps femoris, the semimembranosus, and the semitendinosus are part of the back thigh muscles. They act as the flexors to oppose the actions of the front extensors by bending the leg backward at the knee. The tendons and lower fibers of the semitendi-

nosus and biceps femoris can be seen distinctly on the outside of the knee joint. All three appear as one mass above the knee.

The remaining inside group of upper leg muscles pulls the leg inward toward the body's center of gravity. These adductor muscles are rarely seen individually on the surface due to fatty deposits in this area.

Two sets of muscles control the hinge of the ankle. The front group, situated on both sides of the tibia, flexes the foot and extends the toes. The opposing back group extends the foot and flexes the toes. The heavy top portion of the tibialis anterior is evident on the surface. Its tendon crosses the ankle and is also conspicuous. On the outside of the leg, the extensor digitorum longus extends or lifts the toes and the peronaeus longus pulls up the foot. The gastrocnemius, or calf muscle, is the principal muscle composing the form of the back of the lower leg. Its two heads most often appear as one mass. The soleus is the other calf muscle, which works with the gastrocnemius to extend the foot and keep the body erect. Both the gastrocnemius and the soleus attach to the thick Achilles tendon, which in turn inserts into the heel bone.

PATCH MODELING THE HEAD WITH SPLINES/NURBS

Splines and NURBS can be used to model very detailed and accurate figures. The patch modeling method in which sections of the figure are created allows the greatest amount of control possible. Some of the most visually pleasing 3-D models have been produced with this method.

ADVANTAGES OF PATCH MODELING

Sections of the character are pieced together to form one unified whole. It is similar to stitching a patchwork quilt (Figure 4-1). There are many advantages to patch modeling, such as the following:

1. Complicated parts of the figure can be broken up into sections. One has the freedom to change the direction of the spline mesh anytime it is needed. This is important when modeling complex objects such as humans, composed of various masses moving in every direction.
2. You can choose to hide every part of the model except for the patch you are currently working on. This makes it easier to see and to concentrate on specific parts of the character.

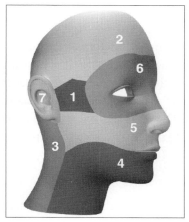

Fig. 4-1 Various patches are modeled separately to make a composite face. The numbers correspond to the order in which each patch was modeled.

3. Since the splines and NURBS can change direction with each separate patch, it is simpler to make openings for the eye, mouth, and ear.

RULES FOR PATCH MODELING

In order for patch modeling to work, several rules need to be adhered to:

1. All edges of the patches have to share points with adjoining ones. If the end points of one patch do

not occupy the same space as the points of the neighboring patch, holes or gaps will show up on the model.

2. When using spline cages that will be surfaced with polygons later, each section of the spline cage mesh must have four or fewer points around it. Sections with more than four points will have holes in them when they are surfaced with polygons.

3. If the patches are modeled with NURBS, adjoining points at the edges will have to be stitched. Sections that are not stitched will show gaps when the mesh is deformed during animation.

4. If your method is to create points first and then connect them to make splines, use the existing points of the neighboring patch as the starting items. This will help you avoid the extra effort of trying to match adjoining patch points.

PREPARATION FOR MODELING

Before starting the modeling process, it helps to bring in templates. These can be in the form of sketches, photos, and/or three-dimensional models.

Since it is very difficult to estimate three-dimensional forms on a flat screen, some people might find it useful to start with photos and/or sketches and use these to block out a quick 3-D model.

The masses of the head, chest, pelvis, and limbs can be conceived of as blocks. Each block or set of planes exists in relationship to the others. Rather than placing them symmetrically, they are oriented on the x, y, and z axes in various degrees.

All of this presents a great opportunity to the 3-D artist. Working with simple primitives or polygons, one can quickly construct a general representation of the body to use as a kind of mannequin (Figure 4-2).

Fig. 4-2 Creating a simple 3-D template of the head. The front- and side-view photos were used as a template for the blocky head.

Subdivision modeling is an excellent way to make the rough 3-D template. When artists have mastered both subdivision and spline/NURBS patch modeling, they then become modelers of a higher order. They are no longer limited to one technique but are fluid in both methods. This allows them to switch back and forth between the two with ease.

Once you have a rough polygon model, a more detailed and curved version can then be modeled on top of this (Figure 4-3). For those who are just starting out, there are various two-dimensional and three-dimensional templates on the accompanying CD-ROM in the "2DTemplates" and "3DTemplates" folders, respectively. Once the procedure for patch modeling is understood, you should be able to work from your own sketches, photos, and simple 3-D templates.

Creating the primitive head to use as a template will probably take about one half hour. You will probably need about two and a half days to complete the patch-modeled head. If you use the templates on the CD-ROM, the head will be finished much faster.

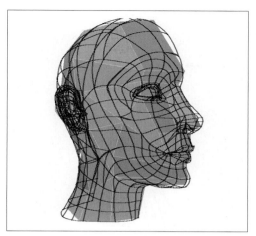

Fig. 4-3 The wireframe shows how the patch model is built on top of the primitive blocky head.

SPLINES/NURBS PATCH MODELING PROCEDURE

Although this section concentrates on the use of splines and NURBS, patch modeling can also be accomplished with polygons. The following directions can be adapted to polygon modeling simply by creating sections of polygons in an order similar to that outlined for splines and NURBS.

Since humans have bilateral symmetry, only half of the figure needs to be modeled. A vertical line extending down the middle of the body divides the head and torso into equal opposite parts. Therefore, be sure to model your character so that the center-half points always lie on the 0 x axis. If these points are moved by accident, you will need to apply a set value to move them back to 0 before mirroring the body. The duplicate middle points of the two halves will then merge to make a seamless human.

As you work through the various steps, you can use the matching templates found on the CD-ROM inside the Chapter 4 folder. They are labeled to correspond with all the following steps.

Patch modeling means that you can divide the face into any number of patches as well as change the order in which the patches are modeled. Therefore, you do not have to follow the steps outlined here. Some of you may decide to study them as a general outline but then proceed to divide the face into sections that you deem best. The Chapter 4 folder on the CD-ROM contains an entire half-face template that you can still use as a guide if you wish.

The following steps begin with simple patches and gradually build up to the most difficult parts. These are the eye area and the ear. By the time you get to them, you should have a fairly good understanding of patch modeling.

The Female Head

Step 1.

As with most tasks, it is usually best to start simple, so the first spline mesh shown in Figure 4-4 defines the temple area. Vertical or horizontal splines are placed along this part and either they are lofted or the points are selected in order and connected. A template of this first step as well as the subsequent ones

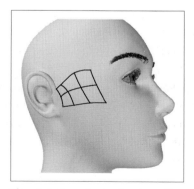

Fig. 4-4 Step 1. A simple spline patch is made in the temple area. The light gray head shows the location of the spline mesh.

can be found in the Chapter 4 folder on the CD-ROM. The poly lines of the template are also named for easier identification and can be found under "Polygon Statistics."

Step 2.

Figure 4-5 shows how new splines are made that shape the cranium. These new splines share points with parts of the previously made splines from Step 1. There should not be any gaps present when neighboring splines share end points. Select the new points on the cranium splines in the right order and make open splines. If you are using NURBS-based modeling software, then loft the curves.

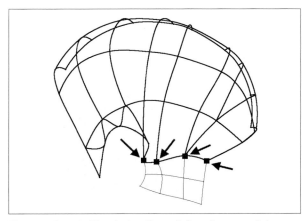

Fig. 4-5 Step 2. The darker lines define the part of the cranium that is modeled next. The arrows indicate the points that are shared between the two patches.

Step 3.

Continuing with the fairly easy sections of the head, model another patch for the lower skull and back of the head (Figure 4-6). Notice the negative space that is beginning to form where the ear will be made later. These points will be utilized at a later stage to shape that complicated part of the head.

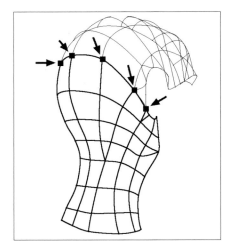

Fig. 4-6 Step 3. The back of the neck and lower skull, shown as darker lines, are made by using the previously made patch points (arrows) and creating new splines.

Step 4.

The jaw and front neck patch is the next section to be completed (Figure 4-7). The existing points from the previous steps are selected in order and used to make the first spline that ends at the corner of the mouth.

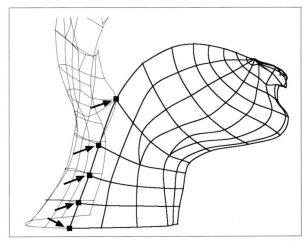

Fig. 4-7 Step 4. Points are selected along the previously made neck part and used to make splines for the jaw and front of the neck (dark lines).

Step 5.

Splines that define the cheek, lower nose, and upper lip make up the next segment of the face (Figure 4-8). There are three previously made patches next to this one. This means a lot more points to merge or stitch. The two most difficult patches, the eye area and the ear, have been saved for last.

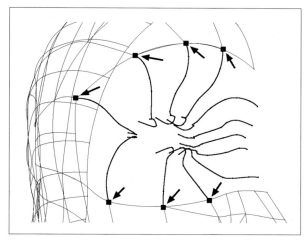

Fig. 4-9 Step 6. The darker radiating lines indicate the beginning of the eye area. Existing points along the previously modeled patches are utilized for these.

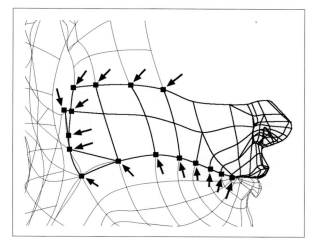

Fig. 4-8 Step 5. The cheek, lower nose, and upper lip are modeled next. Notice how many points (arrows) are now sharing the same space with adjoining patches.

Step 6.

The section around the eye is modeled as the next patch (Figure 4-9). You can create radiating splines that go into the eye socket. The points at the perimeter can serve as the starting region for some of these. Closed circular splines connect many of them (Figure 4-10).

Step 7.

The ear, which is the most complicated part, was saved for this step. If you have been toughing it out by not using the templates on the CD-ROM, then at this

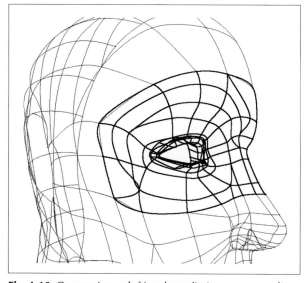

Fig. 4-10 Connecting or lofting the radiating eye area splines produces the next-to-final patch (dark lines).

point you might want to make an exception. Figure 4-11 shows how splines radiate outward from inside the ear and end at the points around the ear opening. It

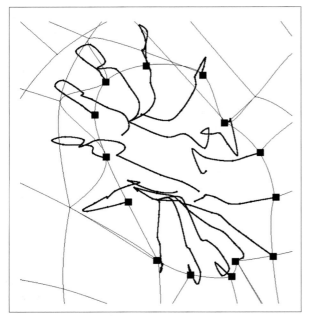

Fig. 4-11 Step 7. The existing points around the ear hole are used as the ends of the radiating ear splines.

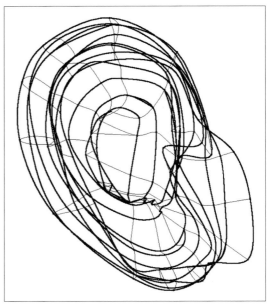

Fig. 4-12 Either the ear splines are lofted or the points are connected with closed splines to finish the ear.

is important to use the same points around the ear to avoid getting gaps between the ear and the rest of the head. Figure 4-12 illustrates how the radiating splines are connected either by lofting or by selecting points in order and connecting them with closed splines. The ear and its placement against the head can be seen in Figure 4-13. The head and ear should match seamlessly since the points at the outer perimeter of the ear occupy the same space as the ones on the head mesh. The shaded view of the ear can be seen in Figure 4-14.

The spline cage mesh can now be made into one seamless head by merging all the points that share the same space at the edge of each patch. Surfacing the spline mesh with polygons in a program like Lightwave can be accomplished by applying the Auto-Patcher plug-in. The AutoPatcher setting can be as low as 0 if you are planning to convert the polygons

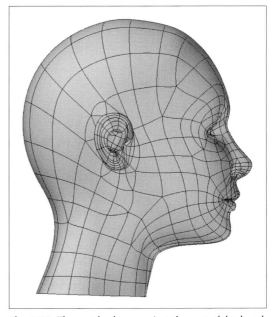

Fig. 4-13 The patched ear against the rest of the head.

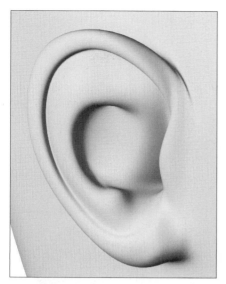

Fig. 4-14 A shaded view of the completed ear against the rest of the head.

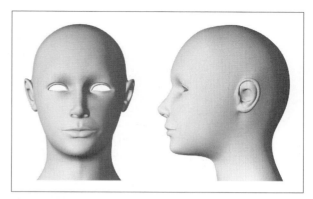

Fig. 4-15 The female head at this stage of the modeling process.

into subdivision surfaces. Make all the surface normals one-sided and align them to face outward.

Rather than merging the spline cage, some may prefer to autopatch each individual section and then separate the polygons by cutting and pasting them into another layer. After making all the surface normals face one direction (outward), the polygon patches can then be merged into one. If your software has subdivision capabilities, check that all your polygons are either three- or four-sided. Delete any one- and two-point polygons and split up any that have more than four sides. Merge all duplicate points and polygons and then turn on subdivision mode to smooth all the edges. Your patch division should not have to be set any higher than three.

If you have been working with NURBS and have completed all the stitching of the various patches, you should now have a joined wire mesh head.

Figure 4-15 shows the female head at this stage of the modeling process.

The Male Head

You can follow the previous patch modeling directions to model the male head. Figure 4-16 illustrates the seven patch sections that make up the total head. The divisions are very similar to the ones on the female head.

If you are using the male templates from the CD-ROM, you should notice that the features on the male head are more pronounced (Figure 4-17). Compared to the female, the male usually has larger brows, a more discernible nose, a strong chin, and an Adam's apple.

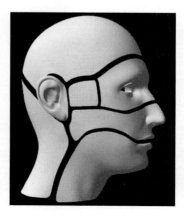

Fig. 4-16 The patch sections for the male head.

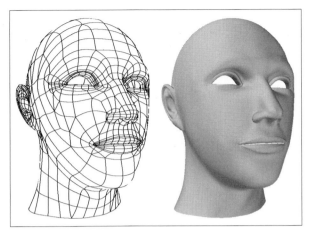

Fig. 4-17 Wireframe and shaded views of the male head.

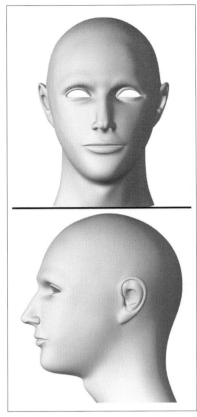

Fig. 4-19 The finished male head.

Figure 4-18 compares the wireframe views of the male and female heads. The female has delicate features, while the male appears to be more rugged.

Figure 4-19 shows several views of the final male head. If you want to continue patch modeling the rest of the female or male, then turn to Chapter 5. Those of you who are using subdivision or box modeling can follow the steps in the next section.

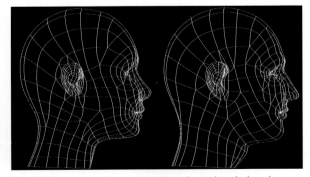

Fig. 4-18 A comparison of the female and male heads.

SUBDIVISION MODELING THE HEAD WITH POLYGONS

Subdivision modeling is a procedure for creating smooth models while keeping the total polygon count at a low level. Point counts are small so that the sculpting process is less confusing.

The following steps will take you through the process of modeling a human head. Your software should have the capability to bevel-extrude polygons and to implement subdivision surfaces. As with most subdivision modeling techniques, you start with a box.

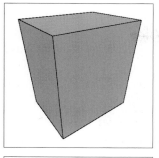

Fig. 4-20 Step 1. Making a box.

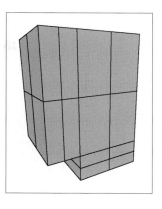

Fig. 4-22 Step 3. Dividing the head into even smaller polygons.

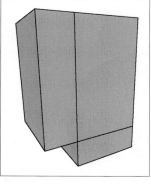

Fig. 4-21 Step 2. Dividing the box.

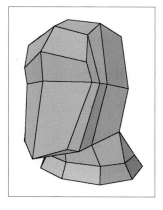

Fig. 4-23 Step 4. Making the general shape of the head.

Step 1.
Make a box (Figure 4-20).

Step 2.
Subdivide the box with the knife tool (Figure 4-21).

Step 3.
Subdivide the head once more like the one in Figure 4-22.

Step 4.
Start shaping the head by moving points (Figure 4-23). Work back and forth between subdivision mode and the low-poly model. The nose will be modeled later.

Step 5.
Delete half the head and use the knife tool to split the polygons near the edge of the cut end (Figure 4-24).

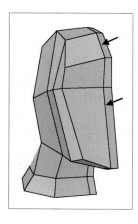

Fig. 4-24 Step 5. After deleting half the head, polygons are split vertically near the middle (arrows).

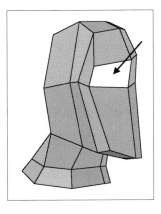

Fig. 4-25 Step 6. Creating an eye hole by deleting a polygon.

The points at the cut have to line up at a value of 0 on the x axis.

Step 6.
Delete the polygon around the eye area (Figure 4-25).

Step 7.
Select the points around the eye opening, copy them, deselect them, hide everything, paste the points, and use the stretch tool to move them in. Show everything, select four points at a time, and make a polygon out of them (Figure 4-26). Incidentally, this is another method of subdivision modeling. Points are made one at a time, selected in order, and made into polygons.

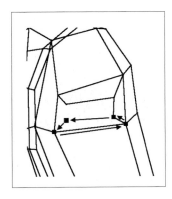

Fig. 4-26 Step 7. Points are made, selected, and turned into polygons for the inside portion of the eye.

One can build an entire human this way, but it is very slow and tedious work. When you consider that one half side of a typical low-polygon human can have over 1300 points . . . well, you get the idea.

Another approach is to copy the points into another layer, make the first layer visible underneath, move the points to the right position, paste them back to the first layer, and then select four at a time and make polygons out of them. Continue building extra polygons inside the eye opening. Use a knife tool and insert the point tool to split larger polygons into smaller ones. Move the points to shape the eye area, including the eyelids (Figures 4-27 and 4-28).

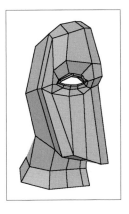

Fig. 4-27 The eye area is split into smaller polygons and shaped.

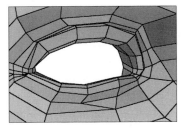

Fig. 4-28 A close-up view of the eye area in low-polygon mode.

Figure 4-29 shows the eye area in subdivision mode. Make sure none of the polygons have more than four points around them. Get Polygon Statistics to select and get rid of one- and two-point polygons.

Fig. 4-29 The eye opening in smooth subdivision mode.

Step 8.

Give the overall head more detail and a better shape by splitting up polygons and moving points. Work in both low-polygon and subdivision modes. Check your polygon statistics to get rid of any unwanted two- and three-point polygons. Any polygons that have more than four sides will have to be split up.

Use the knife tool to divide the polygons around the mouth area. Delete the polygons to make an opening for the mouth (Figure 4-30).

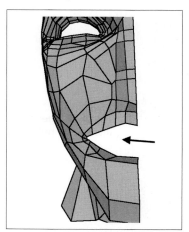

Fig. 4-30 Step 8. Polygons around the mouth are divided and some are eliminated to make the mouth opening.

Step 9.

Select the points around the mouth opening, copy them, deselect them, hide everything, paste the points, and use the stretch tool to move them in. Show everything, select four points at a time, and make a polygon. Continue making new points for the lips and make poly-

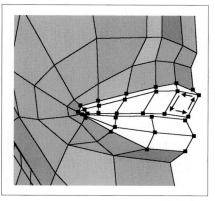

Fig. 4-31 Step 9. Making polygons out of points for the lips and the inside part of the mouth. The black points and connecting lines indicate where new polygons will be created for the lips.

gons out of every four. The corner of the mouth will most likely require three-sided polygons (Figure 4-31).

Step 10.

Continue building extra polygons to make the lips. Once you have the general shape, split the lip polygons to refine the mouth (Figure 4-32).

The inside walls of the mouth, in which the teeth and tongue will be placed, can be made by selecting the points along the inside edge of the lips, making a polygon, and extruding it back. The extruded polygons can then be divided and shaped to make the hol-

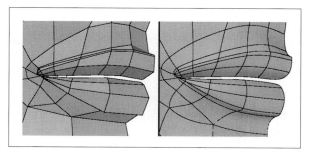

Fig. 4-32 Step 10. The lips are refined by splitting polygons and moving points. The left view shows the low-polygon lips, while the right one is in subdivision mode.

low of the mouth. Select the inside mouth polygons, name them, and flip the polygons inward (Figure 4-33). Figure 4-34 shows the head in subdivision mode, so far. The nose will be modeled next.

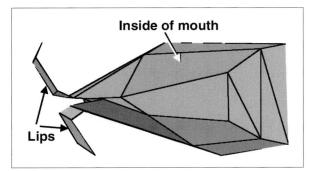

Fig. 4-33 Polygons are flipped inward for the inside part of the mouth.

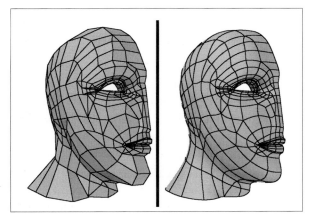

Fig. 4-34 The head at this stage of the modeling process, in both low-polygon (left) and subdivision mode (right). The nose and ear will be modeled next.

Step 11.

Now it is time to bevel out the nose. Before you can do this, you will need to merge the polygons at the nose so that only one large one is beveled out. Temporarily, you will have a nose polygon with more than

four sides. Select the polygon where the nose is located and bevel it out. Shape it somewhat like the one in Figure 4-35. Make sure the points of the nose in the middle of the head are at 0 x value.

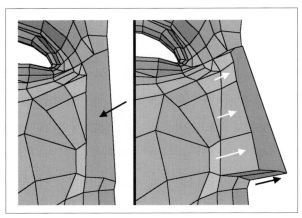

Fig. 4-35 Step 11. Beveling out the nose. The illustration on the left shows how polygons in the nose are merged into one. The image on the right displays the polygon as it is beveled out.

Step 12.

Delete the polygon of the nose that is at the 0 x axis so that the face still looks hollow from the side view (Figure 4-36).

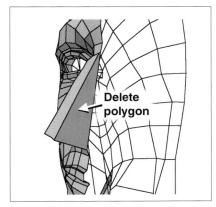

Fig. 4-36 Step 12. Deleting the inside nose polygon at the 0 x axis.

Step 13.

Split the polygons on the side of the nose into smaller ones and begin shaping the wing of the nose by either beveling out a polygon in that location or pulling points out. Work back and forth between the rough polygon display and subdivision mode (Figure 4-37).

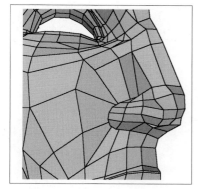

Fig. 4-37 Step 13. Splitting the nose polygons and moving points for more detail.

Step 14.

Now it's time to make the nostril. Select the polygons that will form the nostril hole and merge them into one (Figure 4-38). For the moment, the nostril poly-

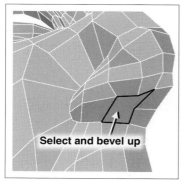

Select and bevel up

Fig. 4-38 Step 14. The polygons for the nostril are merged into one and beveled up.

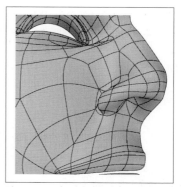

Fig. 4-39 The beveled nostril polygons are split into smaller ones.

gon will have more than four points around it. Select and bevel this polygon up into the nose. Select only the inside nostril polygons and split them near the opening into smaller ones (Figure 4-39). Select points and move them to fine-tune the shape of the nose. Split any polygons that have more than four sides into ones with three or four sides. Work back and forth in subdivision and low-polygon modes.

Step 15.

Before starting work on the ear, give the head a better shape. The polygons should follow the direction of the facial muscles. You can do this by splitting polygons and moving the new points in both subdivision and low-polygon modes. Select the polygons at the bottom of the neck and delete them so the head is hollow when seen from the bottom and the side.

When shaping the head in subdivision mode, try pulling points in the perspective window with Wireframe Shade on. Figure 4-40 shows the head just before working on the ear.

Step 16.

There is an old saying that one can often judge a drawing by the manner in which the ears and hands

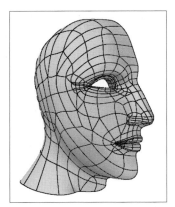

Fig. 4-40 Step 15. Improving the shape of the head by pulling and pushing points.

were executed. This holds true with 3-D modeling. Often a face will look fine until one looks more closely at the ear. This is where you will usually find the weakness in a model. The manner in which the ear is delineated consists of a complex cartilage of concavities and elevations. It is no wonder that many 3-D artists are baffled when it comes to making an ear.

Figure 4-41 illustrates the beginning of the ear. After merging polygons in that section, the points

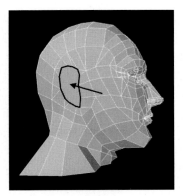

Fig. 4-41 Step 16. Polygons in the ear section are merged and points around it are moved to make the general outline of the ear.

around it are moved to form the outline of the ear. For the time being, the ear polygon will have more than four points. The ones around it will have either three- or four-sided polygons.

Step 17.

Select the ear polygon and bevel it out like the one in Figure 4-42.

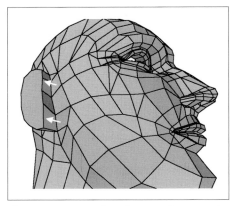

Fig. 4-42 Step 17. Beveling out the ear polygon.

Step 18.

Split the extruded polygons located on the side of the ear and next to the head. Work back and forth between low-polygon and subdivision mode to shape the ear somewhat like the one in Figure 4-43.

Step 19.

Split the large extruded ear polygon into four-sided ones. Work in subdivision mode to give the inside and outside ear a general shape (Figure 4-44).

Step 20.

Refer to photos and anatomy illustrations or have someone pose for you while you shape the front of the

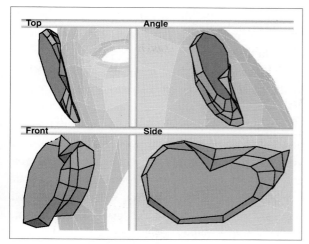

Fig. 4-43 Step 18. The outer part of the ear is split into smaller polygons and points are moved to make the general shape.

ear. Start by splitting the polygons into smaller ones and then pull the extra points. Some points are tucked under others to model the various contortions of the ear's cartilaginous structure.

After a while you will most likely have to push and pull points mostly in subdivision mode since the low-polygon view will be too confusing to try to make sense of. The low-polygon mode can still be useful for finding certain points. More polygons will probably have to be added for shaping the cartilage. Inserting extra points and splitting the polygons in key areas will add to the confusion but are necessary parts of finalizing the ear. Figure 4-45 shows the the ear in low-polygon mode. The final ear can be viewed in Figure 4-46 as a subdivision object.

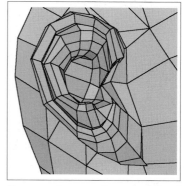

Fig. 4-45 Step 20. The ear is refined even more by continuing to split polygons and moving the resulting extra points.

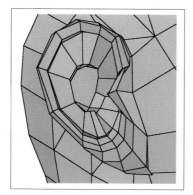

Fig. 4-44 Step 19. Defining the inside and outside of the ear by splitting polygons and moving points.

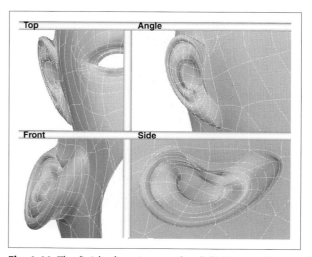

Fig. 4-46 The finished ear in smooth subdivision mode.

95

Step 21.

Select all the points in the middle of the face and use Set Value to move them all on the x axis to a value of 0. Mirror the half head at 0 value on the x axis. Figure 4-47 shows the final half head in subdivision mode.

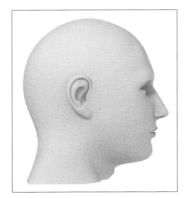

Fig. 4-47 Step 21. The finished subdivision head.

This completes the low-polygon-count subdivision head. Instructions for starting the body can be found in Chapter 5.

If you created a head using the patch modeling method and have converted it into a polygon mesh, your software may allow you to make it into a subdivision object. The simplest way is to just turn on subdivision mode. A preferable way is to go back into your model and simplify it by reducing the polygon count. Merge the smaller polygons while testing your model in subdivision mode. You will find that small polygons often make parts of the object redundant. Why use four polygons when one will yield the same results?

Reducing the polygon count will simplify the later task of modeling morph targets for facial expressions. It will also speed up screen redraws and rendering times since using fewer polygons reduces calculation time on the computer.

MODELING THE TORSO WITH SPLINES/NURBS

Continuing with the figure, the patch modeling technique will now be used to make the torso. Remember, to use this method successfully all edges on the patches have to share points with each of the neighboring ones. The female torso will be modeled first. If you decide to use templates you can find them in the "2DTemplates" and "3DTemplates" folders on the CD-ROM.

THE FEMALE TORSO

Step 1.

The torso will be broken up into several sections. The first one will be the lower neck, clavicle (collarbone), and sternum (breastbone). Open the previously modeled head. Select the points on the lower edge of the neck. Copy these to another layer. They will serve as the starting point of the upper torso. Remember not to move those points because they have to share the same space as the ones on the neck section of the previously modeled head. Figure 5-1 shows the points that were used from the neck and how they will be part of the upper

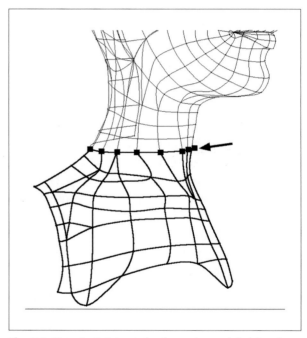

Fig. 5-1 Step 1. Points at the formerly modeled head are selected to serve as a start to the upper torso shown here with darker lines.

torso. Figure 5-2 shows how either the vertical lines are lofted or their points are connected to make the upper torso mesh. Note the curved shape at the bottom, which begins to outline the perimeter of the breast.

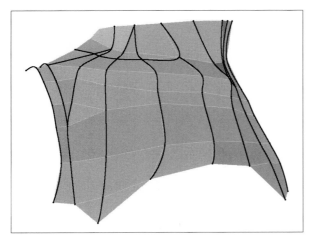

Fig. 5-2 Either the darker vertical lines for the upper torso are lofted or their points are connected to make cross-sectional splines.

Step 2.

Starting with the points at the bottom of the previously made upper torso, radiating splines are drawn that outline the shape of the breast (Figure 5-3). These lines are then lofted or their points are connected to make closed circular splines around the breast. Figure 5-4 shows the two sections shaded. You can see that since they share points, they appear seamless. These mutual points should be either stitched or merged.

Step 3.

The front lower part of the torso is modeled next. Figure 5-5 shows the long splines that extend down to the groin and the top of the leg. As before, existing points located at the bottom of the last patch (Step 2) are utilized for the top patch of Step 3. Extra points will be needed around the belly button area.

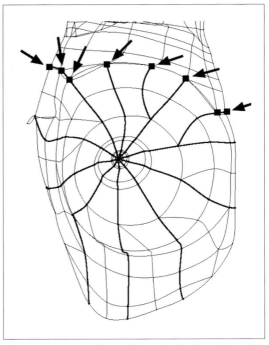

Fig. 5-3 Step 2. Radiating lines (darker lines) form the breast. The arrows point to the vertices that share space with the previously modeled upper torso.

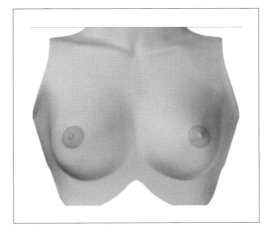

Fig. 5-4 A shaded view of the first two sections. For the sake of clarity the two patches were mirrored.

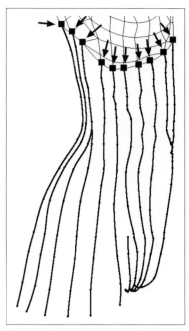

Fig. 5-5 Step 3. Drawing long vertical splines for the front lower torso. Note the arrows pointing to the vertices that share space with the previously modeled patch.

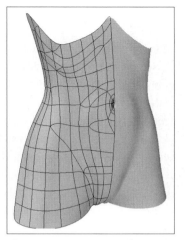

Fig. 5-6 Connecting splines are generated by either selecting points in order and making open splines or lofting the original vertical splines.

Figure 5-6 shows how the vertical splines are connected with horizontal ones. As mentioned in previous steps, software such as Lightwave that utilizes spline cages will let you select points in order and create open splines. Software such as Maya™ that uses NURBS will allow you to loft the vertical splines.

Once you are satisfied with the patch, you can either merge points or stitch them. Figure 5-7 shows the completed front part of the female torso after all the patches have been welded together.

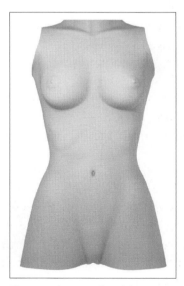

Fig. 5-7 The completed front part of the female torso after the three patches had their points merged or stitched. Mirroring the half front torso makes it easier to see if middle points on the 0 x axis need to be adjusted.

Step 4.

The upper back of the torso is the next patch that will be modeled. Since the back is less complicated than the front, only two patches will be needed to complete the torso. Figure 5-8 shows how points on the side are selected from the previous front torso and the back of the neck patches. New points will have to be made along the back arm opening. These can also be seen in Figure 5-8. Once you have the points, you can create a series of horizontal splines across the back. Except for the opening of the arm, the end points of these splines should occupy the same space as the end points of the previously made front torso and back of the neck.

The back is completed by connecting the horizontal splines with vertical ones. Extra splines are added for details such as the spine and shoulder blade (Figure 5-9).

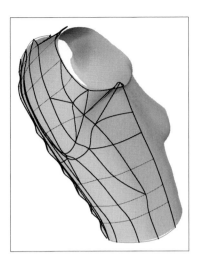

Fig. 5-9 The horizontal splines are connected with vertical ones. Note the extra splines that define the scapula (shoulder blade).

Depending on the type of female that you are modeling, you may decide to add extra splines for some of the ribs (Figure 5-10). The spine can also be shaped more by pulling up every other point on the middle back spline. This will shape the spline into a wavy line to bring out the vertebrae.

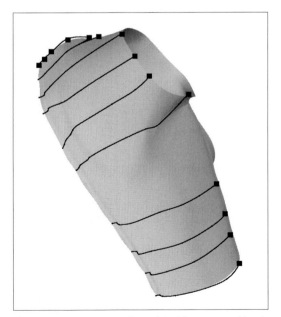

Fig. 5-8 Step 4. Points along the side seam and back of the neck are selected and copied to be used for the upper back torso patch. The light gray shape shows which part of the torso will be modeled for this patch.

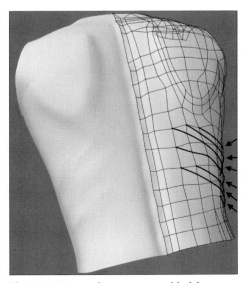

Fig. 5-10 Extra splines are are added for some of the more prominent ribs.

Step 5.

Using the points along the edges of the patches created for Steps 3 and 4 (upper back and front lower torso), create new vertical splines for the buttock (Figure 5-11).

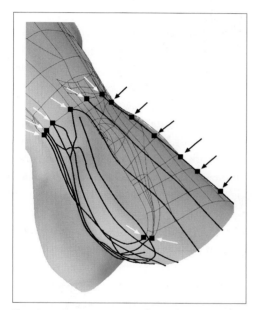

Fig. 5-11 Step 5. Points along the previously modeled upper back and the front lower torso are selected (arrows) and used to make vertical splines of the buttock.

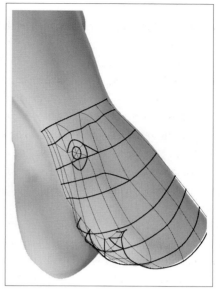

Fig. 5-12 The vertical splines are connected with horizontal ones by either lofting or selecting points in order.

Figure 5-12 illustrates the horizontal splines that are made by either connecting points or lofting the vertical splines.

One detail that should not be ignored is the slightly depressed area to the right and left on the upper part of the buttocks. These two dimples are caused by the angle of the iliac crest of the pelvis. Figure 5-13 shows the extra splines that are inserted to form this depression. Figures 5-14 and 5-15 show the finished female torso from the back and front. These can also be seen

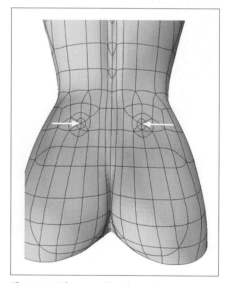

Fig. 5-13 The two dimples at the sacral triangle are formed by the back of the iliac crest on the pelvis. Extra splines are inserted to shape the depression.

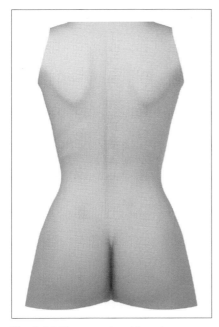

Fig. 5-14 The completed female torso viewed from the back.

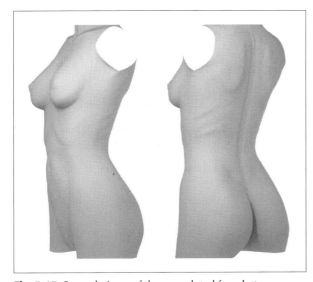

Fig. 5-15 Several views of the completed female torso.

in color in the Chapter 5 folder of the CD-ROM as CD5-14 and CD5-15.

THE MALE TORSO

The differences between the male and the female body will now become more obvious. Aside from the sexual organs, the ideal male body will have less fat than the female one. Unlike the smooth contours of the female, the male is more angular. The muscles on the male are more visible because, unlike the female muscles, they are not hidden by fat deposits. This means that the male model often requires more splines than the female one.

As before, only half of the torso needs to be modeled. Make sure the points along the center seam are lying on the 0 x axis. A command such as Set Value at 0 x Axis should move them there.

Step 1.
Similar to the the female model, the male torso will also be broken up into several sections. Each part will share points with adjoining ones. If you are using templates, you can find them in the "2DTemplates" and "3DTemplates" folders on the CD-ROM.

Starting with the lower part of the neck, select front bottom points and copy and paste them into another layer. Select the points in order and make an open curve out of them. Duplicate this curve and move it down. Continue making new horizontal curves as you work your way down the torso. Some of these will be longer and will require more vertices.

Figure 5-16 illustrates this front part of the torso and the points it shares with the neck. These starting curves that move mostly in a horizontal direction are connected or lofted with vertical ones. Extra splines are added to help define the muscles.

Before moving on to the next bordering area, you may decide to patch the spline cage with polygons.

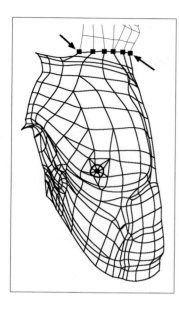

Fig. 5-16 Step 1. The front upper part of the male torso shares vertices with the front bottom section of the neck.

torso (Figure 5-17). Copy and paste these vertices into another layer. Select them in order and make an open curve out of them. You can now continue working toward the bottom of the torso by making new curves out of points, duplicating the first one, or drawing new splines. These splines that run mostly in a horizontal direction define the beginning shape of the lower torso.

Connect the horizontal splines with vertical curves. Extra splines will have to be added to define muscles and other details.

This completes the front part of the male torso. Figure 5-18 illustrates the front section.

If you do this, be sure to separate the polygons from the spline cage by cutting and pasting them into another layer. It is in this layer that you can keep bringing in new sections to build the polygon model. After pasting each polygon mesh in this layer, merge points so that all the separate sections that share vertices at their borders will become one contiguous mesh.

Those of you who are working with software that supports subdivision surfaces may want to implement it on the polygon mesh. As long as all the polygons are only three- or four-sided, you can turn on subdivision mode to further smooth the mesh. As you build your polygon model, it is recommended that you merge smaller polygons. Let subdivision surfaces smooth the curves rather than wasting computer memory on unnecessary polygons.

Step 2.

The front lower section of the male torso is started by selecting points along the bottom of the upper front

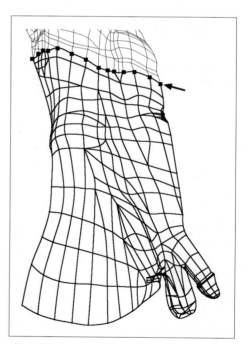

Fig. 5-17 Step 2. Points along the top of the upper torso section are used to start the lower front torso.

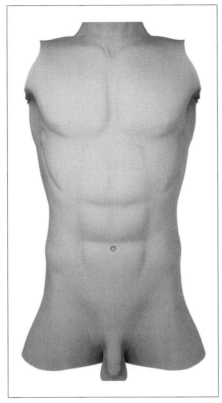

Fig. 5-18 A shaded view of the front torso section.

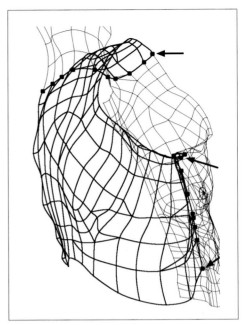

Fig. 5-19 Step 3. The upper back part of the torso shares points with the back of the neck and upper front of the torso.

Step 3.

The spine and scapula (shoulder blade) are the most prominent features of the back upper torso. Figure 5-19 illustrates the points that are shared with the back of the upper neck and the top and the side of the front upper torso segments. Vertices from these previously modeled sections are used to start this upper back piece.

Connecting splines complete this area. Check to make sure that each section has only three or four points around it. One more patch will complete the male torso.

Step 4.

The buttocks and spine are the most prominent sections of the lower back part of the torso. Begin modeling them by using the points along the bottom spline of the upper back and the ones along the side of the lower front torso (Figure 5-20).

Curves that run mostly horizontally define the main form of this patch. Long vertical curves connect these splines. Be sure to add extra curves to make all sections three- or four-sided. Additional curves are also used to shape the dimple caused by the angle of the iliac crest of the pelvis.

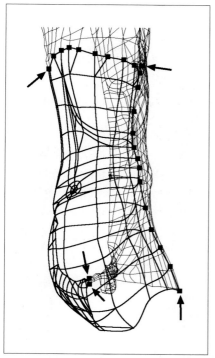

Fig. 5-20 Step 4. The lower back of the torso shares points with the lower front and upper back torso sections.

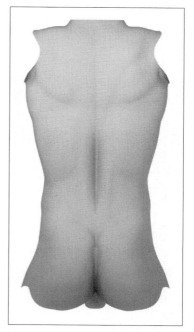

Fig. 5-21 A shaded view of the back torso section.

This completes patch modeling of the male torso. Figure 5-21 shows the back of the torso, and Figure 5-22 depicts some angled views of the male torso. Color images of these can be viewed in the Chapter 5 folder on the CD-ROM.

Chapter 6 continues patch modeling, with instructions for creating the arm, hand, and fingers.

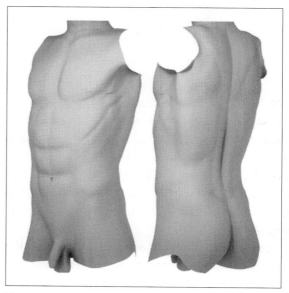

Fig. 5-22 Some angled views of the completed male torso.

SUBDIVISION MODELING THE TORSO WITH POLYGONS

Continuing from Chapter 4, which had you build a polygonal head, the torso will now be modeled using bevel extrusion techniques as well as moving points. Since subdivision mode multiplies polygons internally to smooth the mesh, there is no need to use too many of them to make the torso. The basic form will be sculpted first and then details such as the muscles will be added afterwards.

Step 1.

Open your previously modeled polygon head. Select the points at the bottom of the neck in order, and make a polygon (Figure 5-23).

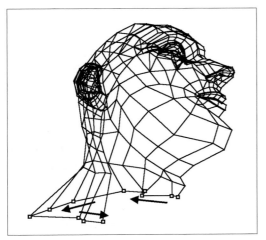

Fig. 5-23 Step 1. Points along the bottom of the neck are selected in order and made into a polygon.

Step 2.

Bevel the bottom polygon down a few times and then bevel it one more time all the way down to the groin area of the figure (Figure 5-24). Use a set value on the middle points to move them on the 0 x axis.

Step 3.

Use the knife tool to split the polygons in the torso (Figure 5-25).

Step 4.

Delete the polygons on the inside of the middle area (Figure 5-26).

Step 5.

Move points to shape the torso both in subdivision mode and in low-poly mode (Figure 5-27). Try working mostly in the perspective window. At this time you are not trying to model muscles and other details. Those will come later after the general form of the torso has been modeled.

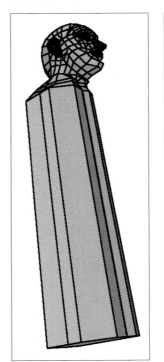
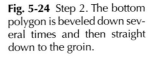
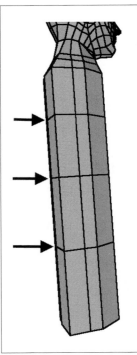

Fig. 5-24 Step 2. The bottom polygon is beveled down several times and then straight down to the groin.

Fig. 5-25 Step 3. The torso is split into several sections horizontally.

Step 6.

Once you have the general shape of the torso, use the knife tool to subdivide it some more and move points to refine the shape of the torso and begin shaping the muscles (Figure 5-28). Places where the skeleton is visible such as the scapula (shoulder blade), thorax (rib cage), spine (backbone), and clavicle (collarbone) are also modeled. Again, work back and forth between subdivision and low-polygon mode.

Step 7.

Details such as muscles basically involve further dividing polygons and moving points. It takes a lot of time and patience to sculpt the muscles, but if you're willing to make the extra effort you will learn a lot

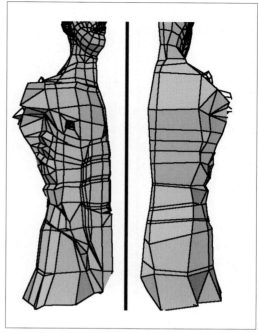

Fig. 5-28 Step 6. The front of the torso is refined by splitting polygons and moving points. The back still needs work.

about modeling and anatomy. Figure 5-29 shows the front and back half torso after sculpting the details. The subdivision or smooth version of the same torso can be seen in Figure 5-30.

HELPFUL HINTS FOR MODELING DETAILS

As you work back and forth pushing and pulling points between low-polygon and subdivision mode, you may want to try a couple of these helpful hints. These can be applied to other parts of the body as well as to the torso.

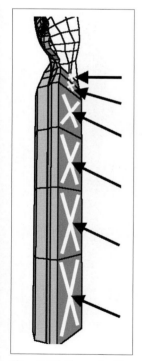

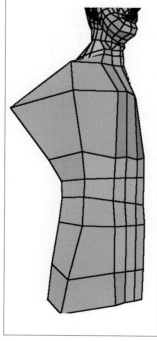

Fig. 5-26 Step 4. The inside polygons at the 0 x axis are deleted.

Fig. 5-27 Step 5. The torso is roughly shaped and polygons are split up more.

1. Do most of your sculpting in the Single Perspective Wireframe Shade window. Create a numeric

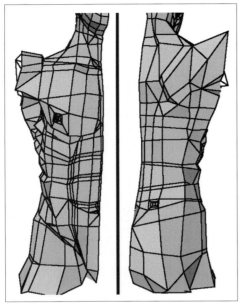

Fig. 5-29 Step 7. The low-polygon version of the finished front and back half torso.

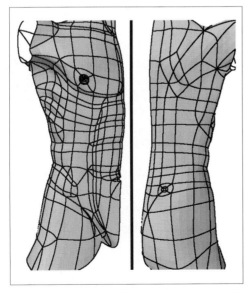

Fig. 5-30 The front and back half torso in subdivision mode.

keyboard shortcut for this view and be sure to turn *off* Show Cages and Show Grid. Show Guides should be *on*. Set the background to a medium green color. Now when you work in subdivision mode in this single-view window, look for the light blue guidelines. Clicking at the end of these guidelines lets you easily select and deselect points. Of course, all this depends on what is available in your software package.

2. If you move any of the points that lie along the middle seam, then be sure to move them back on the 0 x axis. This will ensure that when you mirror-duplicate the half torso, it will merge points along the seam. Vertices that do not rest on the 0 x axis will cause holes and unnatural creases in the middle of the figure.

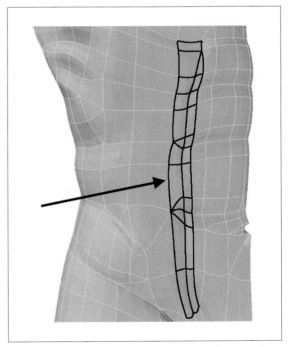

Fig. 5-31 Parallel lines are made to define furrows along the edges of muscle groups.

3. Insert extra points so that they follow the direction of the various muscle groups. When you split polygons, you will, in effect, connect these points, yielding natural curves and lines. Groups of two or three parallel lines are useful for creating grooves where two muscles meet. Split polygons near the furrows so that you have three lines running along the depressions. Pulling in the middle line should suffice to give you the indentation where two muscle groups meet. Figure 5-31 shows a detailed section with three lines in which the middle line is pulled back so that the two outside lines are raised. Most of the creases for the various muscle groups were modeled this way.

4. To get the most control, insert extra points where needed, select the new points in order, and connect them by splitting the polygons. Use both low-poly and subdivision modes to shape the muscles.

COMPLETING THE SUBDIVISION TORSO

The back of the torso is somewhat easier to model than the front. The scapula, or shoulder blade, is pronounced enough to be seen under the skin. The points at the end of the back (0 x axis) are pulled in a little to form the groove along the spine.

Be sure to define the neck muscles. The trapezius muscle starts at the base of the head and extends at an angle down to the scapula (shoulder blade). Its shape sug-

gests a four-sided star. The sternomastoid muscle in the front of the neck suggests a V shape.

When you are finished modeling the torso, mirror the half body and make some adjustments to parts of the body such as the groin area. Points will probably

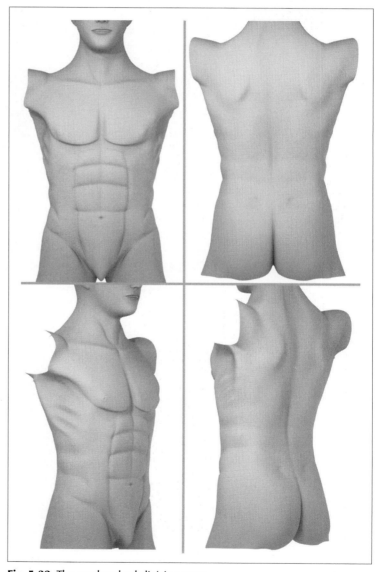

Fig. 5-32 The rendered subdivision torso.

109

have to be pushed and pulled at the center (0 axis). Neighboring points will most likely also need adjusting. Figure 5-32 shows the completed torso in subdivision mode. A color image can be viewed in the Chapter 5 folder of the CD-ROM.

When you are finished adjusting points, delete one half of the body so that you can continue working on details without having to repeat the process for the other half. Be sure to set a value of 0 on the x axis to any points that were moved along the middle seam.

You can continue modeling the low-polygon body by following the directions in Chapter 6. The section for subdivision modeling will have you create the arm, hand, and fingers.

MODELING THE ARM AND HAND WITH SPLINES/NURBS

After completing the torso, the arm will be modeled next. Since the upper arm shares points with patch steps 1, 2, and 4 of the torso, it will be our beginning item.

The female arm will be modeled first. If you decide to use templates you can find them in the "2DTemplates" and "3DTemplates" folders on the CD-ROM.

THE FEMALE ARM

Step 1.

In order to have a seamless transition between the torso and the upper arm, you will need to load in the upper front and back torso as well as the breast patches (Steps 1, 2, and 4). Figure 6-1 shows the points that are selected along the arm opening of the upper torso. These points are made into a closed spline.

The closed spline is then duplicated and positioned along the length of the upper arm. In this case the upper arm extends beyond the elbow joint into part of the lower arm. This will allow us to model the protrusion of the elbow knob along with the rest of the upper arm.

To shape the upper arm you can use a template from the CD-ROM and/or refer to an anatomy book

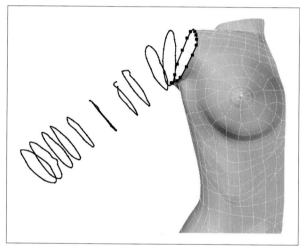

Fig. 6-1 Step 1. The points along the arm opening of the upper torso are selected and made into a closed curve. This is duplicated a number of times and spaced along the upper arm.

and other illustrations. After setting up the closed curves, you can select corresponding points on them and make open splines out of these (Figure 6-2). With some software packages you can simply loft the oval curves.

At this point the upper arm will most likely lack muscle definition. One technique that can help you shape the muscles is to sketch some splines on top of

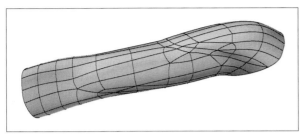

Fig. 6-2 Long connecting splines that run the length of the upper arm are the result of either connecting the closed curves or lofting them.

the upper arm that follow the direction of the muscles. When you do this, you might want to use an anatomy book for reference. As you sketch the lines for the muscles, be sure to move their points so that the lines are placed correctly on the arm (Figure 6-3).

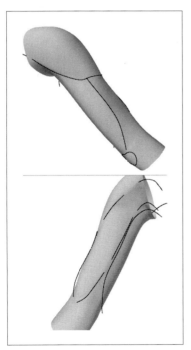

Fig. 6-3 Drawing guidelines helps one visualize the direction and placement of muscles.

After you finish placing these lines put them in another layer. Now you can move points on the arm as well as insert extra splines that follow your previously sketched splines. Figure 6-4 shows some of the extra splines that have been added to the upper arm. By running two to four parallel lines next to each other you can bring out the distinct muscle groups. Since muscles are usually not as distinct on a female as they are on a male, only a couple of lines are paired next to each other. To make the furrow between two muscle groups more distinct just pull down the points along the line between the two. Special attention should be paid to the elbow. Referred to in medical terms as the *olecranon process,* it is a blocky mass at the start of the ulna (lower arm bone). It is in horizontal alignment with the medial and lateral epicondyles of the humerus (upper arm bone). You can feel and see these protuberances. Adding extra splines to shape the elbow is an essential part of modeling the arm.

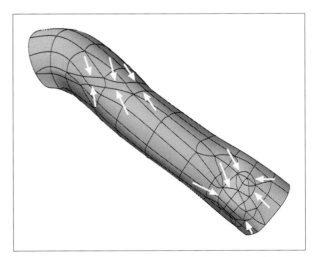

Fig. 6-4 Extra lines that run along the depression between muscle groups are added to the spline mesh. The previously sketched splines were used as templates for these.

Step 2.

To start the lower arm, select the closed curve on the end of the upper arm, copy/paste it, and move the duplicate curve down to form the next segment of the lower arm (Figure 6-5). The curve that was selected in the first place is shared between the upper and lower arm to make a seamless transition.

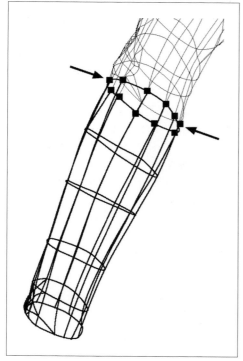

Fig. 6-5 Step 2. The points indicate the end of the upper arm. The closed curve at this junction is duplicated and moved down to make the lower arm splines.

The closed curve is duplicated a number of times to make the supports for the lower arm mesh (Figure 6-6). After scaling and shaping these ovals, connect them by lofting or selecting corresponding points in order.

Fig. 6-6 Duplicate oval splines are connected either by lofting or by selecting points in order.

A distinct feature of the lower arm that should not be ignored is the head or distal end of the ulna (the larger of the two lower arm bones). Located just above the wrist, this small rounded knob can be seen clearly protruding from the little finger side of the forearm. Figure 6-7 shows how closed curves define this area. The middle point is then pulled up.

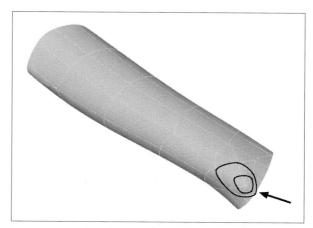

Fig. 6-7 Closed oval curves define the rounded knob at the distal end of the ulna.

113

Once you have completed the lower arm, stitch the points that are shared to the upper arm. Depending on your software, you could also weld or merge these points. Figure 6-8 shows several views of the completed upper and lower arm.

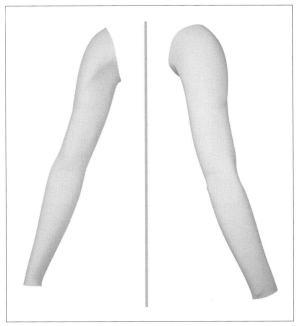

Fig. 6-8 The female arm at this stage of the modeling process.

will simplify the task of making five openings for the thumb and fingers.

For the first step, points along the previously modeled lower arm patch are selected. These are located along the upper half of the wrist (Figure 6-9). The top half of the hand mesh will be modeled in a way that places points along the upper half of the thumb and finger openings (Figure 6-10). Once the half-oval open curves are made, they are lofted or their points are connected to make the upper hand patch (Figure 6-11).

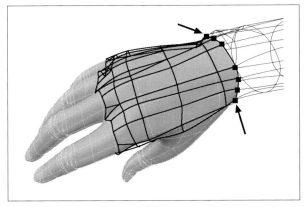

Fig. 6-9 Step 1. Points on the top half of the wrist oval are used to make splines for the upper part of the hand.

THE HAND

Step 1.

Branching is one of the hardest tasks to accomplish in 3-D modeling. When modeling the hand, one has to consider how the fingers and thumb will branch off from it. One way to accomplish this is to split the hand into two halves: the upper and bottom parts. This

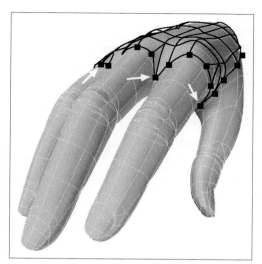

Fig. 6-10 The top halves of the finger and thumb openings are part of the upper hand mesh.

Step 2.

The bottom half of the hand can also be started by selecting points from the end of the lower arm patch. This time you select the bottom-half points including the two middle points that were previously part of the upper hand. This is to ensure that both halves match each other (Figure 6-12).

Figure 6-13 shows some of the points at the boundaries of the upper and lower hand patches that are shared by these patches. In the middle of the web

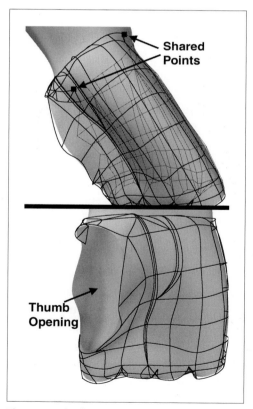

Fig. 6-12 The bottom half of the hand is also started at the wrist. Note the two shared points with the upper half of the hand.

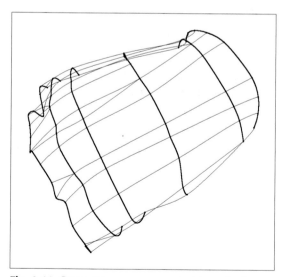

Fig. 6-11 Open curves are connected to make the top part of the hand.

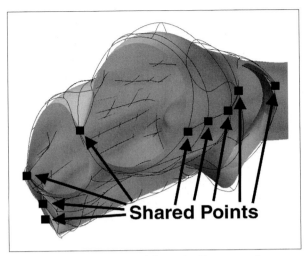

Fig. 6-13 Viewing the hand from the finger openings, one can see the points that are shared at the borderlines of the upper and lower hand.

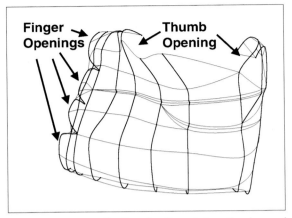

Fig. 6-14 A series of half-oval splines defines the shape of the palm side of the hand. These splines are then connected to complete the mesh. To make creases, extra parallel splines can be inserted.

part of the hand, between the fingers, one can find the points that define both the upper and the lower halves of the fingers.

To start the lower hand patch, create a series of half-oval curves. The first curve shares points with half of the wrist spline at the end of the lower arm. Once you have the curves that define the shape of the lower hand and the area around the thumb and finger openings, connect the splines to make the second hand patch (Figure 6-14). You can also add extra splines for details such as the furrows in the palm. When you are finished modeling the two halves of the hand, merge or stitch the points that are shared by the patches. Once both patches have been made into one mesh, you can merge, weld, or stitch the points to the lower arm. The vertices of both the hand and the lower arm should share the same space at the wrist.

Step 3.

The points that are found around the opening for the thumb will now be used to model the thumb (Figure 6-15). These points are part of the upper and lower hand patches.

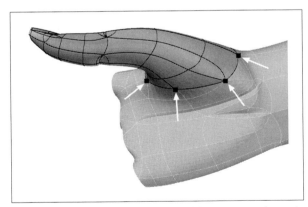

Fig. 6-15 Step 3. The thumb is started from previously made points of the hand. A series of these vertices encircles the opening for the thumb.

Once you have selected the points around the opening of the thumb, you can make them into a closed curve. Duplicate closed curves of varying sizes can now be placed along the length of the thumb (Figure 6-16). The next step is to connect these curves.

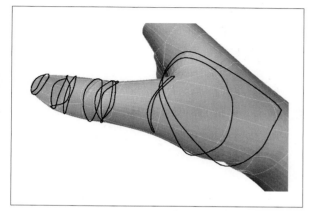

Fig. 6-16 A series of closed oval-shaped curves defines the shape of the thumb.

Figure 6-17 shows the completed thumb mesh after connecting the first oval splines. Extra splines are added for detail. Figure 6-18 shows the completed thumb and nail.

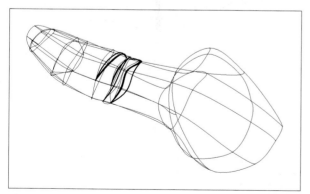

Fig. 6-17 The closed curves are connected and extra splines are inserted (dark lines) to make creases around the joint.

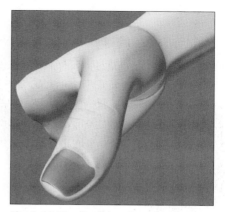

Fig. 6-18 The final thumb and nail.

Step 4.

The index finger, which is next to the thumb, is also modeled by starting with shared points located at the opening of the hand (Figure 6-19). The first oval can then be duplicated a number of times to make the cross sections of the index finger (Figure 6-20).

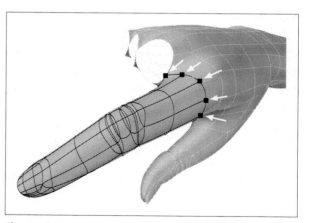

Fig. 6-19 Step 4. Points along the opening for the index finger are selected and made into a closed curve.

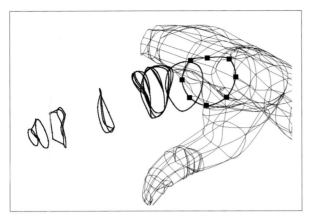

Fig. 6-20 A series of oval closed curves delineates the index finger.

The closed curves are then connected to make the finger mesh. Extra splines are added for details such as the nail and wrinkles (Figure 6-21). The final step for the finger is to merge, weld, or stitch the points to the hand.

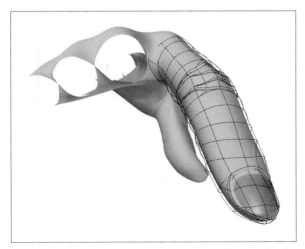

Fig. 6-21 The closed curves are connected to make the index finger.

Step 5.

The middle finger is the next object that is modeled. It is done in a similar fashion as the previous index finger. Figure 6-22 shows how points are selected around the opening and made into the first closed curve.

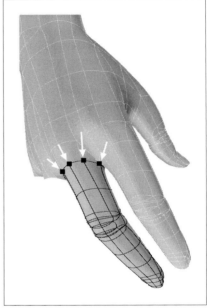

Fig. 6-22 Step 5. The middle finger is modeled like the other digits by first selecting points along the opening.

Steps 6 and 7.

The ring finger and pinky finger complete the hand. Previously made points around these two finger openings on the hand are selected and made into closed curves. Figure 6-23 illustrates the wireframe mesh on top of the shaded view of the hand. The process for modeling these last two digits is the same as for the previously shaped middle and index fingers.

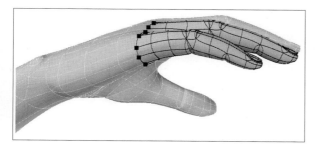

Fig. 6-23 Steps 6 and 7. Completing the hand with the ring and pinky fingers.

Once you complete all the fingers, be sure to merge the points that are shared with those on the hand. Since each of the fingers, the thumb, the hand, and the lower and upper arm share points at their borders, welding, merging, or stitching points should not be a problem. Figure 6-24 shows some rendered views of the finished hand.

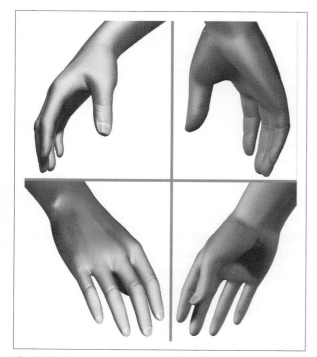

Fig. 6-24 Some rendered views of the hand.

Most of the female has now been modeled. All that is left are the leg and the foot. Figure 6-25 depicts front and back rendered views of the half female.

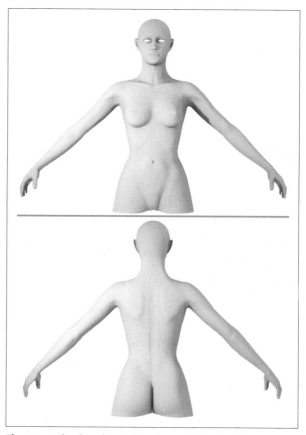

Fig. 6-25 The female at this phase of the modeling procedure.

THE MALE ARM

The process for modeling the male arm is similar to that for the female one. Since there are more muscles that can be seen on the surface, a greater amount of splines will have to be used. Modeling the male hand involves the same process as outlined for the female. To avoid redundancy, only the steps for the upper and lower arm will be discussed here. Refer to the section on modeling the female hand, but use the male hand templates if you need to.

Step 1.

The previously modeled male torso has an opening for the arm. It is there that points are selected in order and made into a closed curve (Figure 6-26). The resulting spline can be cut and pasted into its own layer so that you can build the upper arm separately.

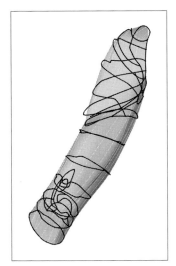

Fig. 6-27 Step 2. The closed curve is duplicated, moved, and shaped to make the structure of the upper arm.

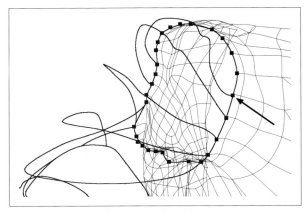

Fig. 6-26 Step 1. Vertices at the shoulder opening of the torso are utilized to make the first closed curve on the upper arm.

As always, it is important not to move the points of the first curve since they have to share the same space with the torso vertices. Later on, the polygons of the upper arm and torso will be unified into one mesh by merging those points. Those of you who are working with splines/NURBS can stitch or weld these points.

Step 2.

After making the first closed curve at the shoulder opening, duplicate it a number of times, move the curves down the length of the arm, and shape each one to make the framework of the upper arm (Figure 6-27). The last closed curve ends just below the elbow.

Points will have to be moved in and out to give the arm a more chiseled look. Consider the pairs of points that will run parallel down and across the arm to outline the neighboring muscles.

Step 3.

Select corresponding points along the closed curves and connect them with open ones (Figure 6-28). These long splines should follow the contours of the muscles. To complete the upper arm, insert extra open curves so that each section has only three or four points around it. Figure 6-29 illustrates various views of the male upper arm. Some may find these useful as a guide for showing the direction of the curves.

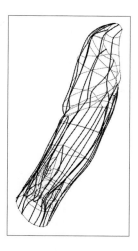

Fig. 6-28 Step 3. Long open curves that run mostly in a vertical direction connect the closed curves.

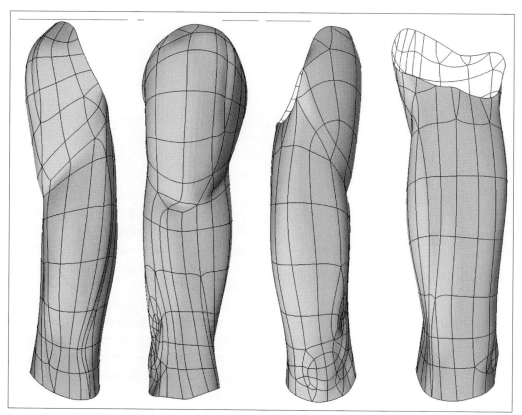

Fig. 6-29 The completed male upper arm. The black lines show how the lines follow the contours of the muscles and the elbow.

If you are planning to patch the spline cage with polygons, then you should do so now to check for holes. As before, separate the polygon mesh from the spline cage. Align all the polygons so they face in the same outward direction.

Step 4.

Start the lower arm by selecting points from the bottom of the upper arm (Figure 6-30). After making a closed curve from these, duplicate them a number of times while positioning each one along the length of the lower arm. Shape these cross sections to make certain muscle groups more prominent.

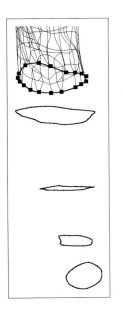

Fig. 6-30 Step 4. Points along the bottom of the upper arm are selected to start the lower arm.

Step 5.

Use open curves to connect the closed ones on the lower arm (Figure 6-31). Some extra curves will have to be added so that each section has only three or four points around it.

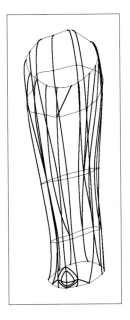

Fig. 6-31 Step 5. Connecting the closed curves with open ones.

This completes the upper and lower parts of the male arm. If you need to patch these sections with polygons in order to see the arm in shaded view, you will most likely want to do so now. It will make reshaping the arm much easier. If you adjust the shape of the arm, make sure that points along the seam where the upper and lower arm meet are not moved until you have merged, stitched, or welded them.

Follow the previous directions for modeling the female hand and apply these to complete the male arm. Figure 6-32 depicts different views of the completed male arm. The almost completed patch-modeled male can be seen in Figure 6-33.

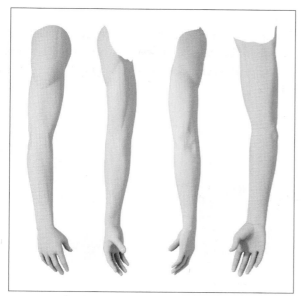

Fig. 6-32 Various views of the completed male arm.

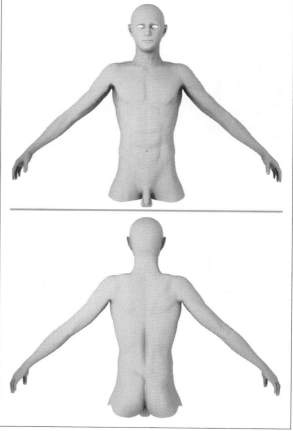

Fig. 6-33 The patch-modeled male at this stage.

Modeling the Arm and Hand with Subdivision Surface Polygons

Step 1.

After finishing the low-polygon torso in Chapter 5 it is now time to make the arm. Using the vertices at the arm opening, select them in order and make a polygon out of them (Figure 6-34).

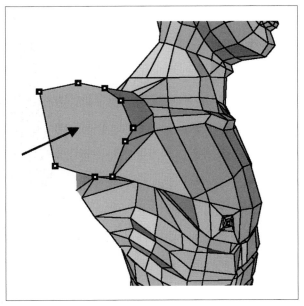

Fig. 6-34 Step 1. A polygon is made from the points at the arm opening. Bevel-extruding it will start the arm.

Step 2.

Bevel or extrude the polygon out. Make the length of the arm to the end of the wrist (Figure 6-35). The hand will be modeled later.

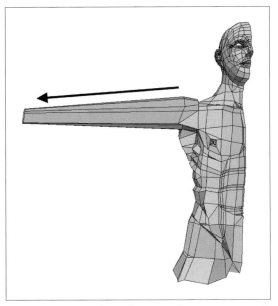

Fig. 6-35 Step 2. The polygon at the arm opening is beveled out to make the length of the arm.

Step 3.

Use the knife tool to slice vertically across the arm. Move the points on the cross sections to shape the arm (Figure 6-36). Do not worry about the muscles yet. They will be modeled a little later.

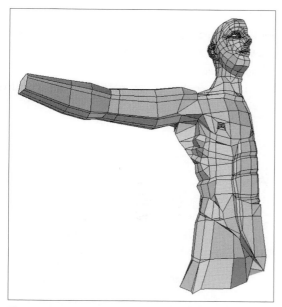

Fig. 6-36 Step 3. The arm is divided into sections by cutting across it vertically. Points are moved to give it a rough shape.

Step 4.

Now it is time to model the muscles on the arm. You can start at the shoulder to sculpt the deltoid, or shoulder muscle (Figure 6-37). The clavicle, or collarbone, should have been modeled when you worked on the torso.

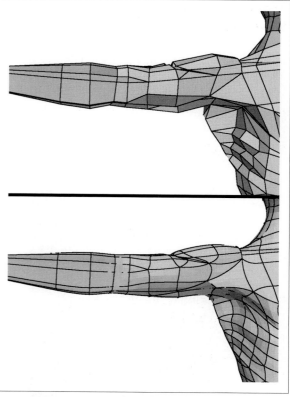

Fig. 6-37 Step 4. Starting the muscles of the upper arm at the deltoid (shoulder muscle). The top image is in low-polygon mode; the lower image shows the model in subdivision structure.

Divide the polygons so that you can pull out specific points. Two lines running parallel and close together can be used to make indentations where two muscle groups meet. One set can be pulled up while the other is pushed down. Use an anatomy book for reference. Work back and forth in low-poly and subdivision modes. Make sure you have only three- and four-sided polygons. Delete any one- and two-point polygons.

Try to move points mostly in subdivision mode using the Perspective Wireframe and Wireframe Shade windows. To keep the arm from looking blocky, you will most likely have to continue dividing polygons.

Step 5.

After completing the muscles on the upper arm, move down toward the lower arm. Just like the upper arm, the lower arm will also need more lines running lengthwise toward the wrist. Insert extra points in places where the muscles are more prominent. Then connect them by selecting them in order and splitting the polygons. Be sure to use some reference material such as an anatomy book that shows the muscles from various viewpoints.

Figure 6-38 shows different views of the finished upper and lower arm in low-polygon mode. Subdivision views of the arm can be seen in Figure 6-39.

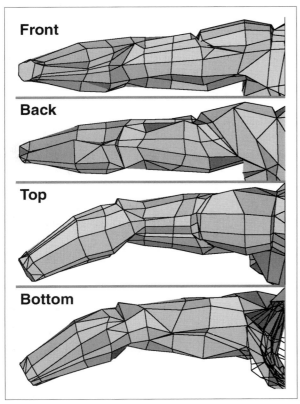

Fig. 6-38 Step 5. The upper and lower parts of the arm in low-polygon structure. The muscles of the arm are now complete.

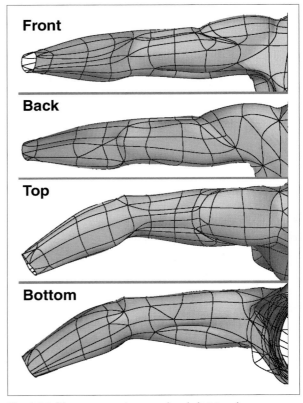

Fig. 6-39 The arm seen in smooth subdivision form.

Step 6.

The next part is to model the hand and fingers. Select the polygon at the end of the wrist and bevel or extrude it out a little (Figure 6-40).

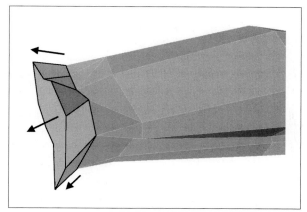

Fig. 6-40 Step 6. Beginning the hand by bevel-extruding at the wrist.

Step 7.

Bevel the hand polygon out several more times. Model a rough approximation of the hand by moving vertices (Figure 6-41).

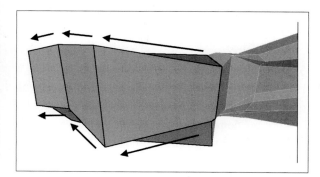

Fig. 6-41 Step 7. Several more bevels create a general shape of the hand.

Step 8.

Refine the shape of the hand in subdivision mode (Figure 6-42). Add extra points and split polygons into smaller ones if you need to.

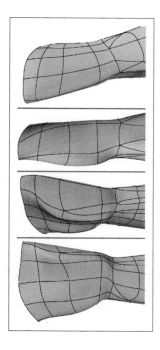

Fig. 6-42 Step 8. Shaping the hand in subdivision form.

Step 9.

Split the polygon on the front of the hand with the knife tool (Figure 6-43). These divisions will be used to bevel-extrude the four fingers later and to shape the hand more accurately.

Fig. 6-43 Step 9. The front hand polygon is divided into four sections for the fingers.

Step 10.

Select the four polygons at the end of the hand and bevel or extrude them out. Do the same with the polygon for the thumb (Figure 6-44).

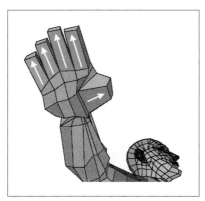

Fig. 6-44 Step 10. Polygons for the fingers and thumb are beveled out.

Step 11.

Use a knife tool to split the polygons on the fingers (Figure 6-45). Start with only two cuts at the joints. Move the points to shape the fingers.

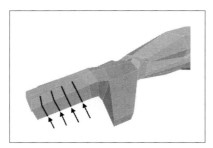

Fig. 6-45 Step 11. Polygons on the fingers and thumb are split into segments for sculpting.

Step 12.

Use low-polygon settings to make the general shapes (Figure 6-46). Switch to subdivision mode to refine them. Split the fingers some more so that you have

extra points for the details. Bend the fingers down into a more relaxed position.

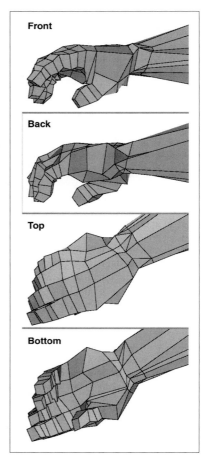

Fig. 6-46 Step 12. Shaping the low-polygon thumb and fingers.

Step 13.

Hand motions are an important part of close-up animation, especially when it has dialogue. To make the hands more convincing, details such as nails should be added. UV mapping can be used later for the creases and wrinkles of the hand.

Figure 6-47 illustrates four steps to modeling the nails:

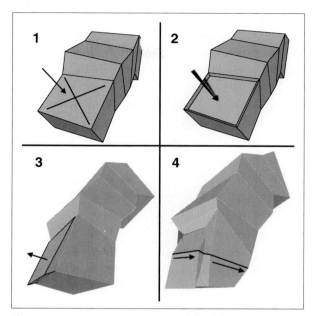

1. Working in low-polygon mode, select the polygon that will be made into the nail.
2. Bevel it down once.
3. While the beveled nail is still selected, bevel it one more time to create another polygon.
4. Move the second beveled polygon up. This will form the nail. Use the knife tool to slice through the middle of the two beveled polygons and the rest of the finger.

Fig. 6-47 Step 13. Four steps to modeling the fingernail.

Select the middle points of the nail polygon and move them up so the nail looks curved.

Extend the two top front points of the nail (second beveled polygon) to give it some length. Tuck the next two lower front points (first beveled polygon) under the nail. Model the rest of the nails on the hand.

Work mostly in subdivision mode as you move points. Figure 6-48 shows the completed nails, fingers, and hand. Assign names, colors, and textures to the nail and the cuticle.

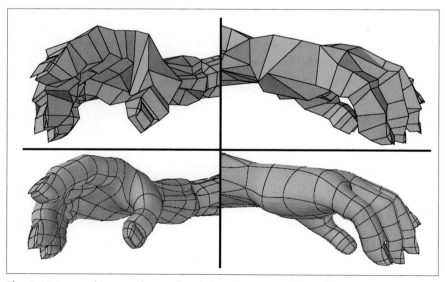

Fig. 6-48 Low-polygon and smooth subdivision views of the completed hand, fingers, and nails.

Figure 6-49 illustrates the subdivision human after completing the head, torso, and arm. Even though the half human has been mirror-duplicated, there is no need to do this yet except to see what it looks like.

Chapter 7 will complete the major part of the human by explaining how to model the legs and feet. Details such as the eyes, the inside of the mouth, hair, and so on, are outlined in Chapter 8.

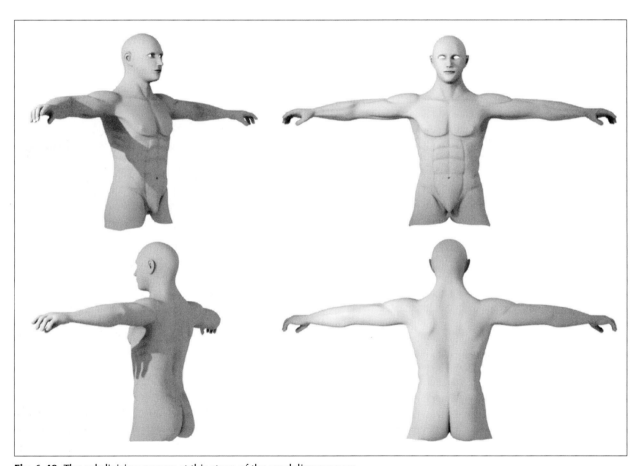

Fig. 6-49 The subdivision person at this stage of the modeling process.

MODELING THE LEG WITH SPLINES/NURBS

Most of the figure will be completed in this chapter. Starting at the bottom of the previously modeled torso, the leg, foot, and toes will be be modeled next.

As mentioned previously, if you decide to use templates you can find them in the "2DTemplates" and "3DTemplates" folders on the CD-ROM.

THE FEMALE LEG

To start the leg you will need to open the previously modeled Steps 3 and 5 for the female torso in Chapter 5 (see Figures 5-5 and 5-11). This is the lower part of the torso, which has the points that you need for the leg.

Step 1.

Figure 7-1 shows the points that you need to select along the lower torso. These should be made into a closed curve.

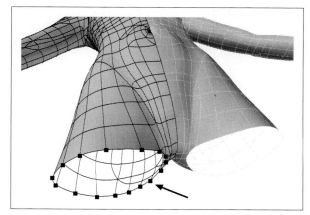

Fig. 7-1 Step 1. Points along the lower torso, which make up the opening for the leg, are selected and made into a closed curve.

A series of closed curves that starts at the upper part of the leg and ends just below the knee is made from the first oval spline (Figure 7-2). Since the top curve shares points with the end of the torso, the leg and torso will fit together seamlessly.

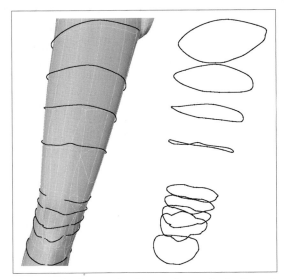

Fig. 7-2 The first oval spline at the top is duplicated, scaled, and shaped into a series of closed curves. These are placed along the length of the upper leg.

The next step is to connect the closed leg curves by either lofting or selecting corresponding points in order and making open curves. Figure 7-3 illustrates the upper leg mesh.

Fig. 7-3 Corresponding points along the closed curves are selected and made into connecting open curves. This can also be accomplished by lofting the ovals.

Around the knee area are a number of prominent parts that delineate the form of the leg. These are the skeletal joints of the knee and the muscle, called the vastus internus. This bulging muscle is located along the inside of the upper leg directly above the knee. Attention should also be paid to the indentations behind the knee formed by the semitendinosus, biceps femoris, and semimembranosus muscles.

Extra splines should be inserted along these conspicuous sections of the leg. Figure 7-4 depicts some views of these parts and the manner in which splines delineate them.

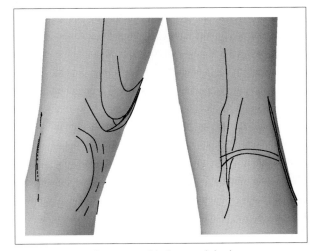

Fig. 7-4 Extra splines are added around the knee area.

Step 2.

Starting the lower half of the leg, points are selected at the bottom of the upper leg and made into a closed curve (Figure 7-5). Duplicates of this first oval can now be placed along the lower leg (Figure 7-6). Notice that the ovals extend below the ankle. This will simplify the process of modeling the foot later on.

Before connecting the ovals, try to shape each one to form the profile of the lower leg. Extra attention should be placed on distinguishing characteristics such as the calf muscle and the outside and inside ankle bones.

Figure 7-7 illustrates the lower leg after connecting the closed curves with open ones. Extra splines should now be inserted for details like the ankle. Figure 7-8 shows some views of the ankle area.

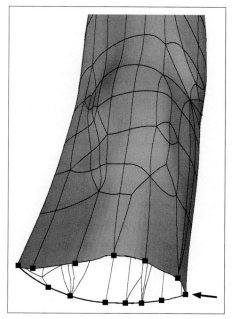

Fig. 7-5 Step 2. Points along the bottom of the upper leg are selected and made into a closed curve.

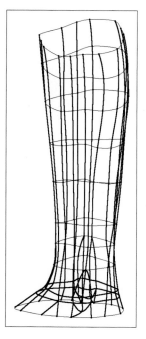

Fig. 7-7 Open curves connect the original closed curves of the lower leg.

Fig. 7-6 The first closed curve is duplicated and distributed along the length of the lower leg.

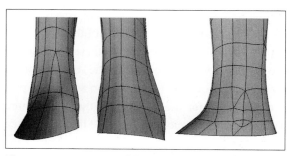

Fig. 7-8 Various views of the ankle area.

Both the upper and the lower leg can now be joined either by merging shared points or by stitching them. Figure 7-9 shows the two leg parts after they were made into one mesh.

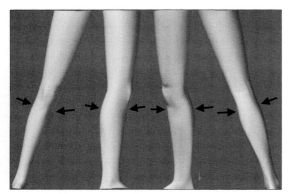

Fig. 7-9 The merged upper and lower leg parts. The arrows indicate the location of the shared closed curve whose points were merged or stitched.

Step 3.

The next step is to model the foot as several pieces. The toes will be added separately in subsequent steps. If you recall, the hand was modeled as an upper and a lower part. This made it possible to have openings for the fingers. The same principle holds true here. Modeling the foot as an upper and a lower part not only simplifies the process but also makes holes for the five toes.

Continuing the seamless patch approach, select the points along the bottom opening of the leg (Figure 7-10). Make an open curve out of these. A series of these closed curves is placed along the structure of the upper foot (Figure 7-11). The bottom spline has partial oval shapes for the top half of the toes. Figure 7-12 shows how the closed curves are then connected with open ones to complete the upper portion of the foot.

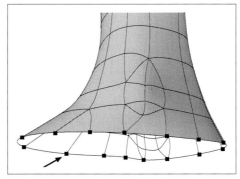

Fig. 7-10 Step 3. Points along the bottom opening of the leg are selected and made into a closed curve for the upper part of the foot.

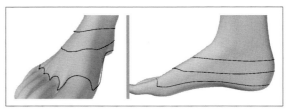

Fig. 7-11 A series of closed curves defines the top half of the foot. Notice the half-oval openings for the toes.

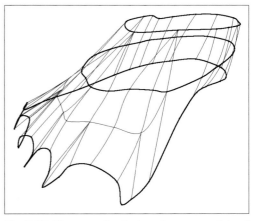

Fig. 7-12 The upper foot's closed curves are joined with open curves.

Step 4.

The lower half of the foot is started by selecting points along the bottom curve of the upper foot (Figure 7-13). After selecting these vertices, a closed curve is made from them, which will then serve as the starting point for the lower half of the foot.

Outlining the bottom of the foot is a series of closed curves (Figure 7-14). The front of the top spline is shaped in such as way as to make the lower-half opening for the toes.

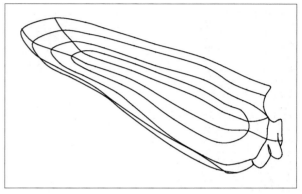

Fig. 7-14 Closed curves define the bottom half of the foot. Notice how the top spline outlines the bottom half of the toes.

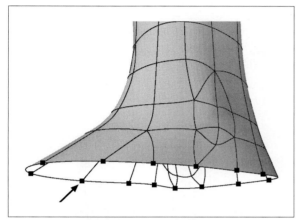

Fig. 7-13 Step 4. Vertices along the bottom curve of the upper foot are selected in order and made into the first closed curve for the bottom half of the foot.

After setting up the closed curves you can connect them with open curves like those in Figure 7-15. The two halves of the foot can now be merged into one mesh. Figure 7-16 illustrates the result of welding, stitching, or merging the shared points. The openings for the toes can now be seen clearly.

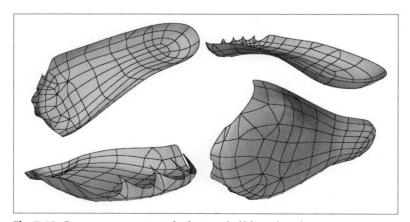

Fig. 7-15 Open curves connect the bottom-half-foot closed curves.

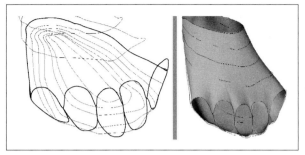

Fig. 7-16 The top and bottom halves of the foot should meet seamlessly. The shared curve also forms the five openings for the toes.

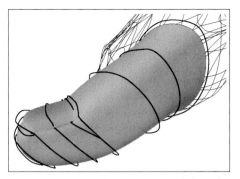

Fig. 7-18 A series of closed curves defines the outline of the big toe.

Step 5.

The big toe will be modeled first. Figure 7-17 depicts the points that are selected around the opening for this toe. A closed curve is made from these.

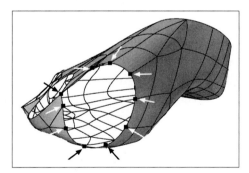

Fig. 7-17 Step 5. Starting the big toe by selecting points around the foot opening and making a closed curve.

A series of closed curves is then made that delineates the form of the big toe (Figure 7-18). These curves are then connected either through lofting or by selecting the corresponding points in order and making open curves (Figure 7-19). Extra splines are inserted for details such as the toenail. The big toe can now be merged with the foot mesh.

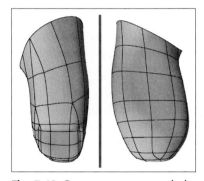

Fig. 7-19 Open curves are made by connecting the original closed ones.

Step 6.

Points located at the index toe opening are selected and made into a closed curve (Figure 7-20). A series of these ovals characterizes the shape of the index toe (Figure 7-21).

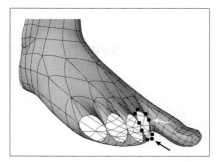

Fig. 7-20 Step 6. The first closed curve for the index toe is also made from points at the opening.

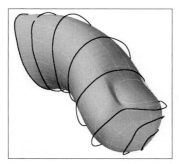

Fig. 7-21 Duplicated and re-shaped curves make up the outline of the index toe.

The index toe's closed curves are then connected with open curves (Figure 7-22). Extra splines are added to define the toenail. This toe is also merged with the foot (Figure 7-23).

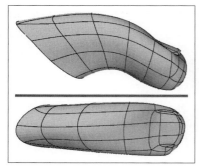

Fig. 7-22 The index toe wire mesh after connecting the closed curves.

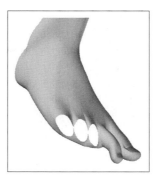

Fig. 7-23 After the index toe is completed, it is merged with the foot.

Step 7.

The middle toe is next in line. Points on the upper and lower foot that form the opening are selected and made into a closed curve. The ovals are then distributed according to the shape of the toe and connected with closed curves. The middle toe is also merged with the rest of the foot (Figure 7-24).

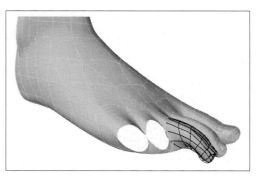

Fig. 7-24 Step 7. After selecting points around the opening, the middle toe is modeled and merged with the foot.

Step 8.

The toe next to the last is also modeled following the previous method. Always start with the points around the opening of the foot. Figure 7-25 illustrates the almost completed foot without the smallest toe.

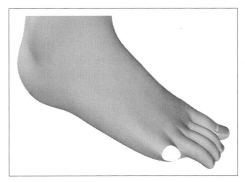

Fig. 7-25 Step 8. The toe next to the pinky toe is modeled in the same manner, starting with points around the opening.

Step 9.

Completing the foot is the small toe at the end, often referred to as the "pinky toe." It is also modeled by starting with the points around the opening and making the first closed curve. Figure 7-26 shows the final foot after merging the pinky toe with it. Various rendered views of the nearly completed female can be seen in Figure 7-27.

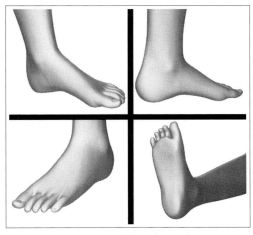

Fig. 7-26 Step 9. Modeling the pinky toe completes the foot.

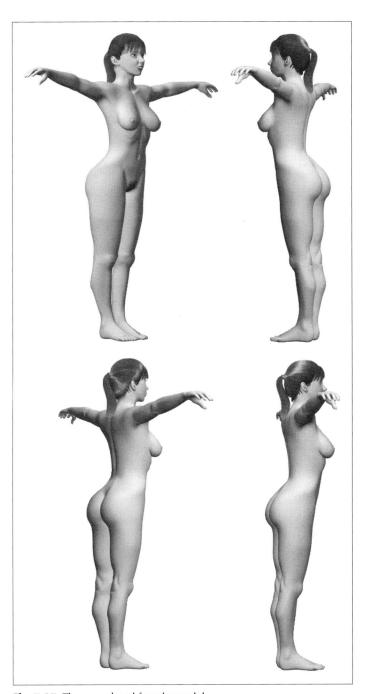

Fig. 7-27 The completed female model.

THE MALE LEG

Templates for the male leg can be found in the "2DTemplates" and "3DTemplates" folders on the CD-ROM. The process is very similar to that used for the female leg except there are more muscles to contend with. The following steps outline the process for creating the upper and lower leg using patch spline/ NURBS modeling. Since the male and the female foot are very similar, it would be redundant to repeat the directions.

Step 1.

At the bottom of the previously modeled torso, you will find the points at the leg opening. Select these in order and make a closed curve out of them (Figure 7-28). If you wish, you may do this in another layer.

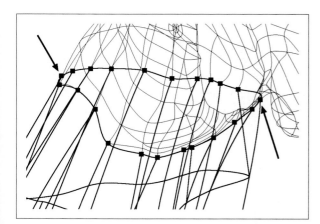

Fig. 7-28 Step 1. Points from the torso at the leg opening are utilized to start the top of the upper leg.

Step 2.

After making the first closed upper leg curve from the shared torso points, copy, paste, and move them down the length of the leg (Figure 7-29). The last closed curve ends below the knee. Shape the leg cross sections by moving points according to your templates, photos, or sketches. The muscles of the upper leg are defined by the manner in which you pull and push groups of vertices. Groups of two or three parallel lines can make the furrows where two muscle groups meet.

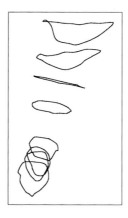

Fig. 7-29 Step 2. Closed curves define the framework for the upper leg.

Step 3.

Connect the closed curves with long open ones like the splines seen in Figure 7-30. Shorter curves will most likely have to be added to divide shapes that have more than four points around them. Continue shaping the muscles of the leg.

Fig. 7-30 Step 3. Vertical open curves connect the closed curves of the upper leg.

If you plan to patch the spline cage with polygons, you do so and thus see a shaded view of the leg as you sculpt it. Your patch setting should be low, such as 0, so that you have the same polygon count as the shapes on the spline cage. Figure 7-31 illustrates the upper leg in shaded view with the splines visible as well. Notice the outline of the various muscle groups formed by the direction of the curves.

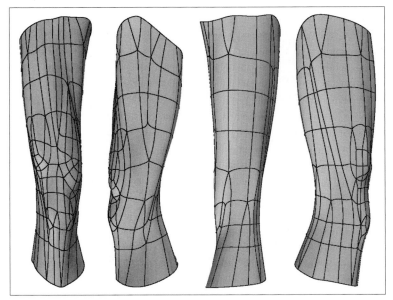

Fig. 7-31 The completed patch-modeled upper leg. The directions of the splines follow the contours of the muscles.

Step 4.

Begin the lower part of the leg by selecting the vertices along the bottom of the upper leg (Figure 7-32). Copy and paste them into a new layer and make a closed curve out of them.

Step 5.

Duplicate the first closed curve of the lower leg and distribute the copies along its length. Shape the cross-sectional curves until they form a framework for the lower leg (Figure 7-33).

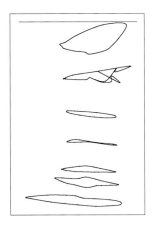

Fig. 7-33 Step 5. Closed curves for the lower leg are duplicated and moved down to the top part of the foot.

Fig. 7-32 Step 4. Vertices along the bottom of the upper leg are used to make the first curve of the lower leg.

140

Step 6.

Select corresponding points along each closed curve and connect or loft them with open ones (Figure 7-34). Insert extra splines to divide any shapes that have more than four vertices around them.

Figure 7-35 illustrates a shaded view of the lower leg and foot with visible splines. These might serve as a guide for the direction of the curves.

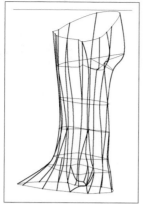

Fig. 7-34 Step 6. Open curves connect the closed ones of the lower leg.

Step 7.

Follow the written directions and illustrations in Figures 7-10 through 7-26 to model the male foot. The procedure is the same as the one for the female foot except you will have to make the foot larger and somewhat wider.

A final rendering of the entire leg and foot can be seen in Figure 7-36. The almost completed spline/NURBS male figure can be viewed in Figure 7-37.

Fig. 7-36 Step 6. Open curves connect the closed ones of the lower leg.

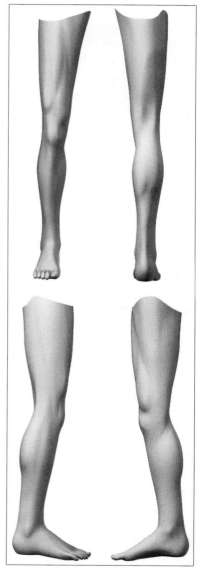

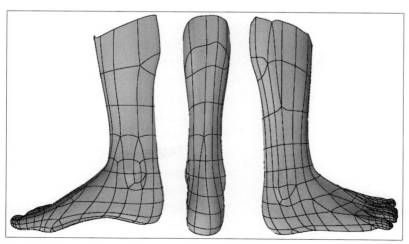

Fig. 7-35 The patch-modeled lower leg and foot, showing the direction of the curves.

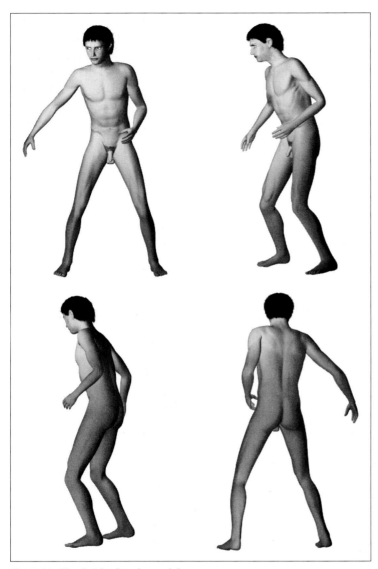

Fig. 7-37 The finished male model.

CONVERTING A SPLINE/NURBS MODEL
FOR SUBDIVISION SURFACE RENDERING

Some artists prefer to build their models with splines or NURBS and then convert them into polygon mod-

els. They may favor finalizing their models in polygon mode since this allows greater flexibility for adding detail and has the advantage of rendering the character as a subdivision object.

Most of the time when a spline/ NURBS object is converted, there are too many polygons. For subdivision surfaces it is best to keep the polygon count to a minimum. The software will divide the polygons into smaller ones during the rendering process. So why slow down your screen redraws during animation or when editing the model? You will also find that developing facial expressions is easier when you have fewer points to contend with.

Although there are plug-ins and stand-alone applications that can automatically convert models into lower-polygon-count objects, they all suffer from one major weakness. Most of the time, key areas on a model require more polygons, while other larger and broader parts can have fewer. Unfortunately, polygon reduction software cannot discriminate between sections of a model that should have more detail and the rest. So they just apply an overall simplification to the entire object. Since they lack the discrimination to select key areas that can be changed into lower resolution while keeping other ones that require better detail in higher polygon count, they are basically useless for preparing a subdivision model.

As with most tasks, there is no substitute for hands-on modeling that requires an artist's sensibilities, discrimination, and creativity. Greater control over the creative process yields a more successful outcome. Most of us would like to reduce the number of mundane jobs, but our endeavor toward perfection forces us to commit to them. Idealists will often become overenthusiastic about computers and software, stating that our lives are now easier since many routine chores have been simplified. Actu-

ally, it is the opposite: Computers and software have made our lives more complicated. Instead of eliminating problems, they have produced new ones. Creating art on the computer is not a simpler process now; it is more complex, requiring great manual dexterity and intellectual skill.

Figure 7-38 illustrates male and female heads that have had their polygon counts reduced manually.

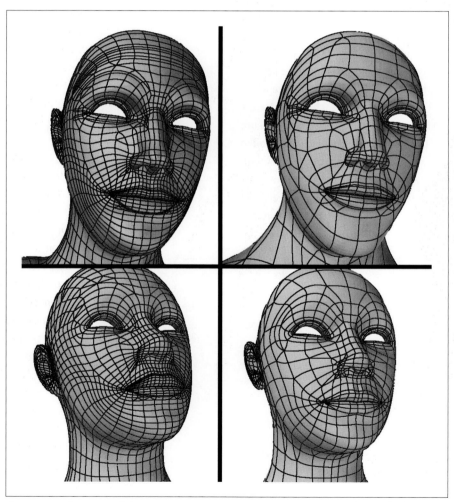

Fig. 7-38 Male (top) and female (bottom) heads that have had their polygon counts reduced manually. Notice that with subdivision surfaces there is no loss of detail.

Notice key areas around the ear, eyes, and nose that have smaller polygons. These are some of the parts that require more detail. Other regions of the model that are less curved can have fewer polygons. Therefore, you will see larger ones there.

Once your model has been converted into a polygon object, select groups of smaller polygons and merge them into one. Delete the extra remaining vertices. Keep merging polygons in the larger and broader areas. You should be able to reduce the polygon count by half or more. Parts of the model that require more detail will have to have less reduction and sometimes none.

During this process you will find that some adjoining regions will end up with polygons that have more than four vertices. This often happens when you have a large polygon next to a group of smaller ones. Be sure to split up all the polygons into three- or four-sided ones. Unless your software can convert polygons with more than four sides into subdivision surfaces, this becomes an essential task. Try to keep the three-sided polygons to a minimum. Usually, four-sided ones work best in subdivision mode.

MODELING THE LEG WITH SUBDIVISION SURFACE POLYGONS

This lesson continues where the instructions for modeling a subdivision torso left off. The general form of the leg will be made, followed by the foot and toes. Details such as toenails and muscles will end the lesson.

Step 1.
Begin modeling the leg by selecting the points at the leg opening of the torso. Make a polygon out of these (Figure 7-39).

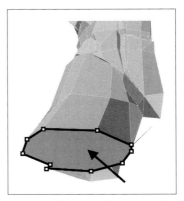

Fig. 7-39 Step 1. Points at the leg opening are selected in order and made into a polygon.

Step 2.
Bevel-extrude it straight down and move the polygon to the side (Figure 7-40). Use a set value to make all the points at the bottom of the leg flat on the ground.

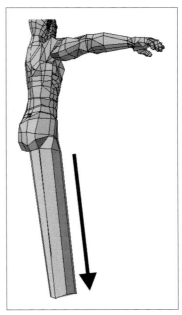

Fig. 7-40 Step 2. The polygon is beveled down for the length of the leg.

Step 3.

With the knife tool, split the polygons on the leg in a horizontal direction (Figure 7-41).

Step 4.

Shape the leg, but save the muscles for later (Figure 7-42).

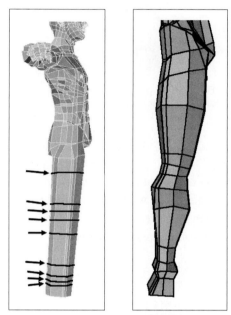

Fig. 7-41 (left) Step 3. The leg is divided into sections in order to begin shaping it.
Fig. 7-42 (right) Step 4. Points are moved to give the leg a general form.

Step 5.

Now it is time to model the foot. The process is very similar to modeling the hand. Select the polygons at the front of the foot and merge them into one (Figure 7-43).

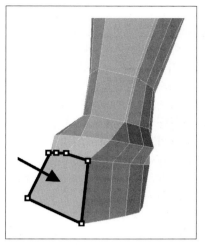

Fig. 7-43 Step 5. Polygons that will be beveled forward to make the foot have to be merged first.

Step 6.

Bevel or extrude the polygon forward to where the toes begin (Figure 7-44). The toes will be bevel-extruded from this same polygon after dividing it.

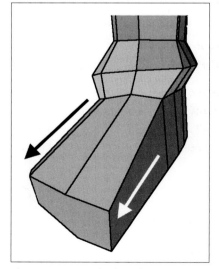

Fig. 7-44 Step 6. The front foot polygon is beveled forward to where the toes begin.

Step 7.

Split the front of the foot polygon into five sections. Figure 7-45 shows the divisions. Make sure you have only four- and three-sided polygons by splitting up any polys that require it. This will yield extra vertices that you can use to further refine the foot in subdivision mode. Delete any one- and two-point polygons. Shape a rough approximation of the foot without the toes.

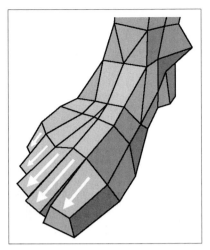

Fig. 7-46 Step 8. The front five polygons are beveled forward for the toes.

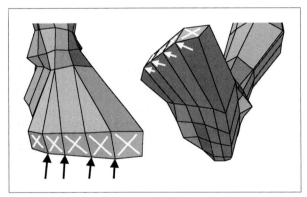

Fig. 7-45 Step 7. Dividing the front polygons into five shapes for the toes. The rest of the foot is also split into three- and four-sided polygons.

Step 9.

Working on one toe at a time, hide the rest of the figure, then split the toe with the knife tool and refine its shape. When you are done with the five toes, they should look somewhat like Figure 7-47.

Step 8.

Select the five polygons at the front of the foot seen in Figure 7-45. Extrude or bevel them forward to make the toes (Figure 7-46).

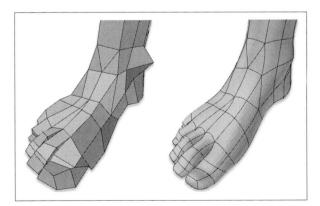

Fig. 7-47 Step 9. The toes are split into smaller polygons. The foot is shaped in both low-polygon and subdivision forms.

Step 10.

The toenails are modeled using the same technique as for the fingernails. Figure 7-48 illustrates the four steps for making a toenail:

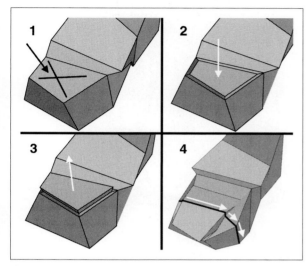

Fig. 7-48 Step 10. The four steps to modeling the toenails.

1. Select the polygon at the top and front of the toe.
2. Bevel it down once. Rotate it up a little.
3. Bevel the newly created polygon again and move the new polygon up. Move the front points forward.
4. Use the knife tool to slice across the middle of the newly created polygons and the part of the toe that they are attached to. Switch to subdivision mode and shape the toe and nail.

Select the toenail, name its surface, and apply a toenail surface to it. Select the cuticle polygon, name its surface, and apply a cuticle surface to it. Figure 7-49 shows the finished foot and toenails in low-polygon and subdivision modes.

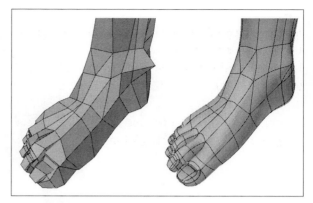

Fig. 7-49 The final foot and toenails seen as low-polygon and subdivision surfaces.

The next set of steps outlines the procedure for finalizing the leg by modeling muscles and other details. Magnify your view of the inside top of the leg near the groin area. Select the four points in order and make a polygon. This will prevent you from getting a hole after the half figure is mirrored.

Step 11.

Modeling the muscles of the leg is a process similar to sculpting the arm muscles. The thigh or upper leg muscles are long and well rounded. As they approach the knee they become more angular. Use the same technique as outlined for the arm, which is to split polygons along the length of the leg. Lines that are close together define two muscle groups and the concave shape between them. The lower leg muscles become round and then taper at the ankle to become more angular.

Figures 7-50 through 7-52 depict the steps for modeling the muscles and the knee of the leg. You might want to refer to an anatomy book that shows all four views of the leg muscles.

147

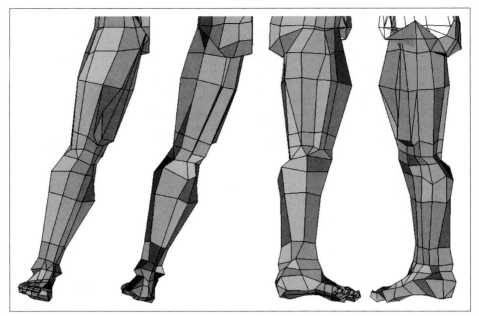

Fig. 7-50 Step 11. Dividing the polygons on the leg to form the muscles.

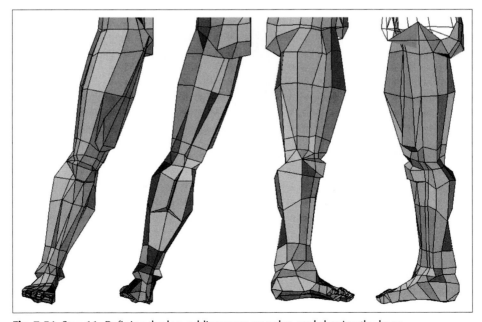

Fig. 7-51 Step 11. Refining the leg, adding more muscles, and shaping the knee.

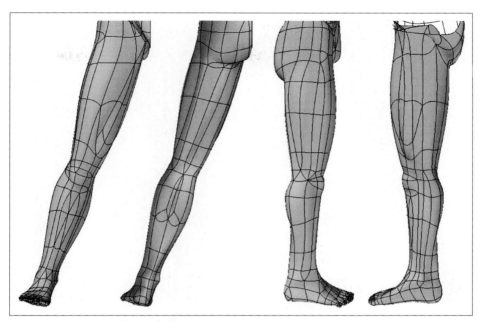

Fig. 7-52 The leg seen as subdivision surfaces.

The final subdivision figure can be seen in Figure 7-53. Details such as the eyes, mouth, hair, and so on, can be modeled next by following the steps in Chapter 8.

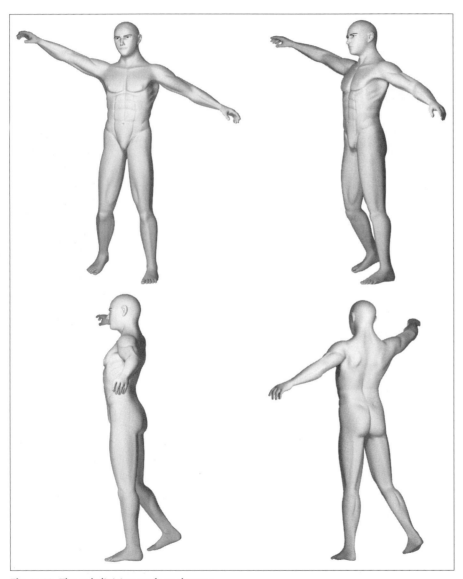

Fig. 7-53 The subdivision surfaces human.

S o far, you have modeled almost the entire body. The additional parts that are covered in this chapter may seem minor, but they will make a big difference in the final appearance of your digital human. The same techniques that were used in preceding chapters are utilized here. The objects can be made from NURBS, splines, and/or polygons. As before, when working with spline cages be sure to patch them with polygons. Templates for each part are provided in the "3DTemplates" folder on the CD-ROM.

The inside of the mouth, the gums, and the tongue only require that half of them be modeled. Mirror these to make the other half. If you have been modeling with the center of the body on the 0 x axis, then be sure to make the centers of these objects also align on the 0 x axis. This will ensure that the right and left sides of these three parts will correspond to one another exactly when mirroring them along with the rest of the body.

THE EYE

Various components with distinct characteristics make up the eye; therefore, it is best to model it in parts. This will simplify the process of assigning precise surfaces to each region.

The cornea, which is the transparent covering for the eye, fits over the eyeball and has a very high specularity and glossiness. Figure 8-1 illustrates the struc-

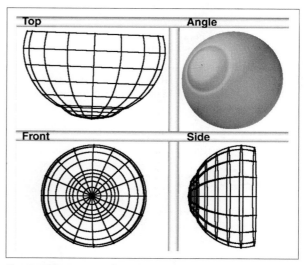

Fig. 8-1 The cornea, the transparent covering of the eyeball, fits over the eye like an old-fashioned watch crystal fits over a watch.

ture of the cornea. Closed curves of varying circumferences can be set up to be lofted or connected. If you need to, autopatch the spline cage. Another modeling method for the cornea is to make a sphere, rotate it so the poles are facing forward, and then truncate it at the back pole. The cornea needs to cover only a little more than half of the front eyeball (Figure 8-2).

The eyeball can be modeled similarly to the cornea except that now it is a full sphere with a hole in the front (Figure 8-3). This hole should be the size of the

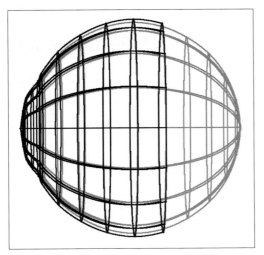

Fig. 8-2 Since the cornea fits like a half sphere over the eyeball, it causes the eye to protrude slightly outward.

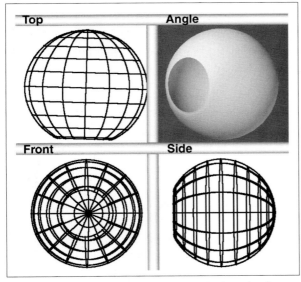

Fig. 8-3 The eyeball has a hole cut into the front for the iris.

iris, which will be modeled next so that it is flush with the front of the eyeball. The eyeball should fit into the previously made cornea, as seen in Figure 8-2.

The iris can be viewed in Figure 8-4. It forms the front part of the eyeball but is a separate object so that it can be textured precisely. You can begin the iris by selecting the front curve of the eyeball. It is located at the perimeter of the eyeball hole. Copy the curve, paste it slightly in front, and scale it down. Repeat the process until you have a series of curves that you can loft or connect. Make sure the iris has a hole in the center for the lens (pupil). If necessary, patch the spline cage with polygons. Figure 8-5 displays the iris.

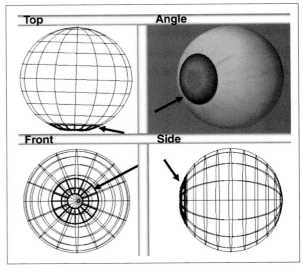

Fig. 8-4 The iris fits over the eyeball as a separate object.

The lens will make the pupil of the eye. It is a simple disklike object that sits behind the hole of the iris (Figure 8-6). A sphere can be reshaped or closed curves can be lofted or connected to make the lens.

The final part is the pink membrane (Figure 8-7) seen in the corner of the eye. It is made up of two

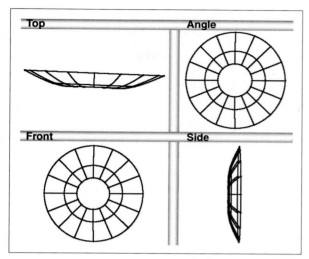

Fig. 8-5 The iris is modeled as a simple disk with a small hole in the center. The hole is for the pupil.

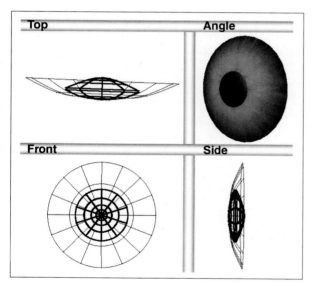

Fig. 8-6 The lens is placed behind and against the iris. The black pupil (lens) can then be seen through the center hole of the iris.

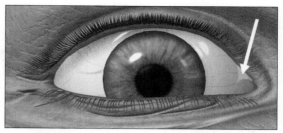

Fig. 8-7 The pink membrane in the corner of the eye is made up of two parts, the inner one being the caruncula and the outer the plica semilunaris.

parts. The larger, outer part is called the plica semilunaris, and the inner one is the caruncula. Figure 8-8 shows the location of the pink membrane on the eyeball. You can model the plica semilunaris as a bent plane that rests against the curve of the eyeball (Figure 8-9). Most of it will be hidden by the eye socket. The caruncula is an amorphous shape that can be created from closed curves or an altered sphere (Figure 8-10). After placing the eye against the eye socket, adjust the shape and position of the pink membrane.

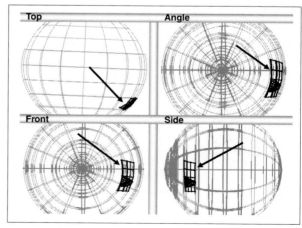

Fig. 8-8 The location of the plica semilunaris and caruncula against the eyeball.

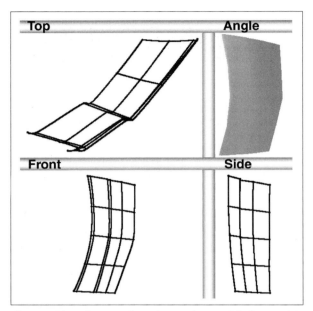

Fig. 8-9 The plica semilunaris can be modeled as a thin membrane that fits against and in the corner of the eye.

THE EYELASHES

You may be tempted to skip this step, but eyelashes are an important part of the final look of your person. They are easy to model but take time to position correctly. A hair generator can often be used to make eyelashes out of fur, but the increase in rendering time may not be worth it.

If you want to do it right, then be prepared to model about 10 different lengths of eyelashes. Placing each one of them correctly along the upper and lower eyelids is what takes up so much time. It may be a painfully tedious process, but the end result will make it worth the effort. You could easily spend 8 to 16 hours just on eyelashes.

Since eyelashes are so small, there is no need to give them more than two or three sides. These are bent and come to a point like the one seen in Figure 8-11. Two or three connected splines or a divided polygon that changes direction on one plane will work.

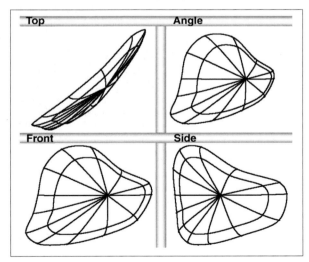

Fig. 8-10 The caruncula is the smaller part of the pink membrane and can be modeled as a kind of kidney-shaped object.

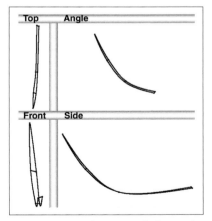

Fig. 8-11 A single top eyelash can be modeled from a couple of splines.

Place copies of the eyelash against the perimeter of the eye socket to make the upper and lower eyelashes. It helps to have some close-up photos of the eye or use a handheld mirror. Figure 8-12 depicts the finished eyelashes.

Fig. 8-14 Single hairs are duplicated, shaped, and arranged for the eyebrow.

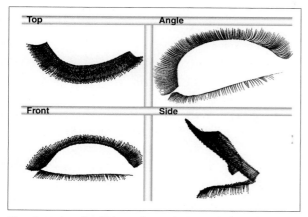

Fig. 8-12 Duplicated single eyelashes are distributed to make the upper and lower eyelashes.

THE EYEBROWS

The eyebrows can be modeled in a similar fashion to that used for the eyelashes (Figure 8-13). After creating one hair fiber, duplicate it, alter its shape, and place it against the skin. Be sure to place one end under the skin. Arranging the eyebrow hairs will take some time, but the effort will be worth it. Figure 8-14 shows the eyebrow hairs.

Some people might prefer painting the eyebrows onto the skin surface. This works fine, especially if your software supports UV mapping. Consult Chapter 10 for more information about surfacing.

This completes the eye. Figure 8-15 shows the final eye, eyelashes, and eyebrow after applying various textures and surface characteristics.

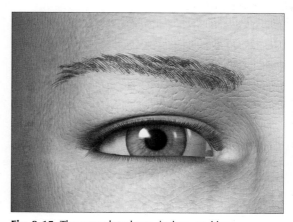

Fig. 8-15 The completed eye, lashes, and brow.

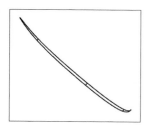

Fig. 8-13 A single eyebrow hair is made from a couple of splines.

THE INSIDE OF THE MOUTH

When you open your character's mouth and you glimpse the inside back of the head, you might realize that it is time to sculpt the inside of the mouth. This object will contain the teeth, gums, and tongue.

In order to match the inside to the outside of the mouth, use the top points along the bottom lip and the bottom points along the top lip (Figure 8-16). Select these points in order and make an open spline. If you already mirrored the half body, then make a closed spline. Duplicate the spline and place copies of it along the boundaries of the inside mouth. The top and bottom points on the duplicate splines will have to be separated more to make the inside mouth wider than they were at the lips (Figure 8-17).

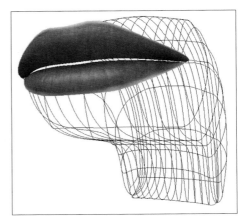

Fig. 8-17 An angled view showing the inside of the mouth mesh against he shaded lips.

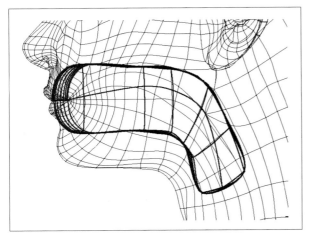

Fig. 8-16 A side view showing the inside of the mouth. Its front points share the same space as the bottom points of the upper lip and top points of the lower lip.

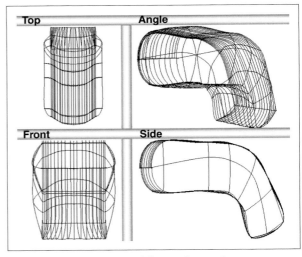

Fig. 8-18 Different views of the inside mouth.

When you are finished arranging the curves, connect or loft them (Figure 8-18). Spline cages will most likely have to be patched with polygons.

If you prefer working with polygons you can also start by selecting the points along the mouth opening, making a polygon, extruding toward the back, and reshaping it.

When you are finished it is very important to turn the surface normals inward. This means flipping the

polygons so that one can see only the inside, and not the outside, of the object. Surface normals that face outward will make the inside mouth object appear solid rather than hollow. Make the inside mouth less obvious by assigning a dark color to it.

THE TEETH

Four different forms will be enough to make the teeth. You can then reshape them a little to make the four incisors, two canines, four bicuspids, and six molars.

Only one side needs to be set up like those in Figure 8-19. The teeth are then mirrored either with the rest of the body or by themselves. Figure 8-20 shows a close-up view of two teeth. One can see that closed curves were arranged and connected or lofted. Subdivision modeling can also be applied to boxlike objects.

THE GUMS

During certain mouth movements, the gums can be seen; therefore, these will be modeled next. Figure 8-21 illustrates the set of open curves that can be used to make the form for the right half of the upper gum. As seen in Figure 8-22, these splines are then connected. The lower gum is a mirror duplicate of the upper one (Figure 8-23).

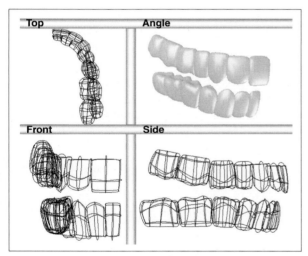

Fig. 8-19 Different views of the teeth on the right side of the mouth.

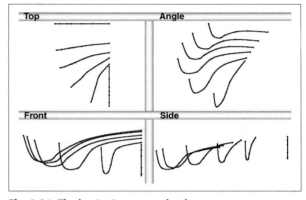

Fig. 8-21 The beginning curves for the upper gum.

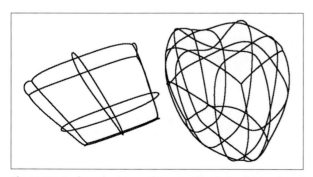

Fig. 8-20 A close-up view of two teeth. Notice how closed curves can be connected or lofted.

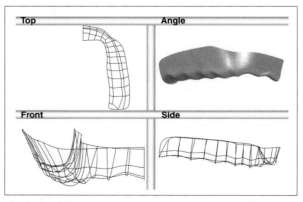

Fig. 8-22 Splines are connected to make the right side of the upper gum.

157

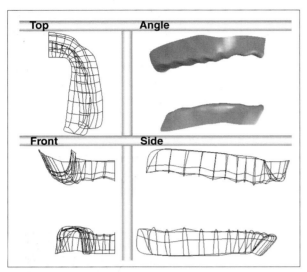

Fig. 8-23 The upper gums are mirrored to make the lower gums.

If you are working only with polygons, a primitive, such as a half sphere, can be sculpted into the gums. In either case be sure to check the position of the gums against the teeth (Figure 8-24). The bottom of the teeth should be inside the gums. To fit correctly, some points along the gums will most likely have to be moved.

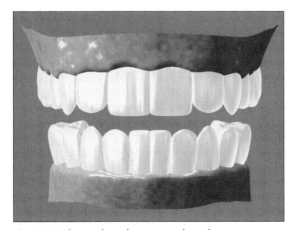

Fig. 8-24 The teeth and gums combined.

THE TONGUE

A simple shape is enough to make the tongue. Figure 8-25 depicts the open curves used to make the right side of the tongue. After connecting them, you can mirror the half tongue (Figure 8-26).

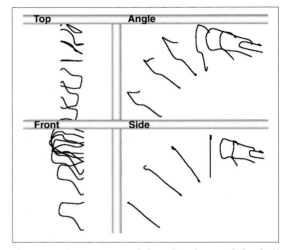

Fig. 8-25 Open curves define the shape of the half tongue.

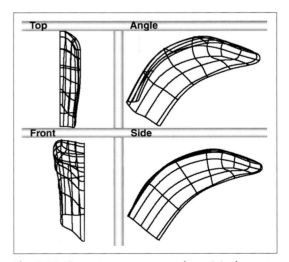

Fig. 8-26 Open curves connect the original tongue curves to make the half tongue.

Another approach to making the tongue is to flatten a sphere and sculpt it into the right shape. The poles of the sphere are in the front and back, not the top and bottom. Figure 8-27 illustrates the finished mouth.

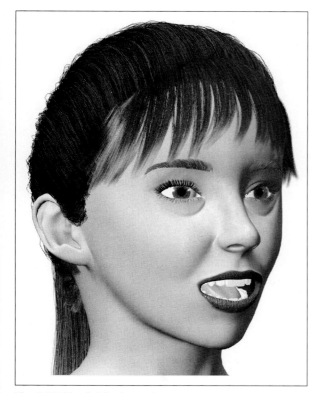

Fig. 8-27 The finished mouth.

THE HAIR

Just as there are many different hairstyles, there are also numerous ways to model the hair. Whether you are modeling hair as an object (often referred to as "helmet hair") or using a hair generator, the following directions will show you how to create both kinds of hair.

Helmet hair renders faster but lacks the realism that hair generators produce. It often takes some creative texturing to get the helmet hair to look somewhat right. Hair made using a fur and hair generator looks a lot better, but it will take extra rendering time. The guides that often have to be set up for longer hair take extra modeling time—sometimes an entire day. The additional time you put into modeling these guides will be well worth it. Figures 8-28 and 8-29 as well as the CD8-29 color image in the Chapter 8 folder on the CD-ROM show the two types of hair.

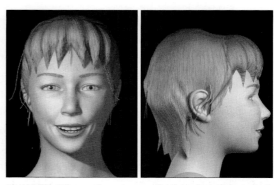

Fig. 8-28 Often referred to as "helmet hair," the wig is a modeled object and random strands are added afterwards.

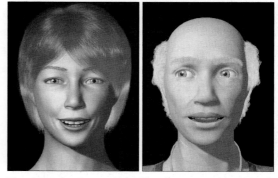

Fig. 8-29 A wig made with a hair generator. Guide geometry was created and bundles of hair were then set to follow them. The eyebrows on the old man also have long hair guides.

METHOD 1: HELMET HAIR

One could create the hair using the previously mentioned subdivision modeling method. A subdivided box could gradually be shaped into the hair object. Another way is to model the outlines of the hair style with splines or NURBS and then connect or loft all of them.

If your software has layers, place the model of the head in the back layer. In the foreground layer, starting at the top of the head, make a series of vertical splines (Figure 8-30). Make sure they each have the same number of points on them. Select in order and connect the corresponding points with open splines. You might want to start with the right front bottom point and then continue selecting the other bottom points until you end with the front left bottom point. You can then work your way up until all the points are connected. If you are using a lofting tool, select the splines in order and loft them. Figure 8-31 shows the connected spline mesh.

To make the hairpiece more intricate, insert extra splines or points to connect.

The spline mesh can be converted to polygons or autopatched. From there you can continue reshaping the wig or add more detail. Other parts such as a ponytail can be modeled and added to the existing hair object. It is also a good idea to model some hair strands. The same method that was used for eyelashes and eyebrows works well for the hair fibers. You can then distribute them randomly around the hairpiece.

Texturing the hair object can be accomplished with UV or spherical projection mapping. All you need is a good hair texture. Surfacing objects is discussed in more detail in Chapter 10.

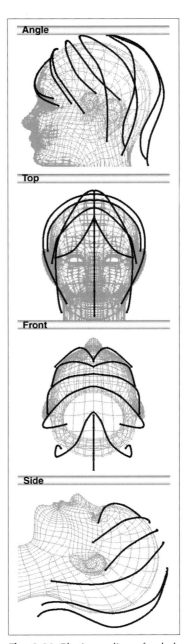

Fig. 8-30 Placing splines for helmet hair. The head model is referenced in the back layer.

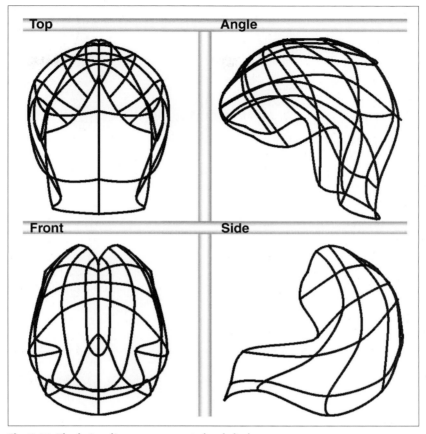

Fig. 8-31 The hair splines are connected or lofted.

METHOD 2: USING A HAIR GENERATOR

When modeling long hair, you will most likely have to place guides so that your software has some direction for the strands to follow. The following technique uses a rail clone tool. This makes it possible to duplicate splines and have them follow along a certain path that is specified with other splines (rails). As long as your software has some kind of cloning tool that allows you to determine the direction of the copies, you should be able to use this method. If your hair generator software requires two-point polygon chains, you will also need a tool or plug-in to convert the splines into guide chains.

The following directions are for creating hair guides using groups of three in each section. Three splines in each group will make soft-body dynamics less computationally intensive. If you do not plan to apply soft-body dynamics (explained in a later part of this chapter), then you might decide to use groups of seven or more splines for fuller hair. When modeling long hair, curves can intersect the body as long as you plan to have a collision object. Once collision detection is activated, the hair strands will sit on top of the skin.

Place your head model in a back layer. Determine where the part on the hair is going to be. Working in the foreground layer, begin drawing an open curve with approximately nine knots (points) on it. Start the spline at the top and front of the head, high up on the forehead where the part begins (Figure 8-32). Make sure the starting point of the spline is inside the skull. This is the root of the hair follicle. You do not want your hair to look like it is floating above the head. Place the next three vertices fairly close to the first one to get a little lift and curve to the hair as it begins to bend away from the skull.

Duplicate or create new splines, with the same amount of points as the first one, and place them one after the other. Let the first curve be the outermost part of the hair, with the subsequent ones gradually arranged lower and closer to the skull. Figure 8-33 illustrates this first group of three splines. Keep in mind that the example is for longer hair. You may decide to model shorter hair and thus use fewer knots on your splines. The direction of your hair will also vary. For example, it may be combed farther back and not even have bangs. Again, make sure each spline starts on the inside of the skull.

Keep the first set of three splines somewhat evenly spaced apart. While the beginning point on each curve starts inside the skull, the end points should be fairly close to the skin but never inside it. Mirror-

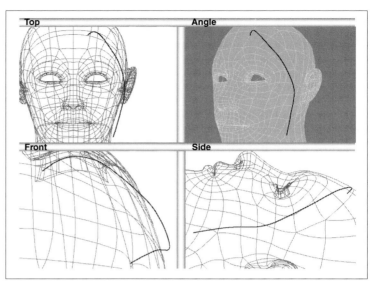

Fig. 8-32 Making guides for a hair generator. The first hair spline starts inside, at the front and top of the skull. The model is lying on her back.

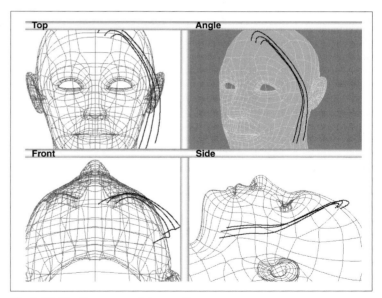

Fig. 8-33 The first group of three splines.

duplicate this first group of three curves and shape them for the other side of the head (Figure 8-34).

Make a second group of three splines by duplicating the first set (Figure 8-35). Move this new group back along the skull, rotate it, and arrange each spline individually. Keep in mind that if your hair is parted, then the first spline of this second group should start at the part but farther back on the head. This first spline also serves as the one that is curved farthest from the skull.

As you arrange this second group, be sure to place the beginning vertex of each spline just inside the skull. If you want thicker hair, bend the curves so they are farther from the head. Keep the shortest ones close enough to the skull so that the hair still lies against the head. Always make sure that none of the splines intersect the skull except at their beginning points. Mirror this second set also for the other side of the skull.

Duplicate all the splines of the second group and move them farther back on the skull. Rotate them and position each strand individually. The beginning point of each starts inside the skull. Bend the curves so that none intersect the skull. Figure 8-36 shows this third set of splines. You may also want to have some of the curves overlap each other so that the arrangement looks more natural. This third group is mirror-duplicated and placed on the other side of the head.

Now it is time to create a fourth group of three splines. You can do this by copying and pasting the third set and then moving, rotating, and organizing the

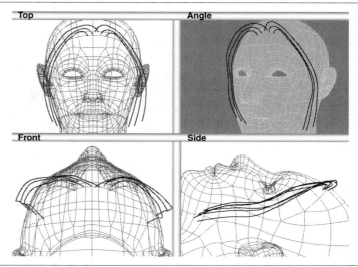

Fig. 8-34 The first group of three splines is mirrored and shaped for the opposite side of the skull.

duplicated splines (Figure 8-37). Mirror the fourth group and arrange and order each curve on both sides of the skull.

Figure 8-38 shows the next group of splines. This set will have to be rotated more than the others since it starts at the back of the head. Mirror the fifth group.

The final group (Figure 8-39) is placed in the middle of the back of the head. This completes all the spline groups. All 11 sets of curves will be enough to create the hair guides for the head. The next step will have you connect them to make the guide rails that are used to rail-clone the curves.

Figure 8-40 shows how the top spline on each of the four groups is selected and the rest are hidden. These are corresponding splines and will now be connected.

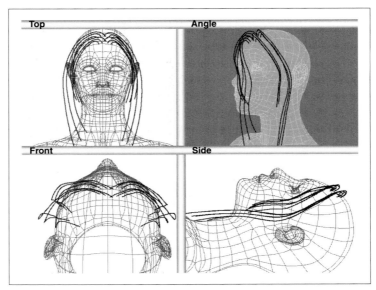

Fig. 8-35 The first set of three splines is duplicated, moved, and organized into the second set. This new set is then mirror-replicated for the opposite side.

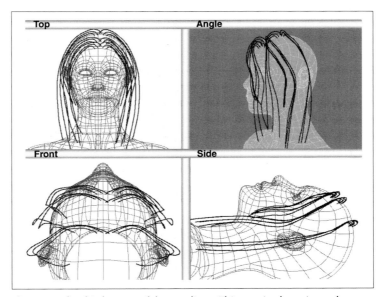

Fig. 8-36 The third group of three splines. This one is also mirrored.

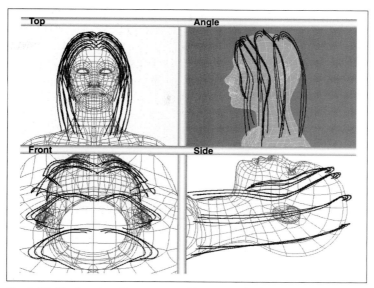

Fig. 8-37 The fourth spline group and its mirror duplicate.

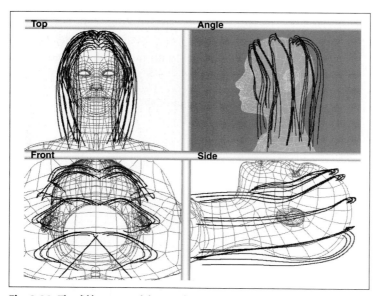

Fig. 8-38 The fifth group of three splines is rotated and mirror-duplicated.

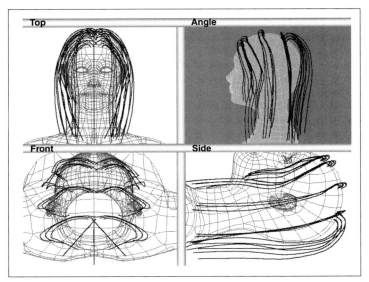

Fig. 8-39 After rotating, the sixth group of three splines is placed at the back of the head.

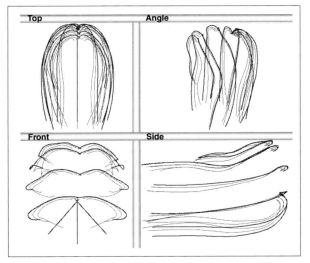

Fig. 8-40 The top spline of each set is selected and the rest are concealed.

Select corresponding points along each curve and connect them with open curves (Figure 8-41). It is also very important that the beginning of each connecting spline start at the first spline that you created at the very beginning of this process. The front-to-back direction of the connecting splines is important. If your software does not allow you to manually connect curves, then loft them.

Display all the splines in the 11 groups. Select the next spline of each group. Be careful to pick the second curve on the first set and the second curves of the other three sets. Hide all the rest of them and connect between the points of the second spline of each group. Just as before, the direction of the connecting curves, from front to back, is important.

Repeat the last steps with the rest of the splines. Pay careful attention to the splines that you are working with. For example, every third curve of each set is connected. Figure 8-42 depicts all 11 sets with each of their three splines connected.

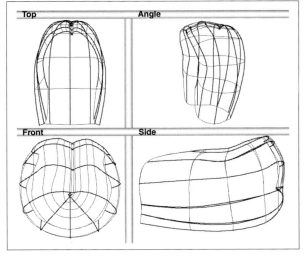

Fig. 8-41 The top splines are connected with open curves.

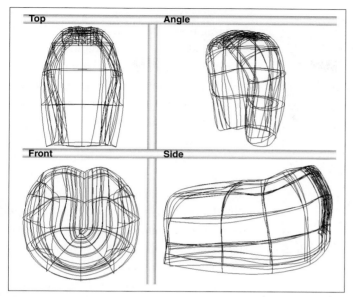

Fig. 8-42 All the rest of the splines in each of the three groups are connected to their corresponding ones.

Rail Clone: Multiple
Segment: Length
Uniform
60 (segments)
Strength: 2.0
Not oriented
No scaling

If you want fewer hair strands just use a smaller number than 60 (segments).

Figure 8-44 shows the result of using a rail clone tool. Cut and paste these new splines into their own layer. Make the head visible behind the 60 rail-cloned splines. Use a magnet tool and/or other modifying tools to change the splines so that they conform to the general shape of the skull. For minute detail work, individual points will also have to be moved one at a time.

All the connecting splines are now going to be used as your guide rails. Select each set of connected splines. Copy and paste them into their own layers. Select the first guide that you created at the beginning of this exercise. Copy and paste it into its own layer. Select only the connecting splines that are part of the first spline. Cut and paste these connecting curves into their own background layer. You should now have one foreground layer with the first spline and one background layer with all the connecting curves that bend around the head (Figure 8-43).

Change your view so that the first curve is in the foreground and its connecting splines are in the background layer. You should now have something similar to what can be seen in Figure 8-43. Select your rail clone tool and use settings similar to these:

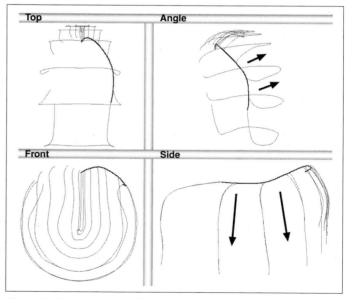

Fig. 8-43 The first curve (black line) is in the foreground layer and only the connecting splines (gray lines) are visible in the background layer. The first curve is now ready to be rail-cloned.

167

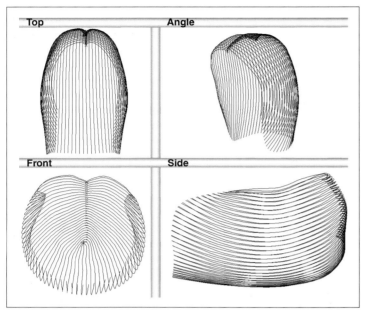

Fig. 8-44 The result of rail cloning the first spline. Sixty new curves have been generated, which serve as the top layer of hair.

like the layers of an onion. These various layers correlate to each other, but you could have some random strands crisscrossing or sticking out. For a layered haircut, try pulling out the bottom back points on the lower layers so that the hair strands stick out from underneath. Figure 8-45 illustrates all three layers, each containing 60 splines.

Copy and paste all the rail-cloned splines into one layer. If necessary, continue shaping the hair while keeping the head in a background layer. In order for the hair not to look too symmetrical, try changing the front of it a little. Another suggestion is to jitter the hair a little so that it looks more natural.

If you plan to apply soft-body dynamics to the hair, it is a good idea to create another set of strands that are very close to the skull. When the hair moves, the short hair against the head will keep the bare skull covered.

So far, you have created the outermost guides for the hair. The inner layers that are closer to the skull will now be made with rail cloning.

In the layer that contains your other two connected splines, select only the second one and paste it into its own layer. Separate the first spline and its connecting curves into two layers. Change your view so that the beginning curve is in the foreground and its connecting splines are in the background layer.

Use the rail clone tool to make 60 copies of the second spline. Use a magnet or other tools to modify these splines.

Repeat this process with the third set of curves. You should now have three layers of hair, with each layer being closer to the skull,

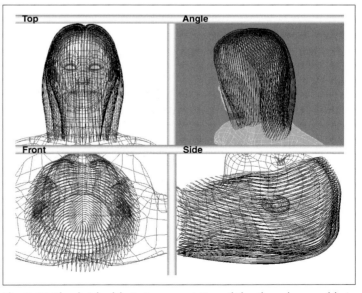

Fig. 8-45 The finished hairpiece consisting of the three layers of hair, which gradually come closer to the head.

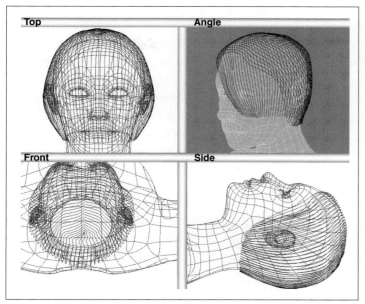

To make this extra hair, you can copy and paste the set of 60 curves that are closest to the skull into another layer. Delete the bottom points to make the curves shorter. Use a magnet tool or any other modifying tool to move points closer to the head. Figure 8-46 illustrates the short hair curves that will remain unaffected by dynamics.

If you are working with a polygon-based software package, the splines will now have to be converted to two-point poly chains. This is either built into your hair generator software or available as a plug-in. Consult the software manual for more information about this.

Your hair guides could also be set up to move in a specific manner. Figure 8-47 illustrates two methods for indicating the amount of flexibility each section of the hair will have when it is affected by dynamics. If your soft-

Fig. 8-46 The short hairpiece that is situated close to the skull. It sits underneath the longer hair, is unaffected by soft-body dynamics, and thus always covers the bare skull.

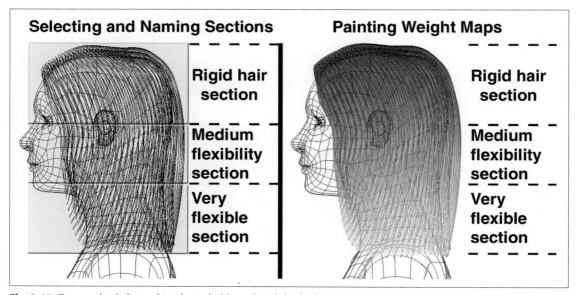

Fig. 8-47 Two methods for making hair pliable with soft-body dynamics. The first one (left) names surfaces that have different degrees of suppleness. The second method (right) uses weight maps and is clearly the superior way of designating degrees of flexibility.

body dynamics engine does not support weight maps then you will most likely have to select parts of the hair and assign names to them. The illustration shows how the hair near the top of the skull moves less than the middle section. The bottom part will have the least resistance to dynamic forces. Painting weight maps on the hair is the most logical way to specify how much each area on the hairpiece will move.

One of the great features of soft-body dynamics is its ability to make use of collision objects. Rather than having your character's hair strands penetrate and go through the skin, you can create a collision object that keeps the hair on top of the surface. The collision object does not have to be detailed since it will be unseen by the camera. Figure 8-48 depicts a low-polygon-count

collision object that sits right on top of the model. Notice that the object extends down to the upper torso. This keeps long hair from sinking into the body.

The collision object is parented to the head bone so that it follows the character's movements. The close-to-the-skull hair and the wig are in turn parented to the collision object or to the head bone.

Figure 8-49 shows what happens when collision detection is turned on. Even though the wig was modeled with parts of it piercing the mesh of the model,

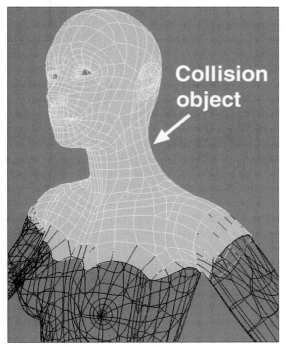

Fig. 8-48 A low-polygon-count collision object (light gray with white lines) sits on top of the character model. It keeps the hair from penetrating the skin during soft-body dynamics.

Fig. 8-49 The collision object is set to be unseen by the camera during rendering. Thus the hair appears to rest against and bounce off the skin.

once the soft-body dynamics engine is activated the hair situates itself above the skin. You can even see where it parts at the shoulder as it reacts to the collision object. A more detailed description of soft-body dynamics can be found at the end of this chapter.

Figures 8-50 and 8-51 illustrate some close-up views of hair generated with the help of guides. The guides themselves are unseen by the renderer so that only the hair that is grown along them can be seen. Figure 8-50 shows the rendered hair on the female model. Figure 8-51 illustrates curly hair on the male model. This was achieved by jittering shorter hair strands. Both images can be seen in color on the CD-ROM as CD8-50 and CD8-51.

HAIR GENERATOR SETTINGS

Hair rendering can sometimes be a confusing task, considering all the options available in some packages. Programs like Sasquatch™ by Worley Labs, Inc., have a dizzying array of settings that require a great amount of time for experimenting with various combinations.

To simplify the process of creating hair, Figures 8-52 through 8-55 illustrate various methods of manipulating it. Color images can be viewed on the CD-ROM as CD8-52 through CD8-55. Each attribute has been rendered at a different percentage or amount. The names of hair settings may differ among hair generators, but the following definitions may help you decide which ones approximate the terms used in your software.

Length Variation. This makes the fibers at the ends change in length. A setting of 0% makes all the fibers the same length, while a setting of 100% makes each a different length, varying from a size 0 to the actual size of the guide (100%).

Fig. 8-50 The final rendered hair.

Fig. 8-51 Curly hair made by jittering the hair guides.

Coarseness. This determines the thickness of the fibers. Small settings make thin hair, while large percentages make thicker hair.

Tip Narrowing. Hair can become narrower at the ends with this setting. Low values keep the hair an even thickness, while high ones make the hair appear wispy at the ends.

Fiber Division. Just like splines that have more vertices on them, hair can also be divided into

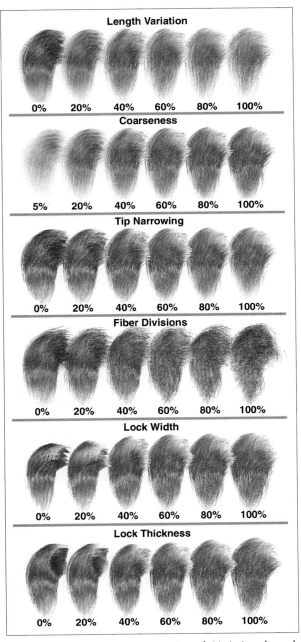

Fig. 8-52 Hair generator settings: Length Variation through Lock Thickness.

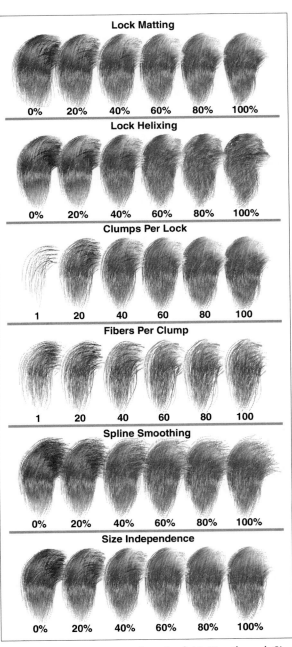

Fig. 8-53 Hair generator settings: Lock Matting through Size Independence.

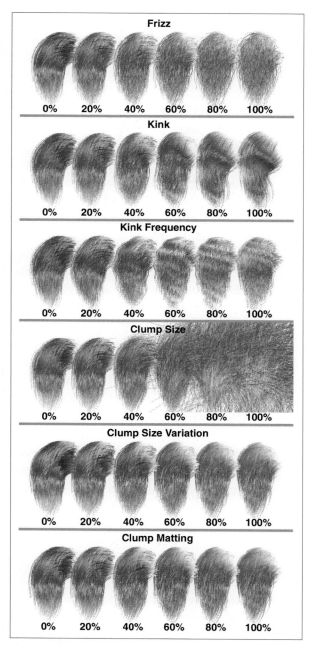

Fig. 8-54 Hair generator settings: Frizz through Clump Matting.

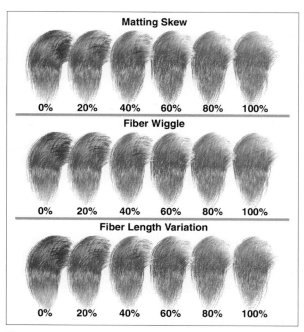

Fig. 8-55 Hair generator settings: Matting Skew through Fiber Length Variation.

smaller segments. This setting is useful for hair that changes direction often, since it helps keep it smooth. High settings can increase rendering time and sometimes cause twisting in the hair.

Lock Width. Hair thickness can be increased by spreading it sideways. If you have a lower amount of guide chains, you can still make the hair appear fuller by increasing this setting.

Lock Thickness. Turning up this setting will make a deeper layer of hair.

Lock Matting. Higher values make the hair grow closer at the tips. This is useful for wet-looking hair. Low values spread the hair at the tips so that it looks dry.

Lock Helixing. Turning up this value will make the hair spiral around the center of the guides.

Clumps Per Lock. This controls how many clumps are made for each guide. If you have a lot of guides, you can use lower settings. Higher values will result in denser hair and longer rendering times.

Fibers Per Clump. Fiber density can be precisely manipulated with this control. If you set larger numbers for Fibers Per Clump, rendering times will increase. To determine how many fibers are generated for each guide, multiply the Clumps Per Lock times the Fibers Per Clump.

Spline Smoothing. This option controls how closely the hair fibers follow the shape of the guide chains. When your guide chains do not have many points, it is useful to turn this setting up to make smooth curves. Rendering times increase with higher values.

Size Independence. You can control the width of various hair fibers by adjusting this setting. Low values will make short and long guides generate the same hair width. High values result in more size independence, meaning that short guides will now generate narrower widths than the long guides.

Frizz. Natural deviation in hair is influenced with this setting. Fibers can be randomly agitated. High values will make hair look wild and out of control.

Kink. When you want long hair to look like it is wavy, try turning up Kink. You can also determine how many waves are in the hair by using Kink Frequency.

Kink Frequency. A higher setting of this option will create more wiggles in the hair. Adjust Kink with Kink Frequency.

Clump Size. With this option, hair can be packed closer together (low values) or spread apart (high values).

Clump Size Variation. This will disturb the arrangement of hair clumps. Small percentages will keep the clumps at a similar scale, while high percentages will make every clump vary in size.

Clump Matting. Increasing Clump Matting makes the fibers gather closer together at the end of the clump. This could be suitable for wet hair. A low value creates a bushy look at the end of the clump.

Matting Skew. This setting works right along with Clump Matting. It determines how quickly the clump of hair packs together. Low values make the clump smaller near its base, medium values make the clump gradually smaller along its entire length, and high values compress them mostly near the tip.

Fiber Wiggle. You can vary the amount that each fiber moves to and fro. Hair appears smooth and straight when the value is low. High values will agitate the hair more. When matting makes the hair compress at the ends, Fiber Wiggle will make the center bulge out a little.

Fiber Length Variation. When you want to make the hair look less even at the bottom, then increase Fiber Length Variation. Low settings create hair that appears to be the same length.

A great variety of attributes can be obtained by changing just a few parameters in the hair settings. Figures 8-56 through 8-64 illustrate different hair qualities and their corresponding values. Figure 8-56 shows the base hair and its properties. Value changes in Figures 8-57 through 8-64 are indicated with bold italic type.

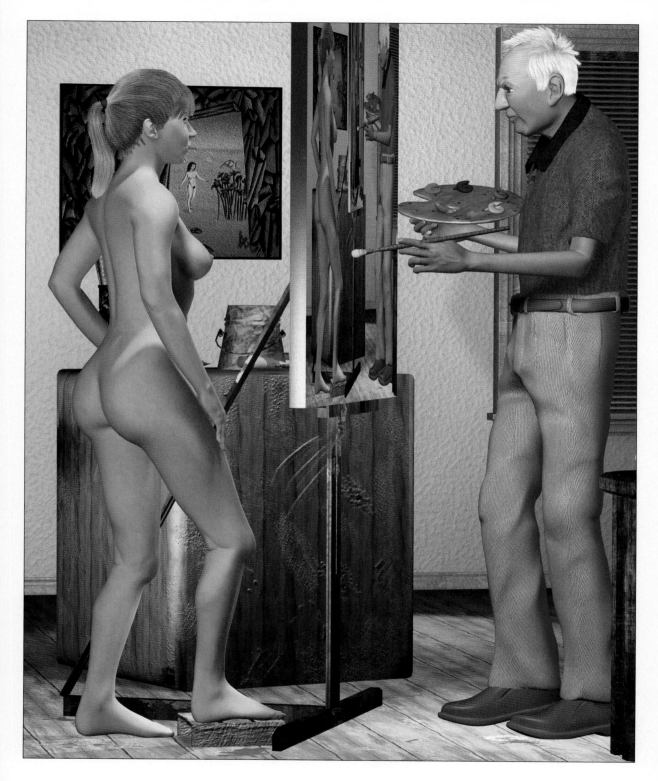

Figure 1 The Digital Artist by Peter Ratner, USA

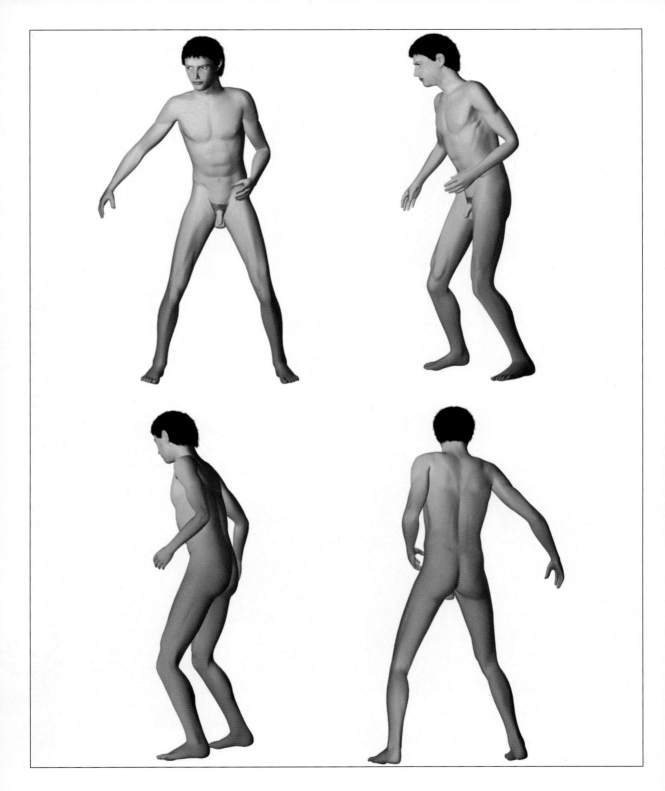

Figure 2 Male Views by Peter Ratner, USA

Figure 3 Windblown by Peter Ratner, USA

Figure 4 Saki_A by Kazuhiro Taneda and Keisuke Takai, Japan

Figure 5 Saki_B by Kazuhiro Taneda and Keisuke Takai, Japan

Figure 6 Yosei by Tetsuya Watanabe, Japan

Figure 7 Girl by Steven Stahlberg, USA

Figure 8 Model by Steven Stahlberg, USA

Figure 9 Hexin by Michel Roger, France

Figure 10 Mankoba by Michel Roger, France

Figure 11 Kaya by Alceu Baptistão, Brazil

Figure 12 A-Muse-Def by Loic Zimmermann, France

Figure 13 Am I Pretty by Park Eun-Kyong, South Korea

Figure 14 Drue by Park Eun-Kyong, South Korea

Figure 15 Jude by Choi Hun-Hwa, South Korea

Figure 16 Blue Girl by Sven Moll, Spain

我が生涯に一片の悔い無し

Figure 17 Samurai by Syunichi Shirai, Japan

Figure 18 Untitled by Syunichi Shirai, Japan

Figure 19 Untitled by Kei Nakamura, Japan

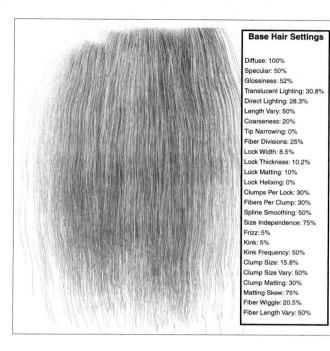

Base Hair Settings

Diffuse: 100%
Specular: 50%
Glossiness: 52%
Translucent Lighting: 30.8%
Direct Lighting: 28.3%
Length Vary: 50%
Coarseness: 20%
Tip Narrowing: 0%
Fiber Divisions: 25%
Lock Width: 8.5%
Lock Thickness: 10.2%
Lock Matting: 10%
Lock Helixing: 0%
Clumps Per Lock: 30%
Fibers Per Clump: 30%
Spline Smoothing: 50%
Size Independence: 75%
Frizz: 5%
Kink: 5%
Kink Frequency: 50%
Clump Size: 15.8%
Clump Size Vary: 50%
Clump Matting: 30%
Matting Skew: 75%
Fiber Wiggle: 20.5%
Fiber Length Vary: 50%

Fig. 8-56 These base hair settings were used as the starting point for different hair characteristics.

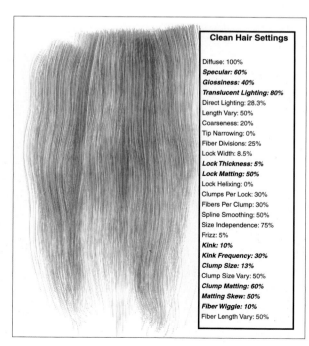

Clean Hair Settings

Diffuse: 100%
Specular: 60%
Glossiness: 40%
Translucent Lighting: 80%
Direct Lighting: 28.3%
Length Vary: 50%
Coarseness: 20%
Tip Narrowing: 0%
Fiber Divisions: 25%
Lock Width: 8.5%
Lock Thickness: 5%
Lock Matting: 50%
Lock Helixing: 0%
Clumps Per Lock: 30%
Fibers Per Clump: 30%
Spline Smoothing: 50%
Size Independence: 75%
Frizz: 5%
Kink: 10%
Kink Frequency: 30%
Clump Size: 13%
Clump Size Vary: 50%
Clump Matting: 60%
Matting Skew: 50%
Fiber Wiggle: 10%
Fiber Length Vary: 50%

Fig. 8-57 Clean hair settings. The bold italic type indicates values that were changed from the base settings.

175

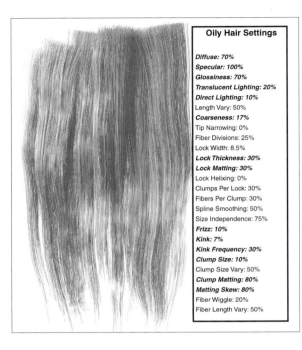

Oily Hair Settings

Diffuse: 70%
Specular: 100%
Glossiness: 70%
Translucent Lighting: 20%
Direct Lighting: 10%
Length Vary: 50%
Coarseness: 17%
Tip Narrowing: 0%
Fiber Divisions: 25%
Lock Width: 8.5%
Lock Thickness: 30%
Lock Matting: 30%
Lock Helixing: 0%
Clumps Per Lock: 30%
Fibers Per Clump: 30%
Spline Smoothing: 50%
Size Independence: 75%
Frizz: 10%
Kink: 7%
Kink Frequency: 30%
Clump Size: 10%
Clump Size Vary: 50%
Clump Matting: 80%
Matting Skew: 80%
Fiber Wiggle: 20%
Fiber Length Vary: 50%

Fig. 8-58 Oily hair settings.

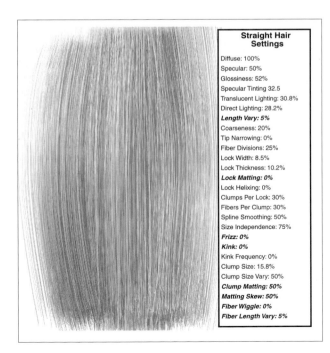

Straight Hair Settings

Diffuse: 100%
Specular: 50%
Glossiness: 52%
Specular Tinting 32.5
Translucent Lighting: 30.8%
Direct Lighting: 28.2%
Length Vary: 5%
Coarseness: 20%
Tip Narrowing: 0%
Fiber Divisions: 25%
Lock Width: 8.5%
Lock Thickness: 10.2%
Lock Matting: 0%
Lock Helixing: 0%
Clumps Per Lock: 30%
Fibers Per Clump: 30%
Spline Smoothing: 50%
Size Independence: 75%
Frizz: 0%
Kink: 0%
Kink Frequency: 0%
Clump Size: 15.8%
Clump Size Vary: 50%
Clump Matting: 50%
Matting Skew: 50%
Fiber Wiggle: 0%
Fiber Length Vary: 5%

Fig. 8-59 Straight hair settings.

Frizzy Hair Settings

Diffuse: 100%
Specular: 50%
Glossiness: 52%
Specular Tinting 32.5
Translucent Lighting: 30.8%
Direct Lighting: 28.2%
Length Vary: 50%
Coarseness: 20%
Tip Narrowing: 0%
Fiber Divisions: 25%
Lock Width: 8.5%
Lock Thickness: 10.2%
Lock Matting: 0%
Lock Helixing: 0%
Clumps Per Lock: 30%
Fibers Per Clump: 30%
Spline Smoothing: 50%
Size Independence: 75%
Frizz: 20%
Kink: 20%
Kink Frequency: 50%
Clump Size: 15.8%
Clump Size Vary: 50%
Clump Matting: 30%
Matting Skew: 50%
Fiber Wiggle: 10%
Fiber Length Vary: 50%

Fig. 8-60 Frizzy hair settings.

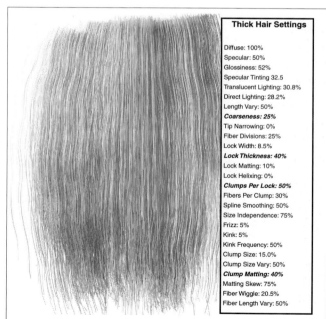

Thick Hair Settings

Diffuse: 100%
Specular: 50%
Glossiness: 52%
Specular Tinting 32.5
Translucent Lighting: 30.8%
Direct Lighting: 28.2%
Length Vary: 50%
Coarseness: 25%
Tip Narrowing: 0%
Fiber Divisions: 25%
Lock Width: 8.5%
Lock Thickness: 40%
Lock Matting: 10%
Lock Helixing: 0%
Clumps Per Lock: 50%
Fibers Per Clump: 30%
Spline Smoothing: 50%
Size Independence: 75%
Frizz: 5%
Kink: 5%
Kink Frequency: 50%
Clump Size: 15.0%
Clump Size Vary: 50%
Clump Matting: 40%
Matting Skew: 75%
Fiber Wiggle: 20.5%
Fiber Length Vary: 50%

Fig. 8-61 Thick hair settings.

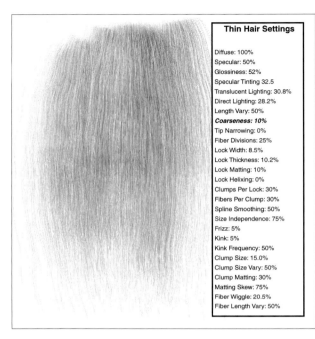

Thin Hair Settings

Diffuse: 100%
Specular: 50%
Glossiness: 52%
Specular Tinting 32.5
Translucent Lighting: 30.8%
Direct Lighting: 28.2%
Length Vary: 50%
Coarseness: 10%
Tip Narrowing: 0%
Fiber Divisions: 25%
Lock Width: 8.5%
Lock Thickness: 10.2%
Lock Matting: 10%
Lock Helixing: 0%
Clumps Per Lock: 30%
Fibers Per Clump: 30%
Spline Smoothing: 50%
Size Independence: 75%
Frizz: 5%
Kink: 5%
Kink Frequency: 50%
Clump Size: 15.0%
Clump Size Vary: 50%
Clump Matting: 30%
Matting Skew: 75%
Fiber Wiggle: 20.5%
Fiber Length Vary: 50%

Fig. 8-62 Thin hair settings.

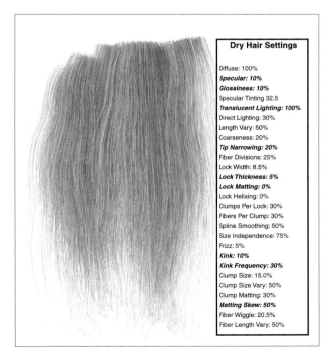

Dry Hair Settings

Diffuse: 100%
Specular: 10%
Glossiness: 10%
Specular Tinting 32.5
Translucent Lighting: 100%
Direct Lighting: 30%
Length Vary: 50%
Coarseness: 20%
Tip Narrowing: 20%
Fiber Divisions: 25%
Lock Width: 8.5%
Lock Thickness: 5%
Lock Matting: 0%
Lock Helixing: 0%
Clumps Per Lock: 30%
Fibers Per Clump: 30%
Spline Smoothing: 50%
Size Independence: 75%
Frizz: 5%
Kink: 10%
Kink Frequency: 30%
Clump Size: 15.0%
Clump Size Vary: 50%
Clump Matting: 30%
Matting Skew: 50%
Fiber Wiggle: 20.5%
Fiber Length Vary: 50%

Fig. 8-63 Dry hair settings.

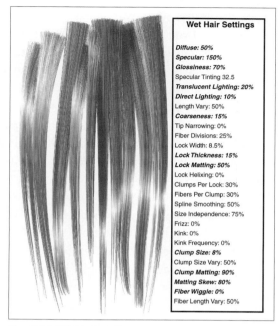

Wet Hair Settings

Diffuse: 50%
Specular: 150%
Glossiness: 70%
Specular Tinting 32.5
Translucent Lighting: 20%
Direct Lighting: 10%
Length Vary: 50%
Coarseness: 15%
Tip Narrowing: 0%
Fiber Divisions: 25%
Lock Width: 8.5%
Lock Thickness: 15%
Lock Matting: 50%
Lock Helixing: 0%
Clumps Per Lock: 30%
Fibers Per Clump: 30%
Spline Smoothing: 50%
Size Independence: 75%
Frizz: 0%
Kink: 0%
Kink Frequency: 0%
Clump Size: 8%
Clump Size Vary: 50%
Clump Matting: 90%
Matting Skew: 80%
Fiber Wiggle: 0%
Fiber Length Vary: 50%

Fig. 8-64 Wet hair settings.

SOFT-BODY DYNAMICS

Soft-body dynamics is a physics emulation software engine that calculates the effects of wind, gravity, and object motions. The object that is affected by these forces becomes a flexible mass. By setting specific parameters, you can simulate cloth, rubber, gelatin, and so on. Normally when the software calculates dynamics it takes into account the effects of motions induced by a skeleton, displacement, inverse kinematics, and other forces applied to the object. Since dynamics calculates the physical effects of specific forces, it is independent of keyframing. For example, the fluttering motions of a flag do not have to be keyframed.

Any software package that implements soft-body dynamics will most likely have its own unique termi-nology. Some general definitions that might be applied to various 3-D software follow.

OBJECT SETTINGS

Target. The elastic body that is influenced by other target or collision objects. In effect, it is the flexible soft body.

Collision Detection. This specifies whether the object itself is influenced by or impacts the flexible object on contact.

Pressure Effect. Objects that are closed and have similarities to spherical shapes can be made to maintain their volume by turning up this set-ting. Higher numbers can make the flexible object appear to be filled with a stiffer gel rather than water.

Fiber Structure. An object that is made to appear as if it is made from a thin fiber material will have higher settings, while a stiffer, thicker material will have lower settings.

SURFACE SETTINGS

Weight. This defines the heaviness of the soft-body material. Higher settings make the object hang down and be less susceptible to move-ment by various forces.

Weight +. Higher numbers add more randomness to the material's weight.

Spring. You can control the elasticity or stiffness of the soft-body object with this parameter. Extremely large values make a clothlike object more rigid, as if it had been starched.

Viscosity. A soft-body object tends to keep its original shape more with higher values. This parameter controls how much impact a colli-sion will have on a soft body.

Resistance. This setting controls the amount of air resistance. A higher setting will make the material stretch more since it has a higher resistance to air flow.

Parallel Resistance. This is used to control the amount of air resistance parallel to the soft-body object's surface. A setting of 100% should yield normal results for falling objects such as cloth or leaves. Lower values will reduce the air resistance and make them fall faster.

Back Resistance. When you want to increase the effects of wind on the back side of the object, then decrease the back air resistance. A value of 100% keeps the air resistance on the back the same as that on the front. When you have overlapping objects, the effects of wind on the back can become weaker since the wind can be blocked by the second object. To increase the effects of the wind on the back, you can then reduce the value of Back Resistance.

Fixed. The object is not affected by soft-body dynamics. It remains rigid and is most often used as a collision object. In the example animation in Chapter 12, it is the flour inside the sack. Many times this collision object is made invisible to the camera.

Substructure. Two-dimensional forms such as a piece of cloth can often become distorted, abnormally stretch, and create unwanted wrinkles. They can also resist bending in other directions, which may result in unnatural motions. A substructure is a form that can be applied to the object, which then restricts its instability as if it had thickness. Higher values help an object keep its normal shape but will result in longer calculation times.

Hold Structure. When you have a 3-D soft-body object and you want to keep it from collapsing during a collision, apply a higher setting to the hold structure. This will help it maintain its original shape. Hold Structure produces a uniform effect throughout the object, while Substructure, which is nonlinear, creates a more natural look. Try using a combination of both settings to achieve the right solution.

Smoothing. When you have an object with two surfaces—one being fixed so as not to be affected by soft-body dynamics and the other acting as the target or flexible surface—you can smooth out the transition between them with this setting. For example, if you have a sail blown by wind and its corner surfaces are fixed so as to keep it from blowing out of your scene, you can apply Smoothing to both surfaces and prevent unwanted wrinkling from occurring between the two areas.

Stretch Limit. A surface can often stretch like rubber. To restrict the amount of stretching, lower the Stretch Limit value.

Compress Stress. This value controls the stiffness of an object under stress. A soft cotton cloth would have a low Compress Stress setting, while a stiffer object such as paper would have a higher Compress Stress setting. When both are dropped on a collision surface, the cloth, with its low Compress Stress setting, would show folds, while the paper, with high Compress Stress settings, would appear more rigid.

Shrink. This parameter can be used to specify how much a fabric should shrink. At 100% there is no shrinkage. At 90%, the size of the surface is reduced to 90%. This option is useful when you want to reduce the looseness of a fabric. Shrink can really slow down calculation time. The more shrinkage that you apply, the longer the calculation time.

Self-collision. This prevents the surface from intersecting or crossing itself. Since the collision detection has to be determined from every angle, calculation times increase dramatically when this is turned on.

Collision Detection. This setting has to be on when you want the soft-body object to be affected by the colliding surface. It will notice when other objects collide with it and adjust its form accordingly. The surface normals of the collision object have to face toward the soft-body object (target) or the soft-body object will pass right through the collision object. For example, if you have a bottle of water and the water object is the soft body (target) while the bottle is the fixed collision object, the surface normals of the bottle will have to face inward to keep the water from leaking out.

Skin Thickness. When Skin Thickness is not set high enough, parts of the target object will penetrate the collision object. Turning up the Skin Thickness setting on the collision object creates a gap between it and the soft-body target. This will prevent any penetration and keep the two surfaces separate from each other during collision.

Friction. This option controls the slickness of the soft-body target surface. If you want the target surface to stick more to the collision object, then increase the Friction value.

Bound Force. You can set some bounce to the target object when it hits your collision object. The higher your settings, the more the object will rebound from the collision surface. Set the Bound Force to the collision object. Higher settings will create a stronger invisible force field around the collision object.

Action Force. This option determines whether or not the colliding soft-body target receives the reaction force at the time of the collision. It does not affect the collision object.

Bind Force. If you want the colliding soft-body target object to stick to the collision surface, then turn up the values for Bind Force. When Bind Force has a setting other than 0, Fix Force becomes available. By applying higher settings to Fix Force, the target object sticks to the collision surface without sliding. With Bind Force and Fix Force on, you can make sticky, rubbery objects like suction cups or any other disgusting viscous substance.

Soft-body dynamics applied to hair is one of the most useful features of this animation tool. Follow-through, the fifth animation principle discussed in Chapter 12, is very noticeable in the movement of long hair. Basically this principle says that when one body incites another, it causes involuntary action by the second body. When a female with long hair shakes her head, it is followed by the motion of her hair.

SETTING UP A SKELETON

In human anatomy, the skeleton carries the weight and serves as the foundation for the body. The muscles are attached to the skeleton with tendons. By contraction, muscles move the bones. The skeleton influences the form of the figure underneath the skin, fat, and muscles. In some parts of the body the skeleton is always discernible on the surface, while in other areas it appears only during certain movements.

While 3-D humans share some structural characteristics with real-life ones, the differences are much greater. The skeleton in animation is used mostly for movement and rarely adds structure to the body. Unless you are using a sophisticated muscular/skeletal system for animation, your character's bones will most likely look like simple geometric shapes. When these are rotated, they affect the polygons, splines, or NURBS mesh.

Any parts of the anatomy that represent skeletal forms appearing on the surface will most likely have been modeled on the mesh itself. The absence of muscles and fat in a digital human accounts for many problems that appear during animation. These are usually found at the joints. During movements, crimping—like that in a bent garden hose—and creases, as well as unwanted protuberances, often appear. There is also a lack of muscular deformation under the skin, which makes it very difficult to create realistic human motion.

At the time of this writing only a few companies use proprietary software capable of realistic skeletal/muscular movement. The rest of us, who are using off-the-shelf software, have to rely on specific techniques to overcome these limitations.

MAKING A SKELETON

In some software packages, gimbal lock occurs when an object no longer rotates correctly around one or more of its axes. This occurs when two rotational axes of an object point in the same direction. The object will no longer rotate the way you think it should.

Any animation system that uses Euler angles will have gimbal lock problems. The reason for this is that Euler angles evaluate each axis independently in a set order such as x, y, and then z. This makes it very easy to have the object point in the same direction on two axes.

Quaternion rotations, on the other hand, evaluate all three axes at the same time to find a direction in which to travel and a fourth value (the w component or up-vector) to tell the matrix how far to travel. Gimbal lock never occurs because all three axes are updated at the same time. The disadvantage to using them is that they are far more complicated to read and conceptualize than Euler angles.

When using an animation system that relies on Euler angles, there are several ways to get around the gimbal lock problem. If your software allows you to change the order of axis rotation, then try to match it to the direction in which your object is moving. For example, when rotating along one axis—for example, y—make the order of axes y, z, x. When rotating down two axes, change the order to correspond with the first and last axes. So if the object is rotated down the x and y axes, change the order of axes to x, z, and y.

Another method that works well for most systems is to make each bone so that it already faces in the direction in which it will be rotated. This means drawing the various bones in different views. For example, if the figure is standing up facing forward on the z axis and you are making the spine bones, then draw them in the front or back views. This will ensure that the spine bones will rotate around the x axis or pitch and tilt where most spine movements occur for bending forward or back. Finger bones are drawn in the top or bottom view so that each digit can rotate around the z axis.

Some of the more flexible software packages allow you to edit the rotational axes of individual bones. Using a kind of Edit Skeleton tool allows you to select a bone and move its bone up-tags so that they face in the direction necessary for most of that bone's rotations.

There are many methods by which to rig a character for animation. The character's shape and proportions determine the skeleton hierarchy, and your software's tools dictate the manner in which it will be implemented. Needless to say, with all these variables there are no right and wrong ways of rigging a 3-D character. The following instructions are meant only as a general guideline and are not meant to be accepted as *the* way to rig a human character.

Figure 9-1 illustrates front and side views of a skeleton placed inside a female character. The hierarchy starts at the groin. The pelvic area is where most move-

ments originate from, so it is appropriate to place the parent bone there. This first bone in the middle of the pelvis will have child bones going in several directions.

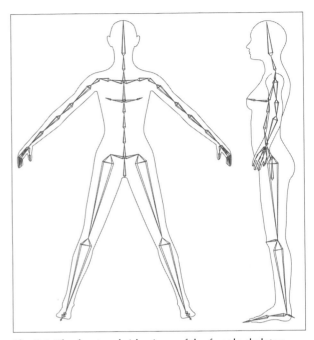

Fig. 9-1 The front and side views of the female skeleton.

If your software orients the rotation of bones according to the view in which they are created and your model is facing forward in the front-view window, then use your skeleton tool to draw the parent bone in the front or back view (Figure 9-2). If possible, work in a separate layer, with the wireframe view of the model in a back layer.

Start at the base of the groin and draw almost halfway toward the belly button. While the parent bone is still active, draw the next bone by clicking on the area toward which you want it to extend. This will be the right hipbone, labeled "2" in Figure 9-2. Click in the middle of the knee to make the third bone, which is for the upper leg. If you need to move or

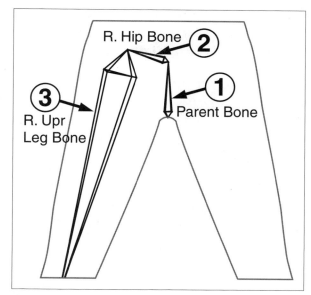

Fig. 9-2 The first bone is the parent at the groin (1). From it comes the child bone. This is the second bone, the right hip (2), followed by the upper leg (3). These bones are drawn in the front view.

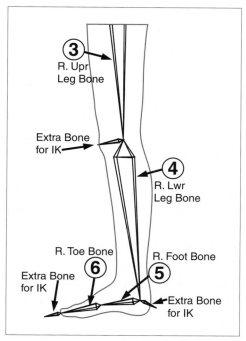

Fig. 9-3 The rest of the leg bones. The small toe tip and knee bones can be used to attach goal objects such as a null for inverse kinematics.

scale a bone, then use the available tools but do *not* weld one bone to another. Instead, make one bone the child of another by going to your skeleton tree, hierarchy window, spreadsheet, or whatever window you have available that lists the order of the bones. Move the child bone under its parent. While you are there, name the bones: Parent, R.Hip, R.UprLeg, R.LwrLeg, and so on.

Figure 9-3 illustrates all the right leg bones. Be sure to name all these bones in the skeleton tree and make certain the hierarchy is correct. Procrastinating on naming bones can lead to confusion later on. You will have many bones and not know what parts of the body they control. As you continue creating and naming bones, you can use the hierarchical skeleton chart in Figure 9-8 as reference.

If your software allows it, start at the top of the leg hierarchy, select the parent bone, and turn on the Edit

Skeleton tool. The small bone up-tags can then be moved to align each bone's rotational axes. Figure 9-4 depicts a view of these bone up-tags. The smaller circle is dragged around to set the bones' rotational axes. Be sure to work in several views. As you can see in Figure 9-4, the leg bones have their rotational axes set to x, or pitch and tilt.

After setting the leg bones' rotational axes, select the hip and all the rest of the leg bones. Use your Mirror tool to copy these along the 0 x axis for the left leg bones (Figure 9-4). You should now have a mirrored duplicate of the right hip and leg bones for the left side of the body.

The left hip and left leg bones will now have to be made child bones of the parent bone. In your skeleton tree window, move these under the parent bone.

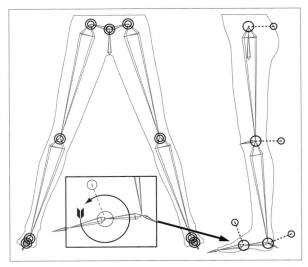

Fig. 9-4 Bone up-tags are used to orient the bones along the right rotational axes. Note the rotation direction indicated by the smaller circles. The right hip and leg bones are selected and mirrored on the 0 x axis.

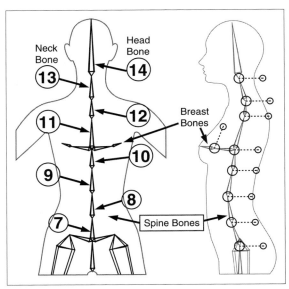

Fig. 9-5 The spine bones. Note the bone up-tags set with the Edit Skeleton tool.

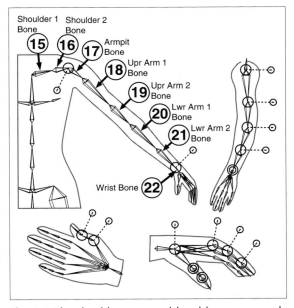

Fig. 9-6 The shoulder, arm, and hand bones are made coming from a spine bone. Note the direction of the bone up-tags.

Rename them L.Hip, L.UprLeg, and so on. Make sure both right and left bones are child bones of the parent bone.

Select the parent bone and, using your Edit Skeleton tool, click below the belly button to make the first spine bone. You can use Figure 9-5 as a guide for creating the spine, neck, and head bones as well as their rotational axes. Figure 9-5 shows their bone up-tags in the side view.

Continue working your way up through the head. If you are modeling a female, make right and left breastbones that are child bones of the chest bone. The bones leading to the breasts are left inactive. They are basically placeholders. The end bones are used to move the breasts.

Situated at a juncture, the spine bone above the breastbones serves as a parent to the neck and shoulder bones. Figure 9-6 depicts the shoulder, arm, and hand bones. A wrist bone controls entire hand movements. The bone up-tags for the arm and fingers can also be seen in Figure 9-6.

Once the entire arm and shoulders are completed, mirror them for the other side of the body. Be sure to set the hierarchy for the shoulder and arm bones underneath the spine bone. Rename the bones for that side of the body.

ASSIGNING WEIGHT MAPS

A number of 3-D software programs allow users the ability to assign values to vertices. These values are often referred to as weights. They control the degree of influence one can exert on specific parts of an object. For example, weights can be painted on an area to control the rigidity or flexibility of the model. One of the most useful functions for weights is the ability to control which bones influence specific parts of a character.

After creating a skeleton, you can assign specific vertices or polygons to each bone. This will ensure that you have more accurate deformations of the body by the skeleton.

Set your view so that you can see the skeleton as well as the wire mesh. If possible, keep the skeleton in a background layer. Select one section of your wire mesh model at a time and assign it a weight name (Figure 9-7). For example, start by selecting the right leg, assign it the weight name R.Leg, and then hide it. In your hierarchical skeleton tree, next to the name of the right upper leg bone and under the heading weight, assign the weight name R.Leg to this part of the skeleton.

Depending on your software, you might be able to do this in its spreadsheet editor, which allows you to make multiple selections of bones and assign a previously determined weight map to them. This would most likely come under the heading "Bone Properties: Influence."

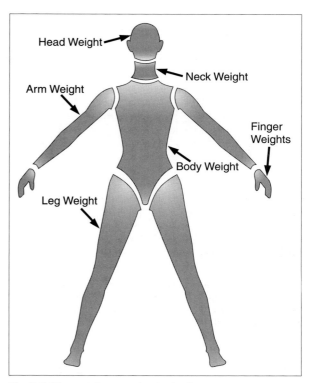

Fig. 9-7 The weight maps for the body.

Use Figure 9-7 as a guide for selecting parts of the wire mesh and assigning weight maps to them. As you can see, the fingers will have their own weight maps. If your software has the capability to automatically assign weight maps according to bone placement, then use it on each hand. Each digit will have a weight map corresponding to its nearest bone. Figure 9-8 shows the entire skeleton hierarchy with the weight maps that have been specified for each bone.

Continue by selecting another section of your human, assign it an appropriate weight name, hide this part, and then designate this weight name to the skeleton hierarchy. You might decide to wait until all the weight maps have been designated before opening the spreadsheet editor to allocate them to the bones.

Female Skeleton Tree

Skeleton	Bone Properties: Influence
Parent -	Body Weight
R.Hip-	Body Weight
R.UprLeg	R.Leg Weight
R.LwrLeg	R.Leg Weight
R.Foot	R.Leg Weight
R.Toe	R.Leg Weight
R.ToeTip -	R.Leg Weight
R.Ankle	R.Leg Weight
L.Hip -	Body Weight
L.UprLeg	L.Leg Weight
L.LwrLeg	L.Leg Weight
L.Foot	L.Leg Weight
L.Toe	L.Leg Weight
L.ToeTip -	L.Leg Weight
L.Ankle	L.Leg Weight
Spine1	Body Weight
Spine2	Body Weight
Spine3	Body Weight
Spine4	Body Weight
Spine5	Body Weight
Spine6	
R.Breast	Body Weight
L.Breast	Body Weight
R.Shoulder1	Body Weight
R.Shoulder2	Body Weight
R.Armpit	Arm Weight
R.UprArm1	Arm Weight
R.UprArm2	Arm Weight
R.LwrArm1	Arm Weight
R.LwrArm2	Arm Weight
R.Wrist	Arm Weight
Neck	NeckWeight
Head	HeadWeight
L.Shoulder1	Body Weight
L.Shoulder2	Body Weight
L.Armpit	Arm Weight
L.UprArm1	Arm Weight
L.UprArm2	Arm Weight
L.LwrArm1	Arm Weight
L.LwrArm2	Arm Weight
L.Wrist	Arm Weight

Female Skeleton Tree Cont. - Hands

Skeleton	Bone Properties: Influence
R.Wrist	Arm Weight
R.ThumbBase	Hand Weight
R.Thumb	Thumb Weight
R.ThumbTip	Thumb Weight
R.PointyFingerBase	Hand Weight
R.PointyFinger	PointyFinger Weight
R.PointyFingerMiddle	PointyFinger Weight
R.PointyFingerTip	PointyFinger Weight
R.IndexFingerBase	Hand Weight
R.IndexFinger	IndexFinger Weight
R.IndexFingerMiddle	IndexFinger Weight
R.IndexFingerTip	IndexFinger Weight
R.RingFingerBase	Hand Weight
R.RingFinger	RingFinger Weight
R.RingFingerMiddle	RingFinger Weight
R.RingFingerTip	RingFinger Weight
R.PinkyFingerBase	Hand Weight
R.PinkyFinger	PinkyFinger Weight
R.PinkyFingerMiddle	PinkyFinger Weight
R.PinkyFingerTip	PinkyFinger Weight
L.Wrist	Arm Weight
L.ThumbBase	Hand Weight
L.Thumb	Thumb Weight
L.ThumbTip	Thumb Weight
L.PointyFingerBase	Hand Weight
L.PointyFinger	PointyFinger Weight
L.PointyFingerMiddle	PointyFinger Weight
L.PointyFingerTip	PointyFinger Weight
L.IndexFingerBase	Hand Weight
L.IndexFinger	IndexFinger Weight
L.IndexFingerMiddle	IndexFinger Weight
L.IndexFingerTip	IndexFinger Weight
L.RingFingerBase	Hand Weight
L.RingFinger	RingFinger Weight
L.RingFingerMiddle	RingFinger Weight
L.RingFingerTip	RingFinger Weight
L.PinkyFingerBase	Hand Weight
L.PinkyFinger	PinkyFinger Weight
L.PinkyFingerMiddle	PinkyFinger Weight
L.PinkyFingerTip	PinkyFinger Weight

Fig. 9-8 A hierarchical view of the entire female skeleton tree. The grid lines should serve as an aid to deciphering the order of each bone.

Eventually all the components of your human model will be hidden and you will know that each vertex or polygon has been assigned to a specific bone. Breaking up every finger and thumb into specific sections at the joints can be tedious, but it's important for making hand animation an easy task. Of course, as mentioned before, some software packages can automatically generate weight maps, simplifying the entire process.

In the animation part of your program, you can now test the various bones to see how well the mesh deforms. If your model is in subdivision mode, then be sure to change the subdivision order to last. This will ensure that your model doesn't have creasing in places where two bones meet. The smoothing effect of subdivision surfaces occurs at the end rather than before some displacement effect. If possible, turn on joint compensation for the bones in the hands, arms, and legs.

ADJUSTING WEIGHT MAPS

Whenever you find that bones do not behave the way they should, then go back to your weight maps and adjust them with an airbrush or weight painting tool (Figure 9-9). Choose only the area that you want to work on and hide everything else. Now select the weight name for the part that you plan to adjust. Set your view window to Weight Shade so that you can see the weight map in color. Let's assume the color red stands for a very strong positive weight influence, light green is neutral, and blue is a strong negative weight influence.

Using your airbrush or weight map painting tool, you will now begin to paint or take away weight. Be sure to bring up the numeric or options box for the weight painting tool and have it open the entire time. This will make it easier to change settings as you work. In the tool's box, select the name of the weight

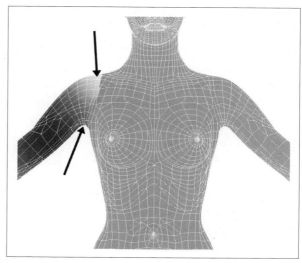

Fig. 9-9 Adjusting the falloff for the right arm weight map.

map that you assigned to the part previously. Set the radius of your brush. You might also be able to do this by clicking and dragging with your right mouse button. Set your airbrush strength. Fifty percent might be a good starting point.

Your software may allow you to use the following shortcuts for painting weights. To add positive values (red = stronger influence), click and drag with your left mouse button. To erase values (light green = no influence), bringing the weight to a neutral setting, hold down the control key while painting with the left mouse button down. To subtract values (blue = negative influence) by painting negative weight, hold down the shift key while painting with the left mouse button down.

SETTING UP AN INVERSE KINEMATICS SKELETON

Unlike hard-body and soft-body dynamics, kinematics is a branch of dynamics that deals with movement separate from considerations of mass and force. Software that requires the user to set up an articulated hierarchical structure and then move parts of the figure starting at the top utilizes forward kinematics (FK). For example, to move a leg, one has to rotate the leg itself, which in turn moves the lower leg and foot.

Inverse kinematics reverses this process and allows the user the freedom to start at the bottom of the hierarchy. For example, to move the foot, simply select and maneuver the foot, and the rest of the leg follows. In some instances it makes things easier for the animator but harder for the programmer. Most 3-D animation software that is used for character animation implements IK in one form or another.

Well-implemented IK should have three functions. The first is the ability to use the IK skeleton as a bone structure that moves the outer shell of the 3-D model. The second function enables a part to be anchored. For example, one could anchor the feet, and thus when the rest of the body is rotated the feet remain stationary and rooted to the ground. The third allows the user to assign limits and parameters to joints. Thus the 3-D figure could have joints with the same freedom of movement, or lack of, as the joints of a real human.

If you decide to create a full IK setup on your skeleton, then refer to Figure 9-10. The illustration shows front and side views of a human female skeleton with the location of goal objects in key areas of the hierarchy. Each of these is used to drive a part of the human.

An anchor is established with the parent bone at the groin by making it unaffected by IK. This is similar in principle to a hoist used for lifting heavy objects—it has to be stabilized somewhere or it becomes a useless tool.

In order to get a rolling motion at the feet for walk cycles, you may also want to parent the goal object located at the ankle to the toe tip goal object. When you move the toe goal object or null, the ankle goal

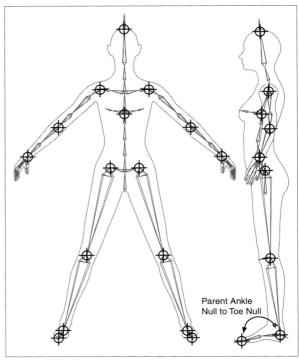

Fig. 9-10 A full inverse kinematics setup. The parent bone located at the groin remains unaffected by IK. The plus signs with circles are the goal objects (sometimes nulls are used) that move parts of the body.

will follow. When the body is moved forward, the toe goal object anchors the front of the foot to the floor, while the ankle goal exerts less influence, causing the back of the foot to lift a little for the rolling action. The ankle goal objects are also used to fine-tune certain foot positions.

Extra child bones that have no strength and can be left inactive are placed at the joints. The goal objects are then assigned to these. The pivot points of these bones become the center of their assigned goal objects.

The goal objects at the knees and elbows are important for adjusting the positions of the arms and legs. Without them, the limbs often snap into undesirable postures during an animation. They also give the animator greater control when moving the limbs.

Goal objects could be placed on the middle and tip of each finger, but this can become somewhat cumbersome. Too many goal objects could even slow down the animation process as the artist hunts around for the right goal object. As mentioned before, IK is not as precise as FK since all the movements on a chain of bones become compressed into a few goal objects. You may find it easier and more accurate to just rotate the fingers with FK or set up morph targets for them.

Figure 9-11 shows a different hierarchical setup using a mixture of inverse and forward kinematics. This option offers the best of both worlds. The feet can stay anchored to the ground while the character walks or simply shifts its weight around. The upper body can

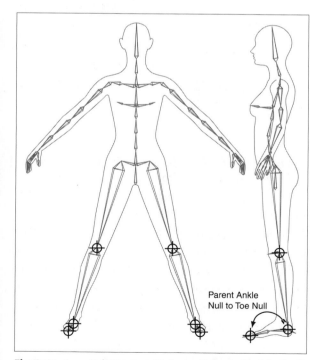

Parent Ankle
Null to Toe Null

Fig. 9-11 A partial IK setup. Only the lower half of the body has IK, while bones are rotated and moved on the upper half.

be positioned accurately by rotating and moving the bones themselves.

To assemble a partial IK hierarchy, start by creating six nulls. These will be the goal objects. Name each of them: R.KneeNull, L.KneeNull, R.ToeNull, L.ToeNull, R.AnkleNull, L.AnkleNull.

Parent the R.AnkleNull to the R.ToeNull. Do the same to the left ankle and toe nulls. Now when you move the toe null, the ankle nulls should follow. Most of the time you will not have to move the ankle nulls, but they are handy for adjusting the position of the foot.

Move each of the six nulls to their respective positions. Place them at the bases (starting points) of the following bones:

R.KneeNull → right knee bone
L.KneeNull → left knee bone
R.ToeNull → right toe tip bone
L.ToeNull → left toe tip bone
R.AnkleNull → right ankle bone
L.AnkleNull → left ankle bone

Select the parent left and right hipbones and in their motion options window turn on Unaffected by IK of Descendants. This will make them independent of the goal objects so that you can move and rotate these bones after IK is turned on.

In the motion options for the rest of the leg bones, set the controllers to Inverse Kinematics. This should apply to all x, y, and z axes (heading, pitch, and bank). Make sure that all rotation axes are on, to avoid limiting the bones' movements. If you wish, you can set some limits to the bones.

Select the right knee bone and in its motion options turn on full-time IK and set its goal object to the R.KneeNull. Assign the appropriate goal object (null) to the left knee, right toe, left toe, right ankle, and left ankle. Be sure to turn on full-time IK for these.

That is it. You can now try out IK by moving the goal objects (nulls). Notice that if you select and move the body, the toe nulls make the feet stick to the ground. This is very important for animating walk cycles or other actions requiring that one foot stay planted to the ground while the body moves forward.

SETTING UP FACIAL EXPRESSIONS

Preparing the human model for facial expressions and dialogue is an essential part of the 3-D animation process. Shape shifting, or the use of morph targets, is the most common method employed for this task. A base model with a neutral expression is the starting point from which a number of different facial aspects are modeled (Figure 9-12).

The base model should have at least three sets of parallel lines for each wrinkle. The locations of these are also indicated in Figure 9-12. During certain facial expressions these creases can be made more prominent by pulling in the middle line(s).

Approximately 56 shapes, or morphs, which include the mouth shapes for dialogue, should be enough for the majority of facial expressions.

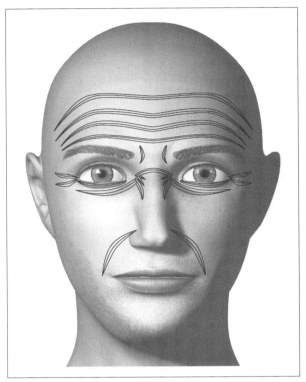

Fig. 9-12 The black lines indicate areas of the face that will wrinkle during certain expressions. Groups of three or more lines should be added there.

MUSCLE GROUPS OF THE FACE

The human face is capable of over 7000 facial expressions. There are 44 muscles, but not all of them are used for changing the visage. Unlike the other muscles of the body, they float freely, giving humans an enormous mobility to create a wide range of expressions.

Figure 9-13 illustrates the major muscles that are the agents for various physiognomies. These also affect the contours and surface characteristics of the face when it is in a neutral position.

Frontalis. This is a broad, flat muscle that wrinkles the brow and lifts the eyebrows.

Orbicularis oculi. This is a circular muscle surrounding the eye, which closes and opens the eyelids, as in squinting.

Corrugator. Beginning at the bridge of the nose, the corrugator is a small muscle that is attached to the skin under the middle of the eyebrow. It has a profound effect on the forehead in frowning or expressing grief. By lowering the inner ends of the eyebrows, the corrugator forces vertical wrinkles of the brow and makes the eyebrows cluster together near the nose.

Quadratus labii superioris. These are three branches of muscles located at the side of the

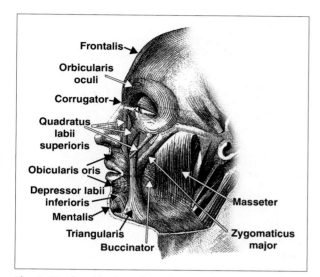

Fig. 9-13 The muscles of the face responsible for expressions.

EXPRESSING EMOTION

There are basic facial expressions that are easily recognizable. Some of these are happiness, sadness, fear, surprise, disgust, joy, anger, and contempt. Other expressions are somewhat more ambiguous and can be difficult to read on a person's face. A few of them are shyness, skepticism, pity, jealousy, disappointment, love, shame, awe, impatience, aloofness, greed, and vanity. Taken out of context, it would be difficult to find agreement among observers as to the nature of these countenances. Figures 9-14 through 9-31 depict some of the more obvious, as well as obscure, expressions. CD9-14 through CD9-31 in the Chapter 9 folder of the CD-ROM show them in color. All of these faces can be made by blending less than 56 morph targets.

nose, which insert into the skin above the upper lip. They pull up the upper lip for sneering.

Orbicularis oris. Encompassing the mouth is another circular muscle, originating from the small muscles at the corner of the mouth. When this muscle contracts, it curls and tightens the lips.

Depressor labii inferioris. Starting at the bottom of the chin and inserting into the lower lip, this muscle pulls down the lower lip.

Mentalis. Located on the chin, the mentalis muscle pushes the lower lip up for expressions such as pouting.

Triangularis. This muscle begins at the lower section of the jaw and inserts into the corners of the mouth. It pulls down the corners of the mouth for frowning.

Zygomaticus major. Starting at the zygomatic arch and extending toward the corners of the mouth, this muscle pulls up the mouth into a smile.

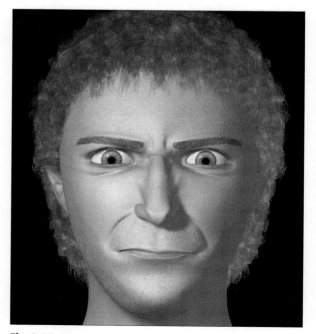

Fig. 9-14 Anger.

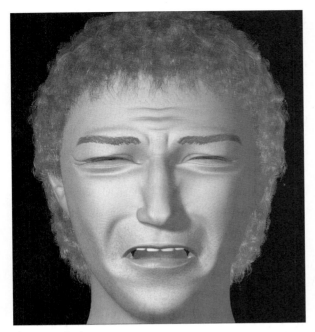

Fig. 9-15 Crying.

Fig. 9-17 Determination.

Fig. 9-16 Debauched smile.

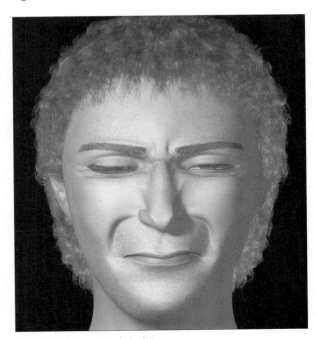

Fig. 9-18 Disgust and disdain.

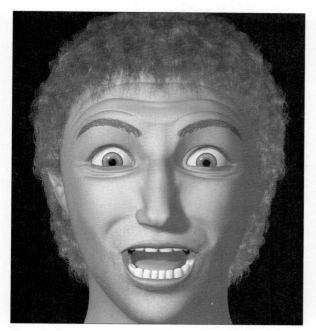

Fig. 9-19 Fear.

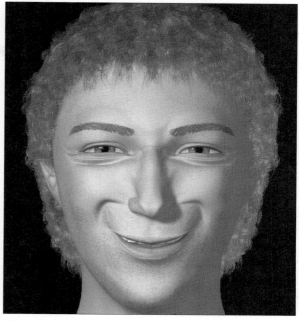

Fig. 9-21 Joy.

Fig. 9-20 Drowsiness.

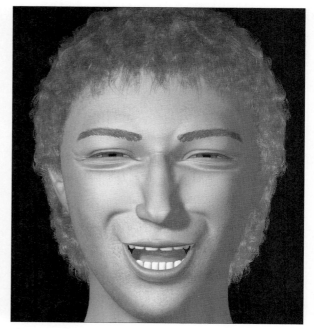

Fig. 9-22 Laughter.

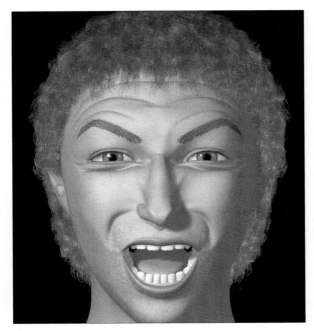

Fig. 9-23 Rage.

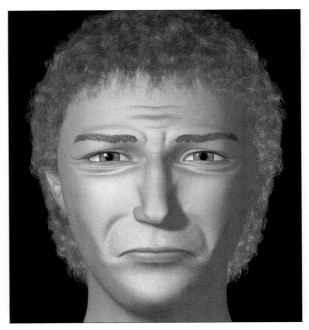

Fig. 9-25 Sadness.

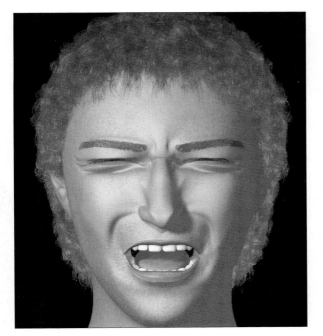

Fig. 9-24 Pain.

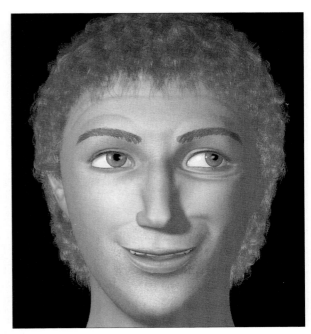

Fig. 9-26 Smile.

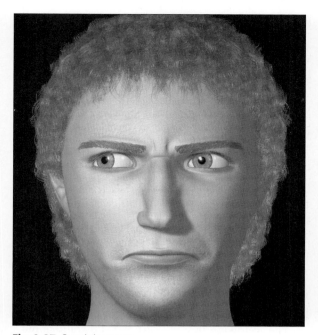

Fig. 9-27 Suspiciousness.

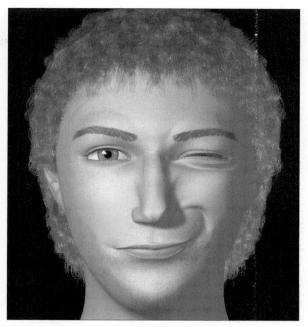

Fig. 9-29 Wink.

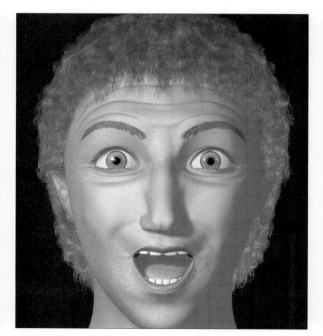

Fig. 9-28 Surprise.

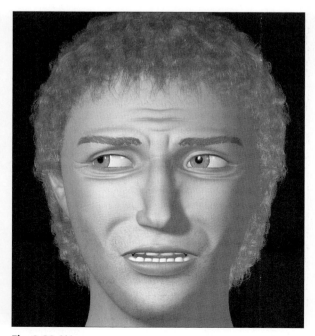

Fig. 9-30 Worry.

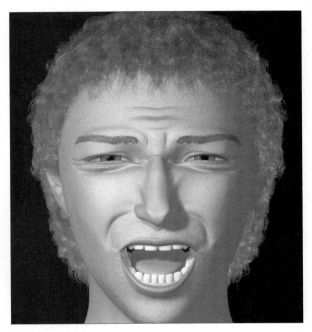

Fig. 9-31 Yawn.

CREATING MORPH TARGETS FOR THE FACE

You can get almost an infinite variety of facial expressions by assigning specific morph targets to individual parts of the face. By blending these, you will have more flexibility than if you had modeled the expressions as a whole. Figure 9-32 shows a sample interface in which separate facial expressions

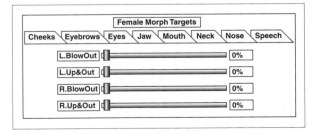

Fig. 9-32 An example of an interface for mixing morph targets for facial animation.

have been assigned to the cheeks, eyebrows, eyes, jaw, mouth, neck, and nose. An extra one for speech was also added.

By moving sliders for each individual expression, you can get degrees of emotions by blending them. For example, if you wanted to show anger, you could move the slider for lowering the eyebrows 100%. Under the mouth tab you would move the lower lip compressed slider to 100%. The upper lip compressed slider would also be moved 100%. To keep the mouth from becoming too symmetrical, you would then move the right sneer slider over to about 45%. Both wings of the nose would be moved up 100%. Separate sliders for the eyes could move them in any direction. Now imagine how much easier this is than having to model thousands of facial expressions or moving bones to deform the face.

The following descriptions and illustrations outline all the morph targets that should fulfill most of your facial animation needs. By blending some of these you can most likely save the transformed model for additional morph targets. As you work through each of them, be sure to use a mirror. Pay attention to the actions of the underlying muscles while you model each expression. Remember, you are isolating each shape, so try not to move points in other areas besides the ones specified.

Cheeks

The cheeks play an important part in many expressions. Smiling, anger, fear, and disgust are just a few aspects that show changes in the cheeks.

1. **Left cheek blows out** (Figure 9-33). For expressions of exasperation, chewing on food, or expelling air, the cheeks are sometimes blown out. Since the cheeks do not have to operate in unison, separate left and right cheek morph targets are

modeled. One of the easiest ways to model the cheek shape is to select the vertices to be moved and then use a magnetlike tool with a falloff to pull the points out. Be sure to close only the left side of the mouth.

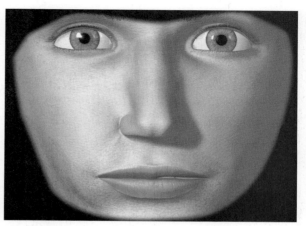

Fig. 9-34 The right cheek blows out morph target.

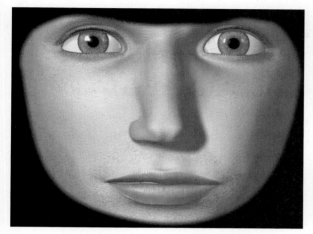

Fig. 9-33 The left cheek blows out morph target.

2. **Right cheek blows out** (Figure 9-34). Points on the right cheek are pulled out. If you want to match the position of the left cheek points, save the transformed left cheek morph target, mirror it, and place it in a background layer as a template. You can then move the left cheek points to match the vertices' positions on the template. Move only the right side of the mouth to close it. Figure 9-35 shows the face when both left and right cheek morph targets are set to 100%, making both cheeks blow out.

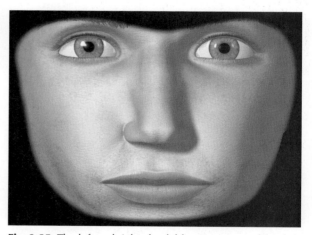

Fig. 9-35 The left and right cheek blowing out combined.

3. **Left cheek up and out** (Figure 9-36). The cheeks are bunched together and moved up to give them that full look during smiling, crying, disgust/disdain, laughing, rage, and other expressions. It is an important shape that should not be neglected.

Select points only on the left cheek and use a magnet tool to move them up toward the left side and out. The crease at the corner of the left side of the mouth and nose wing will also have to be made more noticeable. Moving the cheek up toward the lower eyelid causes wrinkling below and at the corners of the eye. Be sure to model these as part of the morph target.

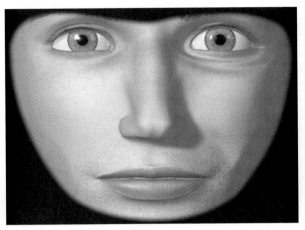

Fig. 9-36 The left cheek moved up and out morph target.

Fig. 9-38 The left and right cheeks moved up and out combined.

4. **Right cheek up and out** (Figure 9-37). The other side is sculpted separately because certain expressions such as the half smile change only one cheek. Figure 9-38 illustrates the two morph targets combined by moving the left and right sliders.

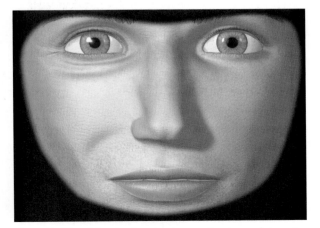

Fig. 9-37 The right cheek moved up and out morph target.

Eyebrows

The eyebrows glide freely up and and down. They change the look of the eye and the bridge of the nose. When raised, they lighten the eyes by admitting light. Lowering the brows darkens and obscures the eyes by shading them.

When modeling the eyebrows, keep in mind that most males have heavier and lower brows than females. In males the eyebrows sit on the downslope of the brow ridge, while in females they are on the upslope. Besides sitting higher, the female eyebrow is also thinner.

5. **Inner ends of eyebrows up** (Figure 9-39). Indications of emotional distress such as crying, worry, and sadness can be made with this morph target. There is no need to model separate left and right morph targets. Points on both sides are moved up, using a magnet tool. Individual vertices are then pulled and pushed to make the furrows.

Fig. 9-39 Both inner ends of the eyebrows are moved up, creating a furrow in the middle of the forehead and creases along the top of the nose.

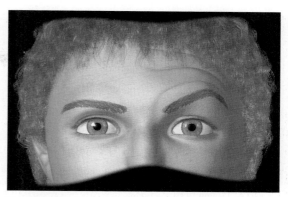

Fig. 9-41 Raising the left eyebrow.

6. **Eyebrows down** (Figure 9-40). Both eyebrows are moved down for expressions of anger, determination, disgust/disdain, pain, suspicion, and so on. Creases above the bridge of the nose will also have to be modeled.

8. **Right eyebrow up** (Figure 9-42). The opposite brow is raised for the other morph target.

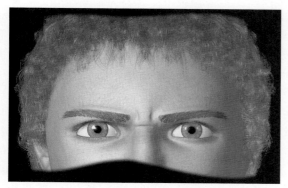

Fig. 9-40 The left and right eyebrows are moved down to shade the eye.

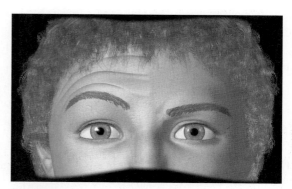

Fig. 9-42 Raising the right eyebrow.

7. **Left eyebrow up** (Figure 9-41). Some people have the ability to raise only one side of the brow. One side remains relaxed while the other moves up for looks of puzzlement and the half smile.

9. **Both eyebrows up** (Figure 9-43). By combining both left and right morph targets and saving them as a transformed object, one can create another morph target. The center points will most likely have to be adjusted. Raising both eyebrows indicates fear, drowsiness, rage, and surprise.

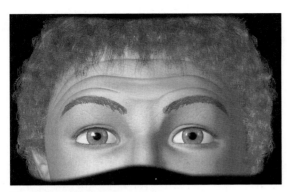

Fig. 9-43 Raising both eyebrows.

Eyes

The eyes move more often than any other aspect of the face. Whether someone is observing outward events or thinking about something, the eyes are usually in motion. In animation, eyes are an indication of what the character is thinking and often telegraph actions before they occur.

10. **Left eye winks** (Figure 9-44). The left upper eyelid is rotated down and the left lower eyelid is rotated up to make the wink or squint. Be sure to model the creases formed at the bottom and corners of the eye.

Fig. 9-44 The left eye winks.

11. **Right eye winks** (Figure 9-45). The right upper and lower eyelids are rotated to make the right wink or squint. Figure 9-46 illustrates both eyes winking or squinting when the left and right morph sliders are moved 100%.

Fig. 9-45 The right eye winks.

Fig. 9-46 Both eyes wink or squint.

12. **Left eye blinks** (Figure 9-47). Blinking is an important part of facial animation. A character will appear lifeless when it does not blink. An interesting trick in animation is to stagger the blink. One eye blinks one frame behind the other. Therefore, the left and right eyes have their own separate blink morph targets. Blinking lowers only the upper eyelid.

Fig. 9-47 The left eye blinks.

Fig. 9-50 The left upper eyelid is raised.

13. **Right eye blinks** (Figure 9-48). The right upper eyelid is rotated down for the right blink. Figure 9-49 depicts both left and right morph targets combined to close the eyes for sleepy expressions.

15. **Raise right upper eyelid** (Figure 9-51). The opposite eyelid is raised. Figure 9-52 shows both left and right morph targets set to 100% for a look of astonishment.

Fig. 9-48 The right eye blinks.

Fig. 9-51 The right upper eyelid is raised.

Fig. 9-49 Both eyes blink.

Fig. 9-52 Both eyelids are raised.

14. **Raise left upper eyelid** (Figure 9-50). Raising the upper eyelid is a common response to the unexpected, such as surprise and fear. The left and right upper eyelids raised are modeled separately for a greater variety of expressions.

16. **Eyes look down** (Figure 9-53). You can take care of most eye movements with only four morph targets. The first of these is to rotate the eyes down.

Fig. 9-53 The eyes look down.

17. **Eyes look left** (Figure 9-54).

Fig. 9-54 The eyes look left.

18. **Eyes look right** (Figure 9-55).

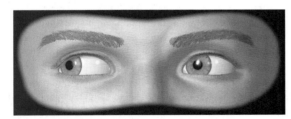

Fig. 9-55 The eyes look right.

19. **Eyes look up** (Figure 9-56).

Fig. 9-56 The eyes look up.

Jaw

Since a majority of the jaw movements are created with the mouth morph targets, only two need to be modeled. These are moving the jaw left and moving it right for chewing motions and other facial nuances.

20. **Jaw moves left** (Figure 9-57). Points on the jaw and lower lip are selected to be moved left.

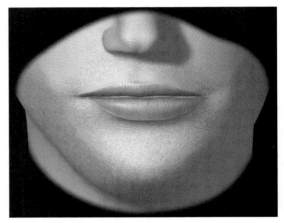

Fig. 9-57 The jaw is moved left.

21. **Jaw moves right** (Figure 9-58).

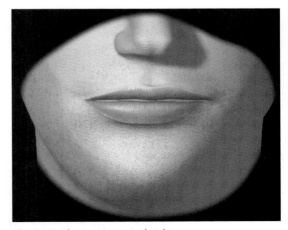

Fig. 9-58 The jaw is moved right.

Mouth

Just when you thought you were making some progress, you have now arrived at the toughest part of all. The mouth has more morph targets than any of the other sections of the face. Approximately seven muscles exert influence on the lips, resulting in a great variety of positions.

The mouth is surrounded by muscles attached on one end to the skull and on the other to the surrounding orbicularis oris. This muscle is freely suspended, making it susceptible to all kinds of forces from the surrounding attached muscles.

Unfortunately, the mouth shapes are also the most challenging to model. Besides the 22 expressions listed under the mouth heading, there are 10 more under the speech heading. In spite of all these, the morph targets by themselves will not provide all the expressions the mouth is capable of. You will most likely find that many shapes have to be a blend of several mouth morph targets in varying degrees.

22. **Bite down on lower lip** (Figure 9-59). Rotate and move points above and on the upper lip. Also move the upper teeth forward and down.

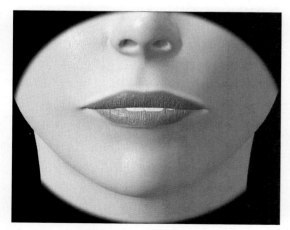

Fig. 9-59 Biting down on the lower lip.

23. **Retract the left corner of the mouth** (Figure 9-60). Points on the corner of the mouth are moved back. A magnet tool works well for this. This expression can be used for puzzlement, resolve, physical exertion, and so on.

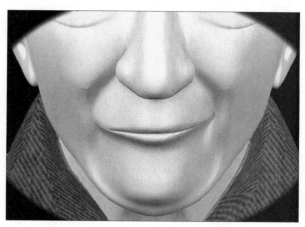

Fig. 9-60 Retracting the left corner of the mouth.

24. **Retract the right corner of the mouth** (Figure 9-61). This target is the same as the previous one, except it is on the opposite side. Figure 9-62 illustrates both left and right mouth corners retracted.

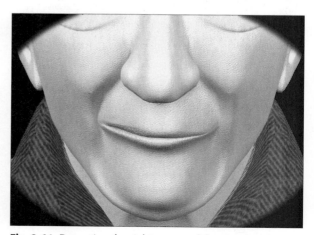

Fig. 9-61 Retracting the right corner of the mouth.

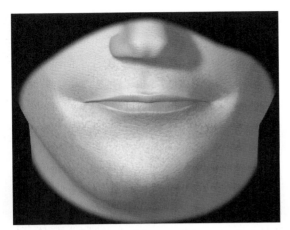

Fig. 9-62 Both corners of the mouth are retracted.

25. **Closed left-sided smile** (Figure 9-63). A Magnet tool can be used to move points up on the left side of the mouth. Individual points will most likely have to be adjusted.

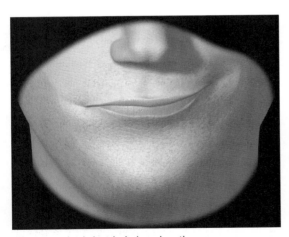

Fig. 9-63 The left-sided closed smile.

26. **Closed right-sided smile** (Figure 9-64). Points on the opposite side of the mouth are moved up to make the right-sided smile. Figure 9-65 shows both sides up for the closed smile. You may need to create a separate morph target for this by saving a transformed object with the left and right closed smile at 100%. You can then modify points until the smile looks correct.

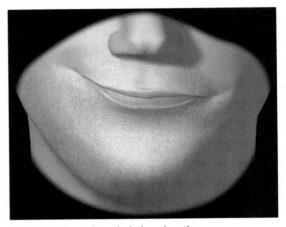

Fig. 9-64 The right-sided closed smile.

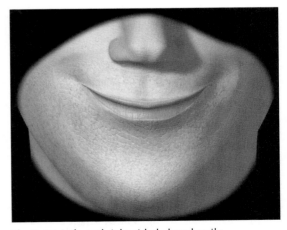

Fig. 9-65 Left- and right-sided closed smile.

27. **Closed mouth** (Figure 9-66). This is one of the simpler expressions to model, but it is used quite often.

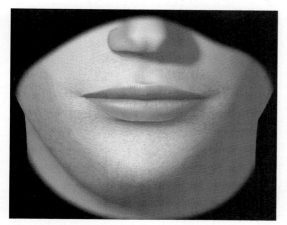

Fig. 9-66 The mouth is closed.

28. **Both corners down** (Figure 9-67). Use the Magnet tool on selected points to make the corners droop.

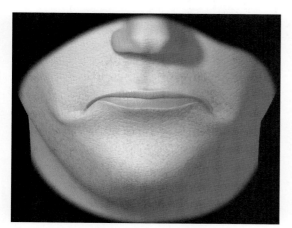

Fig. 9-67 Both corners are turned down.

29. **Left-sided sneer** (Figure 9-68). The left side of the upper lip curls up to reveal part of the upper teeth. This expression can be a snarl or it can exhibit skepticism, disgust, or the like. The Magnet tool should work fine on selected points.

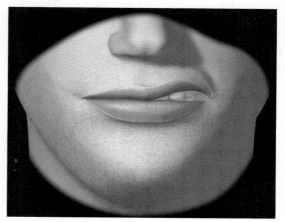

Fig. 9-68 The left-sided sneer.

30. **Right-sided sneer** (Figure 9-69). Points on the opposite side of the upper lip are pulled up.

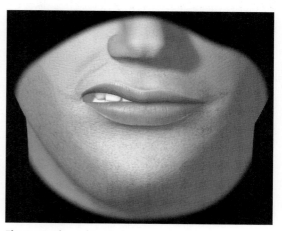

Fig. 9-69 The right-sided sneer.

31. **Compression of the lower lip** (Figure 9-70). The jaw is rotated up to compress and thin the lower lip.

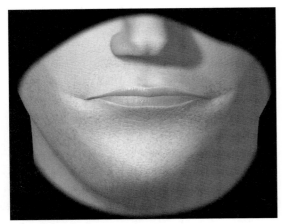

Fig. 9-70 The lower lip is compressed.

32. **Compression of the upper lip** (Figure 9-71). The upper lip points are rotated in and moved down against the lower lip.

33. **The lower lip bulges out** (Figure 9-72). Points along the lower lip are rotated out and spread apart to give it more thickness. This expression can be used to signify serious thinking, grief, holding back feelings, bewilderment, and so on.

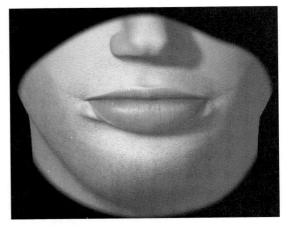

Fig. 9-72 The lower lip bulges out.

34. **The lower part of the mouth is open** (Figure 9-73). The jaw is rotated down to open the mouth wide. The upper lip is stationary. This expression, in combination with another target for moving the upper lip, can signify astonishment, screaming, pain, and so on.

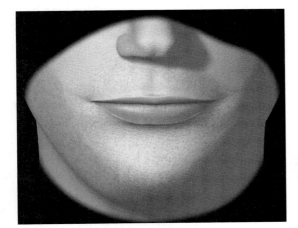

Fig. 9-71 The upper lip is compressed.

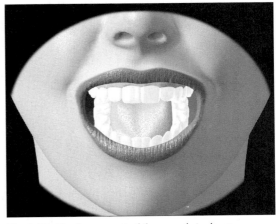

Fig. 9-73 The lower part of the mouth is down.

35. **The upper part of the mouth is open** (Figure 9-74). Points on the upper lip are moved upward.

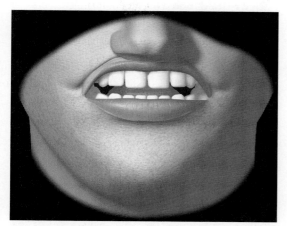

Fig. 9-74 The upper part of the mouth is moved up.

36. **The mouth is opened into a heart shape** (Figure 9-75). This is a useful expression for showing amazement, singing, yawning, and drawing in breath.

37. **Opening the mouth for laughing** (Figure 9-76). This morph target can be modeled from a transformed model that has several different morphs in varying percentages. A Magnet tool can then be used to elevate the corners of the mouth. Points along the lips will most likely have to be lined up.

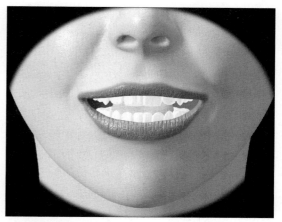

Fig. 9-76 The open laugh.

38. **Pucker in the lips** (Figure 9-77). This is one of the more difficult mouth targets to model. Points on and around the lips are brought closer together as well as moved forward. This expression is useful for showing dread, conniving, or a refusal to speak.

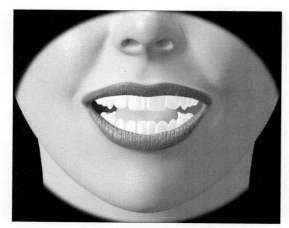

Fig. 9-75 The mouth opens in a heart shape.

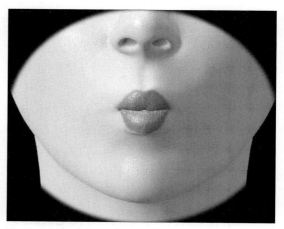

Fig. 9-77 The lips pucker in.

39. **Pucker out the lips** (Figure 9-78). This may be the most difficult expression to model. Both upper and lower lip points are rotated outward, spread apart, and moved forward. It is a look that often appears in speech and can also be a prelude to rage and ill-will.

Fig. 9-78 The lips pucker out.

40. **Left-sided orb** (Figure 9-79). This is another challenging morph target. The lower and upper lips are shaped into a spherelike configuration on

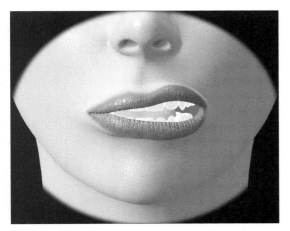

Fig. 9-79 The left side forms into an orb shape.

the left side. This expression is often noticeable in varying degrees during speech.

41. **Right-sided orb** (Figure 9-80). The opposite side of the mouth is formed into an orb shape.

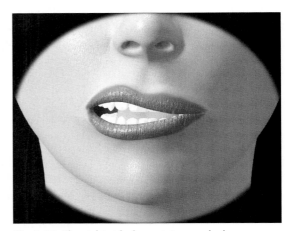

Fig. 9-80 The right side forms into an orb shape.

Neck

42. **Straining the neck** (Figure 9-81). This is the only morph target for the neck. The muscles of the neck are tight from the shoulder to the jaw. The lips are thinned and the muscles on the jaw

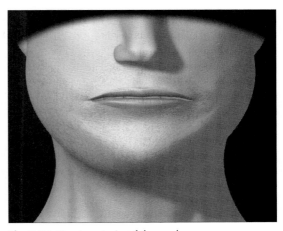

Fig. 9-81 Tension strain of the neck.

are drawn outward. This expression is used to signify pain or tension.

Nose

43. **Raising the right nose wing** (Figure 9-82). The nose has only a few morph targets. The first of these is elevating the right nose wing. If you look in a mirror, you will see this creates several ridges along the cheeks, under the eye, and along the base of the nose. Take time to model these left and right morph targets because they are used often.

Fig. 9-83 The left wing of the nose is up.

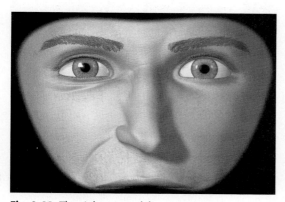

Fig. 9-82 The right wing of the nose is up.

44. **Raising the left nose wing** (Figure 9-83). This is identical to the previous expression except it is on the opposite side. Figure 9-84 shows both nose wings elevated. You may wish to model this as a separate morph target after saving a transformed model of both wings up.

Fig. 9-84 Both wings of the nose are up.

Speech

There are 10 mouth expressions that will suffice to create all the consonants and vowels for dialogue. You can always accent these with any of the other mouth morph targets as well as the various eye, brow, cheek, and nose facial expressions. Blending the assorted mouth expressions and saving them as a transformed object can serve as a useful starting point for these.

45. **A and I** (Figure 9-85).

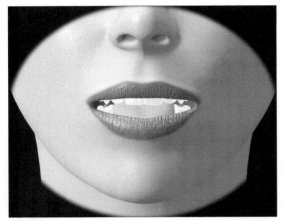

Fig. 9-85 The mouth for speaking A and I sounds.

46. **C, G, H, K, N, R, S, T, Y, and Z** (Figure 9-86).

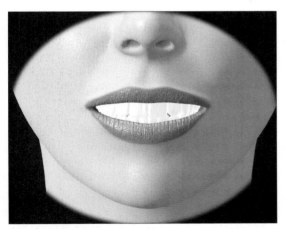

Fig. 9-86 The mouth for speaking C, G, H, K, N, R, S, T, Y, and Z sounds.

47. **D and Th** (Figure 9-87).

Fig. 9-87 The mouth for speaking D and Th sounds.

48. **E** (Figure 9-88).

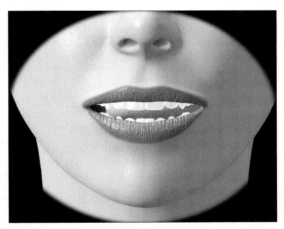

Fig. 9-88 The mouth for speaking the E sound.

49. **F and V** (Figure 9-89).

Fig. 9-89 The mouth for speaking the F and V sounds.

50. **L** (Figure 9-90). The tip of the tongue is placed against the roof of the mouth.

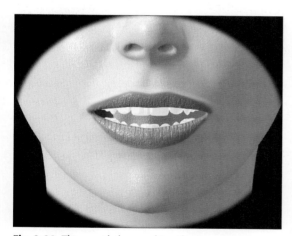

Fig. 9-90 The mouth for speaking the L sound.

51. **M, B, and P** (Figure 9-91).

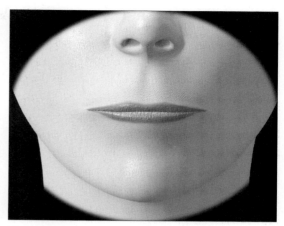

Fig. 9-91 The mouth for speaking the M, B, and P sounds.

52. **O** (Figure 9-92).

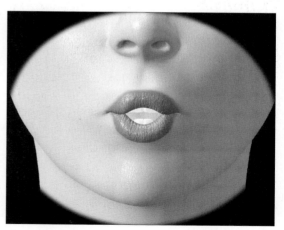

Fig. 9-92 The mouth for speaking the O sound.

53. **U** (Figure 9-93).

54. **W and Q** (Figure 9-94).

Fig. 9-93 The mouth for speaking the U sound.

Fig. 9-94 The mouth for speaking the W and Q sounds.

SURFACING DETAILS

Surfacing a model is a very important part of the 3-D process. Rather than spending a great amount of time modeling details, texturing them onto the object will not only reduce computer memory requirements but will also greatly improve your character's appearance. When it is done right, the texture on the model becomes indistinguishable from the actual surface geometry.

After texture-mapping a model, saving the scene file usually saves the image map data along with the object. Some programs, such as Lightwave, are set up so that you have to save the individual object in order to save the texture information along with it.

Although there are a number of different ways to project an image onto an object, most of the time UV mapping is used for the precise placement of facial textures. Front projection mapping methods consisting of planar, cubic, cylindrical, and spherical types, are based on simple primitive forms. These will work well for general overall textures or for simple shapes such as the spherical eyeball.

UV texture maps work well for irregular shapes. The texture maps are adhered to special points on the object. Since the placement of the texture can be assigned to specific parts of the object, the greatest control possible is now in the hands of the artist. UV mapping can be accomplished in several ways. One of the most common is to unroll and flatten the wire mesh and then paint or assign a texture to it in an image editing program. When the image is saved and assigned to the model, the texture conforms to its shape. Some tweaking will most likely have to be done in order to precisely fit the mesh points to the texture.

Another method is to use a special 3-D paint program and actually paint the textures onto the object. When the object is saved, the UV texture coordinate settings are saved along with it or the texture can be saved for spherical mapping.

VARIOUS IMAGE-MAPPING METHODS

The different types of image projection settings should work well for a large part of the human model. To simplify the process, some of the most common image projection types are illustrated in Figures 10-1 and 10-2.

Cubic image mapping, as seen in Figure 10-1, projects the texture multiple times from all three axes. The advantage to using this type of mapping is that there is little distortion of the image. The disadvantage is that often a seam can be detected between two axes. Cubic image mapping works well for overall textures such as skin color and skin bump maps that

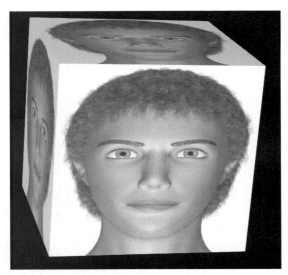

Fig. 10-1 Cubic image mapping projects the image from all three x, y, and z axes at the same time.

have very little surface differentiation. The edges of these types of textures blend well into each other so that the seam is hidden.

Examples of planar, cylindrical, and spherical mapping can be seen in Figure 10-2. Since each of these projects from only one axis, the textures will vary according to which axis one chooses to project from.

Planar mapping can be compared to projecting a slide through a slide projector. Depending on where the slide projector is placed, the image can look like it is the right proportion on the side facing the projector, while appearing stretched on the sides, top, and bottom. On the back, the image is reversed. Planar pro-

jection works well on the iris of the eye. Since the iris is a round lens type of object with most of the visible surface near the front, there is little distortion.

Cylindrical projection wraps a texture only once around an object, similar to bark around a tree trunk. This type of mapping works well for the eyeball, to show the veins near the front and the red area on the back.

Spherical mapping rolls the image as if you were wrapping a skin around a ball. It is not used very often for human texturing.

When using planar, cylindrical, and spherical mapping, it is important to note which axis the model faces toward. For example, if the model faces toward the z axis (front), then you would use planar on the z axis mapping for the iris. On the other hand, if the same model is lying on its back facing up on the y axis, then use planar on the y axis mapping for the iris. Planar on the x axis would be used if the person is standing up facing toward the right or left. Figure 10-3 shows how the mapping changes for each axis, depending on the direction in which the model faces.

If you plan to use planar, cylindrical, spherical, and cubic mapping make sure your object faces toward one of the three axes (Figure 10-3). A model that presents itself to one of the axes at an angle, before texturing, will distort the applied texture since it does not project face-on. After applying the texture to a model that faces straight on to the x, y, or z axis, you can turn it in any direction without experiencing distortion since the image has already been adhered correctly.

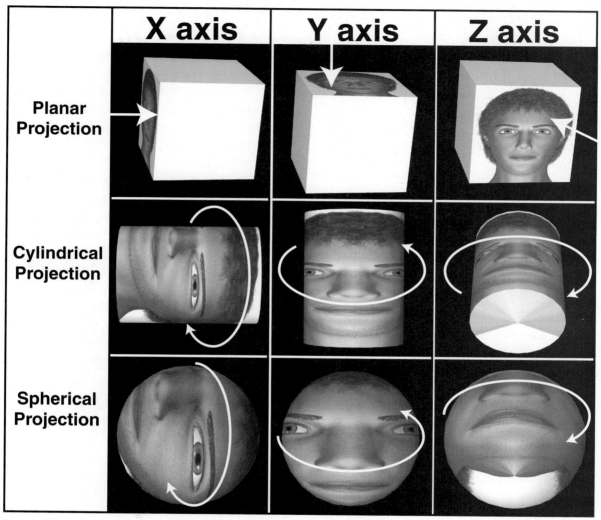

Fig. 10-2 The direction in which an image is projected on the x, y, and z axes when using planar, cylindrical, and spherical mapping.

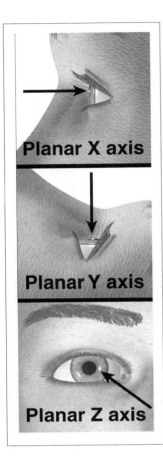

Fig. 10-3 When looking at the model from the front view, the direction in which it faces determines what axis is used for planar mapping.

PROCEDURAL TEXTURES

So far, the discussion has centered on image texture mapping. The other method for texturing is referred to as procedural texturing. It uses a mathematical algorithm to place an image onto an object.

Procedurals often use a filtered noise function that creates an impulse of random amplitude over the surface. A variety of ways are used to distribute and filter the impulses spatially. These methods determine the character of the function and in turn the appearance of the surface. Some common effects that are the result of distribution and filtering are those from phenomena such as fire, smoke, clouds, and marble formation.

Figure 10-4 shows the interface of a procedural texture generator—a texture plug-in named Disgust produced by Worley Labs, Inc. Texture generators such as this one can produce an infinite variety of surfaces, including those with a bumpy appearance. Cellular structures such as skin can be produced procedurally. The texture will map seamlessly and appear never to repeat itself. Since they are mathematically generated textures, they use only a fraction of the memory that image maps do. The disadvantage to using procedurals is that they do not look as realistic as photographic image maps.

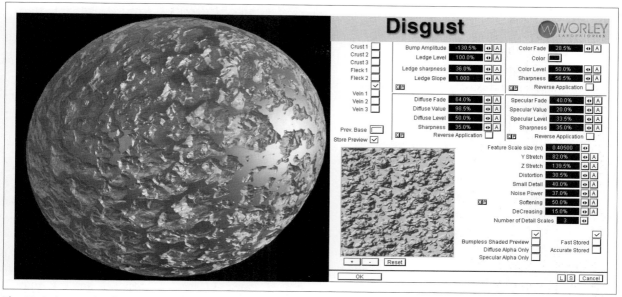

Fig. 10-4 A procedural texture generator by Worley Labs, Inc.

SURFACE FACTORS

In addition to applied textures, the characteristic appearance of a surface is also influenced by color, luminosity, diffuseness, specularity, glossiness, reflectivity, transparency, translucency, and bumpiness. Color, the most obvious surface attribute, is often hidden by a texture. If the texture has transparent areas, then the initial color of the object does play an important role in the appearance of the model.

Luminosity is used to describe a surface that illuminates. Objects with high degrees of luminosity or luster seem to glow with an inner light. Since luminous objects in computer graphics do not have any actual light-emitting properties, a certain amount of glow should be applied to the surface. A luminous object without glow will have hard edges, thus making the object merely appear flat rather than glow.

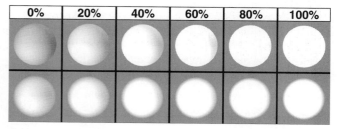

Fig. 10-5 A luminosity chart of various percentages applied to a sphere. The top row illustrates luminosity without glow or edge transparency, while the bottom row has all three.

Figure 10-5 contains a chart with varying percentages of luminosity applied to a sphere. Note how the top row, which displays only luminosity, merely makes the sphere appear flatter and lighter while the bottom row, which in addition to luminosity shows glow and edge transparency, achieves true luminosity by making the sphere appear to glow with an inner light.

Diffuseness or diffusion refers to the manner in

219

which light is scattered over a surface. To make an object appear brighter, use a higher setting for Diffuse. Lower settings are more appropriate for metal or dirt surfaces. Figure 10-6 illustrates various percentages of diffusion applied to a sphere.

Specularity is basically the reflection of light on an object. It is determined by the quality of the surface. If the object is shiny like plastic, then it will have a high degree of specularity. Bright spots in the form of highlights will appear on the surface. The lights that shine on the object will also determine how many bright spots show up on the object. Figure 10-7 illustrates varying percentages of specularity.

Glossiness settings influence the size of the specular highlight(s). Lower settings will spread out the highlight to cover a greater surface area. A higher glossiness setting makes the bright spots smaller. Figure 10-8 shows a chart with varying percentages of glossiness. The Diffuse level was set to 100%.

Reflectivity can be accomplished in several ways. Ray tracing can trace the actual reflections of the environment on the object. Although the ray recursion depth or limit can be turned down for faster renderings, a quicker alternative is to use reflection maps. Ray-tracing the reflections can yield a more realistic animation, especially if the environment changes around the reflecting object. Figure 10-9 illustrates two types of reflections. The top row has spheres with ray-traced reflections and the bottom row of spheres has a reflection map.

Depending on the setting, transparency (Figure 10-10) can make the surface of an object clear. Refraction bends the light in varying amounts according to the characteristics of an item. For example, crystal has a higher refraction index than water.

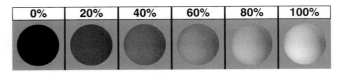

Fig. 10-6 A diffusion chart of various percentages applied to a sphere. Higher percentages mean more light is scattered over the surface.

| 0% | 20% | 40% | 60% | 80% | 100% |

Fig. 10-7 Specularity is the highlight or reflection of the light source. In this case several lights were used. Higher percentages yield brighter highlights.

| 0% | 20% | 40% | 60% | 80% | 100% |

Fig. 10-8 Glossiness sets the size of the specular highlights. Higher settings create smaller bright spots.

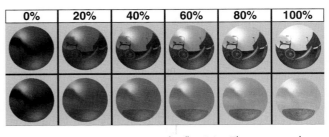

Fig. 10-9 Varying percentages of reflectivity. The top row shows ray-traced reflections, while the bottom spheres use a reflection map.

| 0% | 20% | 40% | 60% | 80% | 100% |

Fig. 10-10 A transparency chart.

Translucency is similar to transparency; when an object is translucent, lighting properties such as color and luminosity will show through. Unlike a transparent object, a translucent object will not let objects be seen through it. A silhouette of objects behind the translucent one can be seen if a light that casts shadows is placed in the background,which is similar to seeing the silhouette of someone who is backlit standing behind a thin sheet. Figure 10-11 shows a shower curtain with translucency applied to its surface. The objects behind it cast shadows, creating silhouettes that become more obvious with higher settings.

Fig. 10-12 Bump mapping simulates the way light reflects from a rough object. The close-up shows how bump mapping does not affect the edges of objects.

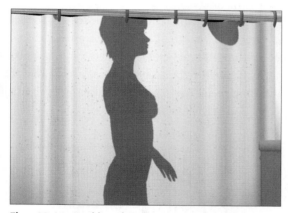

Fig. 10-11 Backlit objects seen with translucency enabled. In this case a setting of 80% translucency was used.

Bump mapping simulates the appearance of a rough surface without displacing the actual geometry. By changing the position of the surface normals during the rendering process, light is reflected from several directions off the surface. One can detect bump mapping by looking at the edges of objects. Only the areas facing toward the camera appear bumpy. Figure 10-12 shows bump mapping applied to the skin and background.

SURFACING A HUMAN CHARACTER

There are a variety of ways to texture a human model. Some prefer to create their own textures by painting them either in an image editing program or directly onto the model using 3-D paint software. Other artists use a combination of both methods.

The textures themselves can also be derived from scanned or digital photos. The process of mapping the images onto the model also requires different approaches. UV mapping serves best for precise placement of textures, while the previously discussed projection methods work fine for either general overall texturing or applying them to simpler forms on the model.

The following directions use both projection and UV mapping. They can be used as a general guide in combination with other techniques such as a 3-D paint program. In order to use these instructions successfully, be sure to have your human character in the side view face up, lying on his or her back. The top view would show the front of the figure. Texturing the human model by individual sections will also simplify the process.

TEXTURING THE EYES

Since the eyes are made of separate sections, each will have a different mapping scheme. The iris and eyeball, which require textures, will have UV mapping applied to them. The rest will need only surface settings.

The Cornea

The cornea is the outer, transparent part of the eye. It projects outward in a manner similar to the way a watch glass does from its case. Figure 10-13 shows the surface settings that can be used for the cornea. The percentages are meant only as a general guide. You may decide to vary them somewhat. For example, the reflection option can be set higher for certain effects. Even though the transparency is 100%, the high specularity setting (400%) will add highlights to the eye. There is no need to apply a texture to the cornea.

The Eyeball

The eyeball sits inside the transparent cornea. It has a texture applied to it. Figure 10-14 shows the surface settings for the eyeball. Most of the settings are turned off since the applied image map is the most important part of it. Figure 10-15 illustrates the texture used and the settings that go along with it. The texture is a simple two-step linear gradient. The bottom half is orange red, which gradually becomes a light off-white color. Thin veins are painted, starting at the top and tapering off at the halfway point.

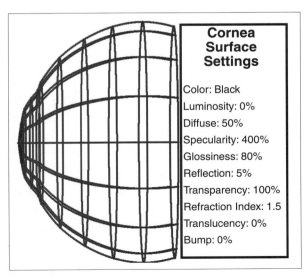

Cornea Surface Settings

Color: Black
Luminosity: 0%
Diffuse: 50%
Specularity: 400%
Glossiness: 80%
Reflection: 5%
Transparency: 100%
Refraction Index: 1.5
Translucency: 0%
Bump: 0%

Fig. 10-13 Cornea surface settings.

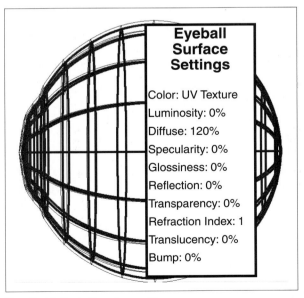

Eyeball Surface Settings

Color: UV Texture
Luminosity: 0%
Diffuse: 120%
Specularity: 0%
Glossiness: 0%
Reflection: 0%
Transparency: 0%
Refraction Index: 1
Translucency: 0%
Bump: 0%

Fig. 10-14 Eyeball surface settings.

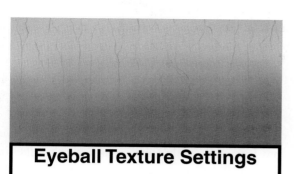

Eyeball Texture Settings

Layer Type: Image Map

Blending Mode: Additive

Layer Opacity: 100%

Projection: UV

UV Map: L.EyeballUV

Image: Eyeball.jpg

Automatic Sizing

Fig. 10-15 Eyeball texture and settings.

Select the left eyeball and name its surface. View it in the UV Texture window and apply a new UV texture to it. The objective of UV mapping is to flatten the sphere so that the texture can be applied with the least distortion and to prevent it from slipping during eye movements. For the UV map settings try the following:

Texture Name: L.EyeballUV

Map Type: Cylindrical

Axis: y

View the new UV map in your UV Texture window. If your model is lying on its back, then the eyeball should be flat. Refer to Figure 10-2 for the

various mapping schemes. Notice that cylindrical on the y axis should unwrap an object such as the eyeball correctly when it is facing up on the y axis.

In your display options, set the background image for the UV Texture window to show the eyeball texture. The blood-red color should be at the bottom, which is the back of the eyeball, while the light color with veins should be seen at the top, which is the front of the eyeball.

In your surface editor, select the left eyeball surface and apply settings similar to those seen in Figures 10-14 and 10-15. Select the right eyeball and repeat the preceding steps, but name the UV map R.EyeballUV.

The Iris

The iris is the most interesting part of the eye. It is a thin, circular muscle suspended behind the cornea and in front of the lens. It has a hole in the center, which is the pupil, for the conveyance of light. The iris contains not only pigment but also fibers and cells. The bundles of fibrous tissue radiate toward the pupil and the numerous branched cells are interspersed between them. In dark eyes they contain pigment granules, but in blue eyes or the pink eyes of albinos they lack pigment. All of this makes for a very complicated texture. Some recommended surface settings for the iris can be seen in Figure 10-16. Image maps for the iris can be found in the Chapter 10 folder of the accompanying CD-ROM. If you can find actual close-up photographs of the iris, you will most likely get the best results. Figure 10-17 shows the iris texture and its color image map settings. To soften the edge of the pupil, a transparency map was applied. This texture can also be found on the CD-ROM and is seen in Figure 10-18.

To UV-map the iris, select the left iris, name it, and open your UV Texture window. Apply a new UV tex-

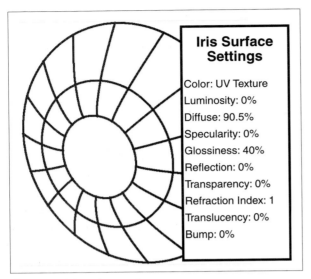

Iris Surface Settings

Color: UV Texture
Luminosity: 0%
Diffuse: 90.5%
Specularity: 0%
Glossiness: 40%
Reflection: 0%
Transparency: 0%
Refraction Index: 1
Translucency: 0%
Bump: 0%

Fig. 10-16 Iris surface settings.

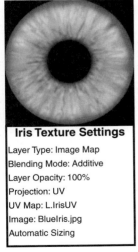

Iris Texture Settings

Layer Type: Image Map
Blending Mode: Additive
Layer Opacity: 100%
Projection: UV
UV Map: L.IrisUV
Image: BlueIris.jpg
Automatic Sizing

Fig. 10-17 Iris texture and settings.

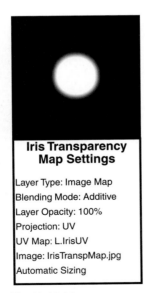

Iris Transparency Map Settings

Layer Type: Image Map
Blending Mode: Additive
Layer Opacity: 100%
Projection: UV
UV Map: L.IrisUV
Image: IrisTranspMap.jpg
Automatic Sizing

Fig. 10-18 Iris transparency map texture and settings.

ture to the iris. Since the iris is an almost flat disk, try the following UV map settings:

Texture Name: L.IrisUV
Map Type: Planar
Axis: y

View the new UV map in your UV Texture window. If your model is lying on its back, then the iris should be flat. Planar on the y axis should unwrap the iris correctly when it is facing up on the y axis.

In your display options, set the background image for the UV Texture window to show the iris texture. The texture should line up with the flattened iris.

In your surface editor, select the left iris surface and apply settings similar to those seen in Figures 10-16 through 10-18. Notice that for transparency the same UV map is used, but the image is the iris transparency map seen in Figure 10-18. Select the right iris and repeat the preceding steps, but name the UV map R.IrisUV.

The Lens

The lens makes up the last part of the eye. It basically serves as the black part seen through the pupil, so it does not need any textures. The surface settings for the lens can be seen in Figure 10-19. A rendered view of the final eye appears in Figure 10-20 and in color on the CD-ROM in the Chapter 10 folder as CD10-20Eyeball. The next section covers texturing the body and the rest of the face.

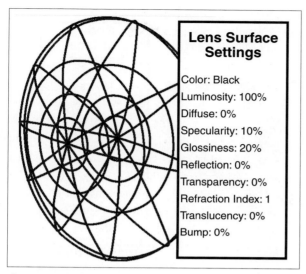

Lens Surface Settings

Color: Black

Luminosity: 100%

Diffuse: 0%

Specularity: 10%

Glossiness: 20%

Reflection: 0%

Transparency: 0%

Refraction Index: 1

Translucency: 0%

Bump: 0%

Fig. 10-19 Lens surface settings.

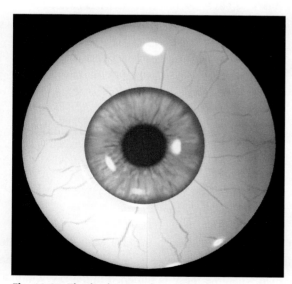

Fig. 10-20 The final textured eye.

TEXTURING THE BODY

It is highly recommended that you start with an over-all color texture that can be utilized for most of the body. This may be obtained by either scanning a photo, downloading an image from the Internet, or even sitting on a scanner. The color map should tile seamlessly. Use an image editing program to make the top and bottom edges and the left and right edges match up. By creating a uniform color texture along all four edges, you should be able to construct a continuous image when tiled. A cloning tool works well for this. Also make sure that there are not any distinct areas on the texture. If a part(s) stands out from the rest it will show up as a sharply defined pattern when repeated.

After preparing the skin color, you will need to obtain a seamless bump map. This is important since it will give the skin a tactile property. Images of leather can work fine for this or you can experiment with various image editing filters.

The Chapter 10 folder on the CD-ROM contains both color skin and bump textures. An illustration of the two textures and their applications on a female model can be viewed in Figure 10-21.

Settings for the body surface, texture, and bump map are outlined in Figure 10-22. The color image and bump maps have width and height tiling rather than being sized to the figure. The bump is also scaled down 25%. This could vary depending on the size of your bump map. Some close-up renderings should give you an indication of how big to make them. Be sure to experiment with your own settings or variations of the ones in Figure 10-22. Later on you will see that lighting has a lot to do with the way the texture shows up.

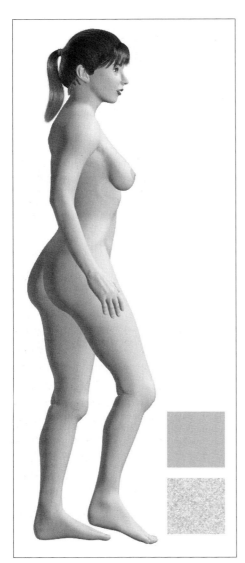

Fig. 10-21 The overall body texture.

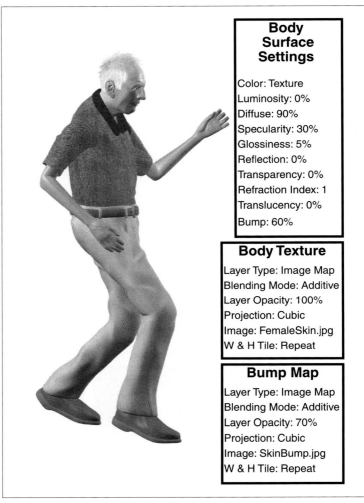

Body Surface Settings

Color: Texture
Luminosity: 0%
Diffuse: 90%
Specularity: 30%
Glossiness: 5%
Reflection: 0%
Transparency: 0%
Refraction Index: 1
Translucency: 0%
Bump: 60%

Body Texture

Layer Type: Image Map
Blending Mode: Additive
Layer Opacity: 100%
Projection: Cubic
Image: FemaleSkin.jpg
W & H Tile: Repeat

Bump Map

Layer Type: Image Map
Blending Mode: Additive
Layer Opacity: 70%
Projection: Cubic
Image: SkinBump.jpg
W & H Tile: Repeat

Fig. 10-22 Settings for the overall body texture and bump map.

TEXTURING THE FACE

UV mapping of the face can be done in several ways. Some people prefer to break up the face into several sections so as to minimize the distortion of the map when the mesh is flattened in the UV window. This approach makes it easier to control the textures. The disadvantage is that the edges of the separate maps have to match their adjoining neighboring textures exactly.

Another method is to try to map most of the face as one image. This can simplify the process of trying to match separate textures but can often lead to stretching and distortion of the original image map. The following instructions explain how to UV-map a face using both techniques.

Method 1: UV-Mapping a Face in Sections

To simplify the UV-mapping process, the upper and lower lips will be textured separately. To get the lip texture you might want to scan a photo of real lips, download a digital image, or paint the lips in an image editing program. In this case a straight-on photo of lips was scanned (Figure 10-23). It can also be found in the Chapter 10 folder of the CD-ROM.

Fig. 10-23 A photo of female lips for UV mapping.

The upper lip will now be separated from the lower one. Select, copy, and paste it into a new document with a transparent background. Open the skin color texture and paste it into the upper lip document. Move the layer containing the skin texture image below the layer with the upper lip (Figure 10-24).

The top edge of the upper lip should be blurred so that it blends gradually into the skin texture. You can do this by selecting the top edge and feathering the selection, or use a selection tool with a feather radius. Delete the narrow, feathered top of the lip selection. Another method is to use a soft-edged eraser set to

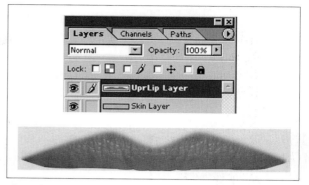

Fig. 10-24 The separated upper lip in the top layer, with the skin texture under it in the bottom layer. Note the blurred top edge of the lip.

airbrush mode. In either case, you should now have a blurry top edge on the upper lip texture. Merge all the layers and save your image.

In your 3-D package, import the upper lip texture. Select only the top lip of your model and hide everything else. Name the upper lip surface. View it in the UV Texture window and apply a new UV texture to it. You might want to give it a name like UVuprLip. After naming the UV texture, select Planar for mapping type. Assuming your model is lying on its back, set the axis to y. This will unwrap and flatten the upper lip.

In your surface editor, select the upper lip surface and apply settings similar to those in Figure 10-25. For specular and bump, you can apply the same upper lip texture that you used for the color.

Another option is to go back to your image editing program, add an empty layer on top of the upper lip color image, and draw thin lines for the creases in the upper lip. Once you complete the thin lines, delete the layer underneath that has the original color map of the upper lip. Save this as your bump map. Inverse the image so that the lines are now white, and save this as your specular map. Back in your 3-D program, use the same UV map for the color, specularity, and bump.

Upper Lip Surface Settings	Specular Texture
Color: UV Texture	Layer Type: Image Map
Luminosity: 0%	Blending Mode: Additive
Diffuse: 90%	Layer Opacity: 100%
Specularity: 30%	Projection: UV
Glossiness: 20%	UV Map: UVuprLip
Reflection: 0%	Image: UprLipSpec.jpg
Transparency: 0%	Automatic Sizing
Refraction Index: 1	**Bump Map**
Translucency: 0%	Layer Type: Image Map
Bump: 120%	Blending Mode: Additive
Color Texture	Layer Opacity: 100%
Layer Type: Image Map	Projection: UV
Blending Mode: Additive	UV Map: UVuprLip
Layer Opacity: 100%	Texture Amplitude: 1.2
Projection: UV	Image: UprLipBump.jpg
UV Map: UVuprLip	Automatic Sizing
Image: UprLip.jpg	
Automatic Sizing	

Fig. 10-25 Surface, color, specular, and bump map settings for the upper lip.

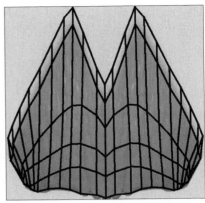

Fig. 10-26 In the UV view window, points are moved on the flattened upper lip so they line up with the upper lip texture.

For image, use the three-color, specular, and bump images for each surface (see Figure 10-25).

For your display options, select the upper lip texture so that it shows up as your background image in the UV window. Your UV view might now look like the one in Figure 10-26. Notice how the mesh lines up with the background lip texture. The top edge of the wireframe lip extends into the background skin color. This will make the top of the upper lip less hard-edged. The rest of the wireframe lip's points are moved within the lip texture. Check your progress by bringing up a full-texture view of the upper lip. You might also want to have both the UV and the texture view windows up at the same time. When you move points around in the UV window, you should see the texture view update.

After finishing the upper lip, the lower lip will now be UV-mapped. In your image editing program, select the lower half of the scanned lips. Select, copy, and paste it into a new document with a transparent background. Open the skin color texture and paste it into the lower lip document. Move the layer containing the skin texture image below the layer with the upper lip (Figure 10-27).

The bottom edge of the lower lip should be blurred so that it blends gradually into the skin texture. Merge all the layers and save your bottom lip image.

In your 3-D package, import the lower lip texture. Select only the bottom lip of your model and hide everything else. Name the lower lip surface. View it in the UV Texture window and apply a new UV texture to it. You might want to give it a name like UVl-wrLip. After naming the UV texture, select Planar for mapping type. Assuming your model is lying on its back, set the axis to y. This will unwrap and flatten the lower lip.

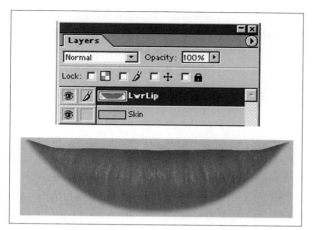

Fig. 10-27 The separated lower lip with the skin texture underneath it in another layer. The bottom edge is blurred to blend into the skin texture.

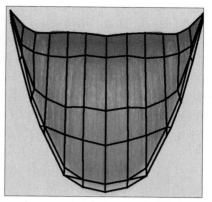

Fig. 10-28 The UV view showing the lip texture behind the flattened lower lip mesh. Points are moved to line up with the image in the background.

In your surface editor, select the lower lip surface and apply settings similar to those in Figure 10-25, except the UV map will be named UVlwrLip and the imported image will be the lower lip texture. For specular and bump, you can apply the same lower lip texture that you used for the color, or paint specular and bump maps as you might have done for the upper lip.

For your display options, select the lower lip texture so that it shows up as your background image in the UV window. Your UV view might now look like the one in Figure 10-28. Notice how the mesh lines up with the background lip texture. The bottom edge of the wireframe lip extends into the background skin color. This will make the bottom of the lower lip less hard-edged. The rest of the wireframe lip's points are moved within the lip texture. Check your progress by bringing up a full-texture view of the lower lip. You might also want to have both the UV and the texture view windows up at the same time. The texture view will update as points are moved around in the UV window.

After completing the lips, the area around the eyes, extending down the nose and into the forehead, will be UV-mapped. The texture around the eyes is very important since this is a prominent part of the face that is very noticeable.

The edges of the texture will be treated in a fashion similar to those of the lips so that they blend into the overall skin texture. This will ensure that all the facial textures blend into one another.

The UV mapping for this part will be a little different from that for the lips. Rather than starting in the image editing program, we will work first with the 3-D software.

Select only the area around the eyes, the forehead, and the nose of your model (Figure 10-29). Hide everything else. Name the surface something like UVtopface. View it in the UV Texture window and apply a new UV texture to it. You might want to give it the same name (something like UVtopface). After naming the UV texture, select Planar for mapping type. Assuming your model is lying on its back, set the axis to y. This will flatten this part of the face. The

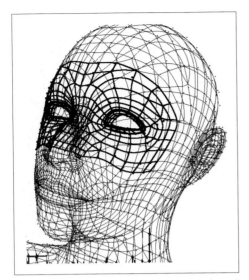

Fig. 10-29 The area around the eyes is selected for UV mapping.

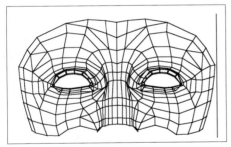

Fig. 10-30 The UV view of the unwrapped part of the face.

as your guide. Depending on how realistic you want the textures, you could also clone images from scanned or digital photos. Be sure to use reference photos and/or a mirror. Figure 10-31 shows the three layers.

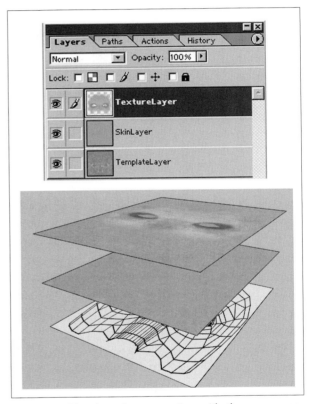

Fig. 10-31 The three layers, starting with the screen-captured UV template, superimposed with the skin texture and ending with the top painted map layer.

UV view of this region of the face might look like the one in Figure 10-30.

Copy or do a screen capture of the UV view. Paste it into your image editing program. Paste the overall skin texture that you have already applied to the body. Add a third layer on top of the skin texture. Hide the skin texture and begin painting the colors and markings in the third layer. Use the bottom-layer template

Let the painted texture fade at the edges so that the skin color in the middle layer takes over at the boundaries. Try using an eraser with airbrush settings or make a feathered selection around the UV template, inverse the selection, switch to the top layer, and delete. Now the margins should have just the skin color that will blend into the overall skin color on the rest of the face and body. Save two versions of this file. One file is saved with all the layers intact in case you decide to change things or add two other layers for the specular and bump maps. The way to do this will be discussed a little later. The other file is going to be your color image map that is applied to the UV mesh. You need only the top layer for this file.

Import the painted texture into your 3-D program. In your surface editor, select the UVtopface name and apply settings similar to those in Figure 10-32. Notice how the surface settings are identical to those for the body as seen in Figure 10-22. This is very important since we do not want this part of the face to be darker, lighter, or glossier than the rest of the person. Unless your person is wearing clothes, the surfaces should look continuous. Also notice that the bump map settings are identical to those for the rest of the body. If

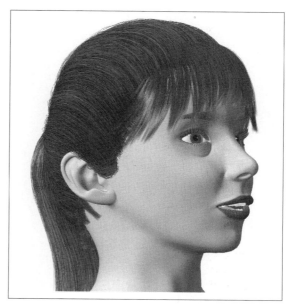

Fig. 10-33 The textured female face.

Upper Face Surface Settings	Color Texture
Color: UV Texture	Layer Type: Image Map
Luminosity: 0%	Blending Mode: Additive
Diffuse: 90%	Layer Opacity: 100%
Specularity: 30%	Projection: UV
Glossiness: 5%	UV Map: UVtopface
Reflection: 0%	Image: UVtopface.jpg
Transparency: 0%	Automatic Sizing
Refraction Index: 1	**Bump Map**
Translucency: 0%	Layer Type: Image Map
Bump: 60%	Blending Mode: Additive
	Layer Opacity: 70%
	Projection: Cubic
	Image: SkinBump.jpg
	W & H Tile: Repeat

Fig. 10-32 The surface, texture, and bump map settings for the top part of the face.

you scaled down the bump map on the body, then be sure to do the same for this part. Figure 10-33 and the CD10-33 color image show the female face so far.

At this point you may decide to stop texturing or to continue by selecting other parts of the face. If you decide to texture other areas, then use the same surface settings as before and have the edges blend into the overall skin color, for uninterrupted tones.

Some of you may want to add some lines or creases to the face. The following directions should help you with that.

In your image editing program, create another layer on top of the previously painted texture that you made for the area around the eyes and forehead. Paint or draw black lines for the creases and wrinkles (Figure 10-34). For deeper lines, draw them darker. Notice that the forehead wrinkles in the illustration have lighter lines. Delete the painted face texture layer

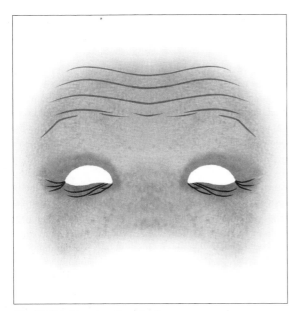

Fig. 10-34 Drawing lines for bump-mapped creases.

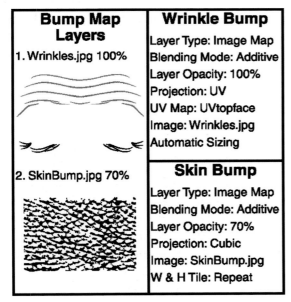

Bump Map Layers	Wrinkle Bump
1. Wrinkles.jpg 100%	Layer Type: Image Map
	Blending Mode: Additive
	Layer Opacity: 100%
	Projection: UV
	UV Map: UVtopface
	Image: Wrinkles.jpg
	Automatic Sizing
2. SkinBump.jpg 70%	**Skin Bump**
	Layer Type: Image Map
	Blending Mode: Additive
	Layer Opacity: 70%
	Projection: Cubic
	Image: SkinBump.jpg
	W & H Tile: Repeat

Fig. 10-35 Settings for the two layers of bump maps. The wrinkle bump map sits on top of the overall skin bump. Since the wrinkle bump map has an alpha channel, the skin bump is visible behind it.

underneath the wrinkle lines. The lines should now have a transparent background. This is important since it will serve as an alpha channel (empty space). When you add the line textures on top of the overall skin bump map, the face will still have a consistent cellular bump map as well as the newly added wrinkle line bump map. Save the line bump map in a format that also saves the alpha channel (psd, tif, pct, tga, etc.).

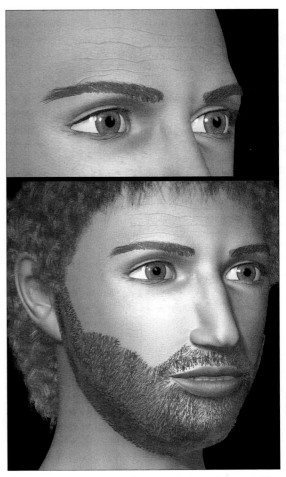

Fig. 10-36 A close-up and a normal view of the wrinkles on a male head.

In your 3-D program's texture editor, select the surface name to which you plan to add the bump name. Since it will already have the overall bump map, add another layer on top of that one. Import the wrinkle line bump map for this new layer. Figure 10-35 shows the settings for the new bump map as well as the old settings for the skin bump map underneath it. A close-up of the wrinkles on the rendered face as well as the final rendered face can be seen in Figure 10-36. It can also be viewed in color on the CD-ROM in the Chapter 10 folder as CD10-36BumpMaleFace.

Method 2: UV-Mapping an Entire Face

Even though the face is mapped as a whole, you will still need an overall seamless skin texture, as discussed in the preceding section. The mapped face should look fine in the front view, but you will most likely see some pulling or distortion in the side view. Figure 10-37 illustrates the UV-mapped face, which can also be seen in color on the CD-ROM in the Chapter 10 folder as CD10-37SingleUVFaceMap.

In your 3-D program, select the front part of the face that extends from the neck up to the end of the forehead and all the way to the sides where the ears begin. In this lesson, the lips are not selected since these will be textured separately. You could go ahead

and make them part of your UV face or follow the directions in the previous lesson to map them individually.

Name this surface UVfrontface. Now make only this part of the face a UV map. If the body is lying down, make the UV map planar on the y axis. In your UV window view, you should now see the face flattened out. Copy or do a screen capture of the UV view. Paste it into your image editing program. Figure 10-38 depicts the screen capture of the flattened UV face.

In your image editing program, open the screen-captured flattened UV face. If you plan to use a photograph, then open that also. Create a separate layer on top of the screen-captured UV face. Using the UV screen capture as a guide, paint or clone parts of the photographed face in the top layer. The screen capture will act as a template to help you locate the various features of the face. Figure 10-39 shows the screen capture guide underneath the painted texture. Notice

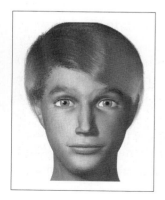

Fig. 10-37 A head UV-mapped with a single face texture.

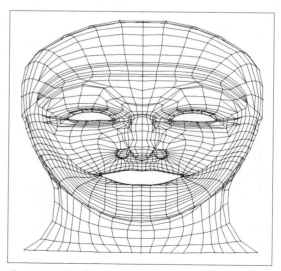

Fig. 10-38 The flattened UV face.

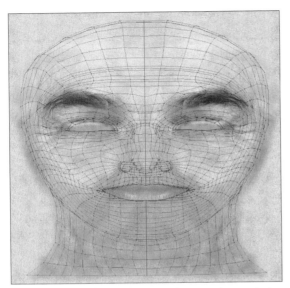

Fig. 10-39 In a separate layer, a photograph or painting of the face is applied over the screen-captured UV face.

In your 3-D program, apply the painted face to the previously named UVfrontface surface. When you bring up the texture as a background image in the UV window view, you should see it match up exactly to the face mesh. If you need to make some adjustments, then manipulate the mesh in the UV window until it matches everything on the background image.

Apply a bump map to the face as described in Figure 10-32. Assign a body texture and bump map as listed in Figure 10-22. The overall skin texture that is a part of the face on the edges is applied to the rest of the head and body. Make sure the surface settings are the same for the face and the body. If the face has more or less specular, diffuse, glossy and such characteristics than the body, it will be noticeable at the edges.

As you experiment with UV mapping you will most likely discover that the combinations of various texturing methods seem limitless. Since UV mapping uses the point coordinates on the model, you should also see that the textures deform right along with the mesh during facial animation. Those of you who do not have UV mapping in your software might find the following technique useful.

how the eyebrows are also painted on the face. If you decided to map the lips separately, then follow the previous directions under the subheading "Method 1: UV-Mapping a Face in Sections."

You will also need to make a seamless overall skin color texture. Blur the edges of your painted face and apply the seamless skin color underneath it in another layer. It should blend seamlessly into the rest of the face and extend all the way to the edges of the image. The overall skin color will be applied to the rest of the head and body so that you should not see any edges between the two separate maps.

The eyeholes can be left hollow since the separate eyeball object will be placed there. When you are done painting the face, delete the layer that has the template of the screen-captured UV face. Flatten the two layers containing the painted face and the overall skin texture.

Using a Texture Guide

Another method for mapping textures to a face is to use a pattern guide. The pattern, when mapped to the face, indicates where parts of the final texture will be placed.

You can create a pattern or use the one included on the CD-ROM, located in the Chapter 10 "Texture" folder (Figure 10-40). Assuming your person is lying face up, map the pattern spherically on the z axis. Be sure to use automatic sizing so that it stretches across the entire head or face. You do not want the texture to tile. Each unique marking on the pattern will then tell you where to line up the final texture (Figure 10-41).

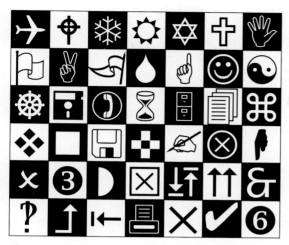

Fig. 10-40 A pattern guide like this one can be used to map parts of the face for texturing.

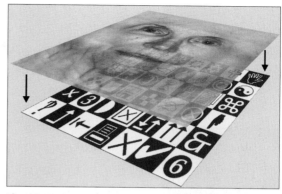

Fig. 10-42 Using the pattern as a guide, the final texture is painted in a layer on top of it. This will ensure that all the features line up correctly when the texture is mapped on the model.

With the pattern mapped to the model, create several renderings showing different views of the face. Use these as your guide when you begin to work on the final texture. In your image editing program, place the original pattern in the first layer and start painting over

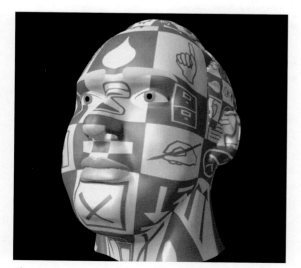

Fig. 10-41 Since the model was lying on its back, the pattern was spherically mapped on the z axis.

it in a second top layer (Figure 10-42). You can make the top layer somewhat transparent so that you can see where to line up the textures. As you paint you will most likely have to stretch and distort some of the facial features. The pattern on the renderings will serve as your guide for where to paint specific textures.

After you finish painting the face map, delete the layer with the pattern. Save only the painted face texture. In your 3-D program, replace the pattern with the newly painted face texture. It should fit exactly the same way as the substituted pattern.

Working with a 3-D Paint Program

Most 3-D paint programs are full-featured applications that allow users to paint directly onto 3-D models. These software packages usually import and export most of the popular 3-D formats. Many have tools similar to those in familiar image-processing programs. When it comes to rotating the model in preview mode, performance varies among the different software packages. Models can usually be viewed with color, bump, and specularity maps.

235

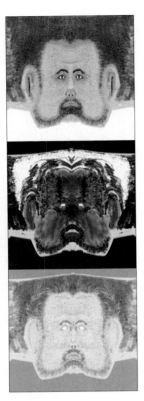

Fig. 10-43 Three image maps exported from a 3-D paint program. The top image is the color map, the middle one is the specular map, and the bottom shows the bump map.

When working in a 3-D paint program, you do not always have to use UV mapping. Your model and the texture can be exported using one of the projection methods such as spherical mapping. Figure 10-43 shows three maps created in a 3-D paint program called Deep Paint 3D™. After painting on a model of the head, the color, specular, and bump maps were exported and applied using spherical mapping on the y axis. Since the model was facing forward in the front view, the texture had a seam running from the top of the head down the back toward the neck.

LIGHTING THE HUMAN MODEL

The one thing to keep in mind when lighting human models is that there are no set rules that you should follow. Each situation requires its own setup. Lighting configurations establish the mood of the scene. Therefore, like everything else in computer animation, lighting takes some planning.

Colored sketches or paintings can be helpful guides in determining the right mood of a scene. Working from preliminary sketches or paintings saves time and brings about new ideas. Without them, one can spend a great amount of time setting up lights, changing them, and rendering test scenes. Even with preliminaries one will still have to make a number of experimental renderings, but it should reduce the amount required.

Figure 10-44 shows a typical lighting arrangement. A color image can also be viewed in the Chapter 10 folder on the CD-ROM as CD10-44LightingSetup. The illustration can be used as a guide and then altered according to each situation. These lights are exclusive to one character; in other words, they should not affect anything else in the setting. Each digital actor has its own lights, and none of them should act upon anything else in their environment. The exception to this is that the light(s) that cast shadows will affect other characters and their surroundings. Spotlights are typically used most often since they allow a greater degree of control and work well with shadow maps.

To make it easier to move all the lights at once, they can be parented to a null or an object. Parenting them to a character works fine as long as they don't affect anything else in the scene. Objects such as the ground, which are not excluded from these lights, will show a change in brightness as the figure travels through the scene.

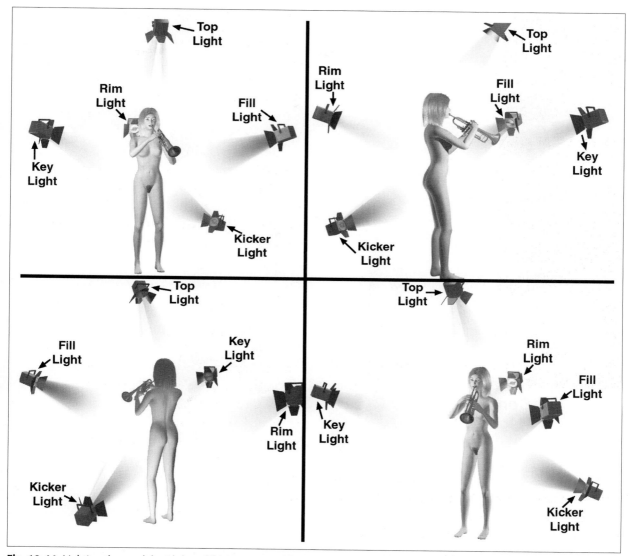

Fig. 10-44 Lighting the model with key, fill, rim, top, and kicker lights. All these are parented to a null for easier control.

TYPES OF LIGHTS

Each light is classified according to its individual function and placement. The basic lighting arrangement seen in Figure 10-45 consists of the following.

Ambient

Overall brightness of a scene is determined by a global light that affects everything. This is a flat illumination that does not create shadows but lightens

237

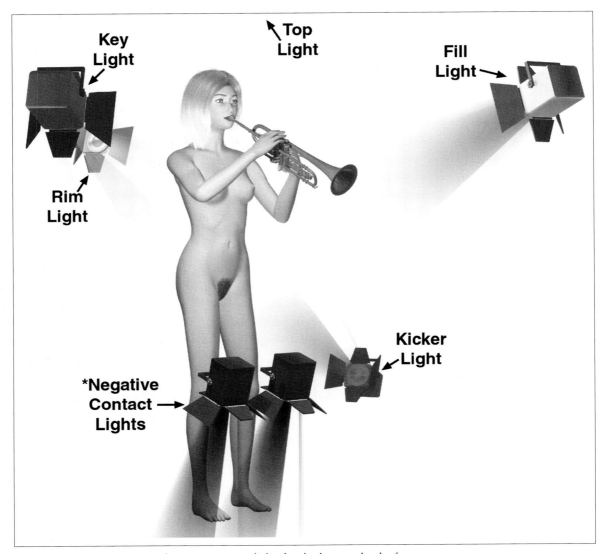

Fig. 10-45 Adding positive and negative contact lights for shadows under the feet.

them. Its quality of unvariedness can make a scene look bland and washed out. A small percentage of ambient light can be applied to prevent absolute black areas.

Key Light

This is the brightest light on a subject. The key light's color as well as its placement affect the mood and dramatic quality of the subject. A green-colored key light can make the person look sickly or menacing. Placing the light on the bottom pointing up can enhance this sinister look. Pointing the light down from the top can add an air of mystery.

Most often the key light is a warm color such as light yellow. It is usually placed slightly above the person or the camera plane and about 30 to 45 degrees to the side.

Since the key light's function is to serve as the principal source of illumination, it can be set to cast shadows. Assigning shadow maps to the key light works well in many situations. Turning up the shadow map size and soft edges (fuzziness) enhances the quality of the shadows. Hard-edged, ray-traced shadows can make a scene look cold, while soft, shadow-mapped ones will add warmth, thus making the image look a little less computer generated.

Fill Light

A key light by itself can create some very dark shadow areas. The paintings of Rembrandt or Caravaggio are superb examples of the dramatic effects that can be achieved with a single source of illumination.

The fill light is a lower-intensity source of illumination that is used to soften and fill in areas of shadows. Assigning a cool color such as blue to the fill light can enhance the appearance of the subject matter. One can also work with complementary colors.

For example, if the key light is yellow, the fill light can be violet.

Traditionally the fill light is placed facing the subject from the other side of the key light. If the key light is placed to the left of the person, then the fill light is positioned on the right side.

The lighting ratio of the key light to the fill light varies according to the situation. A well-lit subject will have more fill light. More dramatic circumstances will have very little fill light and perhaps none at all.

Rim or Back Light

This type of light is placed directly behind the person facing the camera. It can be used as a method for separating the subject from the background. The rim light creates a thin edge of light around different parts of the subject.

Rim lights can be used to establish a romantic mood. The color is usually warm, such as light yellow.

If you are using a hair generator, you will most likely be able to set up key, fill, and rim lights exclusively for the hair. The remaining light strength will vary according to the look you are trying to achieve with the hair.

Kicker Light

The purpose of this light is to enhance the look of the character and add some definition to one edge of the surface. It is usually placed somewhat behind the person, low to the ground, and facing directly toward the key light. The color of the kicker light can vary greatly. Sometimes a complementary color to that of the key light is chosen, while other times warmer hues such as crimson or orange work well with the subject matter.

Top Light

A top light helps define the face and hair of the person. Since most shots would show the upper half more often than the lower body, the top light makes it easier to distinguish those characteristics.

Rather than placing the top light directly above the person, it can be positioned slightly in front, facing down. Its color is usually warm, such as light yellow.

Special Lights

Since most of the lights are set above the midsection of the person, the lower legs are often not as well lit as other areas. To remedy this, one can add an extra light below the key light, facing toward the low-lit area. These two lights should overlap each other. The penumbra, or soft-edge angle, of the lights should be large enough so that one cannot detect an edge between the two lights.

Bounce Lights

Special lights can also refer to other lights that accent parts of the subject and its surroundings. Bounce lights that simulate radiosity can be classified as special lights. They are colored according to the surfaces they are simulating. For example, if a red towel is lying on a white table, a red bounce light can be directed at the table right by the towel. This will make it seem as if red from the towel is reflected onto the surface of the table.

Contact Lights

This kind of light does not add any extra illumination to a scene. Its sole purpose is to add extra shadows. Figure 10-45 and the color image in the Chapter 10 folder of the CD-ROM titled CD10-45FeetContact-Lights show the location of the negative contact lights. Negative lights reduce illumination. Instead of having a positive intensity value, they have a negative one. Contact lights made up of equal negative and positive lights can be set to make shadows under the feet.

To make contact lights, create a positive light and turn on Shadow Map for it. Parent this light to one of the foot bones and point it down on the feet. Clone this light and put a minus in front of the intensity value. Turn *off* Shadow Map for the negative light. Both lights occupy the same space and are facing the same direction. If the light intensity for the positive light is 60%, then the negative one will have an intensity of –60%. Although the positive light casts a shadow, the two lights cancel each other out, thus eliminating any extra illumination.

Clone both lights and parent the second pair to the other foot bone. The feet or shoes will cast shadows underneath them.

Negative lights are also useful for creating dark areas in places such as corners or underneath objects. They can be used to cut back on illumination, especially in areas with hot spots. Negative lights allow a great degree of control over shadows.

Gobos or Cucaloris Lights

Sometimes referred to as a *light gel* or *cookie,* this kind of light can produce abstract patterns or more representative shadows. The light acts as a kind of slide projector, bathing the subject with a specific shape(s). The pattern or picture can be mapped directly to a light as a projection image or mapped to a semitransparent plane that is placed in front of a light.

One can use transparency mapping with an alpha channel to project images as shadows against objects. For example, to have a wall show the shadow of a tree that will never be seen, it is not necessary to model an entire tree. A plane with a silhouette image of a tree mapped onto it and placed in front of a light should work just fine. The image will have to have an alpha channel around and between the tree and its branches.

This alpha channel becomes invisible with transparency mapping.

Freestanding flags are also useful for controlling the shape and placement of light. They can block out unwanted parts of light and delineate specific forms.

Fundamentals of Human Animation 11

If you are reading this part, then you have most likely finished building your human character, created textures for it, set up its skeleton, made morph targets for facial expressions, and arranged lights around the model. You have then arrived at perhaps the most exciting part of 3-D design, which is animating a character. Up to now the work has been somewhat creative, sometimes tedious, and often difficult.

It is very gratifying when all your previous efforts start to pay off as you enliven your character. When animating, there is a creative flow that increases gradually over time. You are now at the phase where you become both the actor and the director of a movie or play.

Although animation appears to be a more spontaneous act, it is nevertheless just as challenging, if not more so, than all the previous steps that led up to it. Your animations will look pitiful if you do not understand some basic fundamentals and principles. The following pointers are meant to give you some direction. Feel free to experiment with them. Bend and break the rules whenever you think it will improve the animation.

SOME ANIMATION POINTERS

1. **Try isolating parts.** Sometimes this is referred to as animating in stages. Rather than trying to move every part of a body at the same time, concentrate on specific areas. Only one section of the body is moved for the duration of the animation. Then returning to the beginning of the timeline, another section is animated. By successively returning to the beginning and animating a different part each time, the entire process is less confusing.

2. **Put in some lag time.** Different parts of the body should not start and stop at the same time. When an arm swings, the lower arm should follow a few frames after that. The hand swings after the lower arm. It is like a chain reaction that works its way through the entire length of the limb.

3. **Nothing ever comes to a total stop.** In life, only machines appear to come to a dead stop. Muscles, tendons, force, and gravity all affect the movement of a human. You can prove this to yourself. Try punching the air with a full extension. Notice that your fist has a bounce at the end.

   If a part comes to a stop such as a motion hold, keyframe it once and then again after three to eight or more keyframes. Your motion graph will then have a curve between the two identical keyframes. This will make the part appear to bounce rather than come to a dead stop.

4. **Add facial expressions and finger movements.** Your digital human should exhibit signs of life

by blinking and breathing. A blink will normally occur every 60 seconds. A typical blink might be as follows:

Frame 60: Both eyes are open.
Frame 61: The right eye closes halfway.
Frame 62: The right eye closes all the way and the left eye closes halfway.
Frame 63: The right eye opens halfway and the left eye closes all the way.
Frame 64: The right eye opens all the way and left eye opens halfway.
Frame 65: The left eye opens all the way.

Closing the eyes at slightly different times makes the blink less mechanical.

Changing facial expressions could be just using eye movements to indicate thoughts running through your model's head. The hands will appear stiff if you do not add finger movements. Too many students are too lazy to take the time to add facial and hand movements. If you make the extra effort for these details you will find that your animations become much more interesting.

5. **What is not seen by the camera is unimportant.** If an arm goes through a leg but is not seen in the camera view, then do not bother to fix it. If you want a hand to appear close to the body and the camera view makes it seem to be close even though it is not, then why move it any closer? This also applies to sets. There is no need to build an entire house if all the action takes place in the living room. Consider painting backdrops rather than modeling every part of a scene.

6. **Use a minimum amount of keyframes.** Too many keyframes can make the character appear to move in spastic motions. Sharp, cartoonlike movements are created with closely spaced keyframes. Floaty or soft, languid motions are the result of widely spaced keyframes. An animation will often be a mixture of both. Try to look for ways that will abbreviate the motions. You can retain the essential elements of an animation while reducing the amount of keyframes necessary to create a gesture.

7. **Anchor a part of the body.** Unless your character is in the air, it should have some part of itself locked to the ground. This could be a foot, a hand, or both. Whichever portion is on the ground should be held in the same spot for a number of frames. This prevents unwanted sliding motions. When the model shifts its weight, the foot that touches down becomes locked in place. This is especially true with walking motions.

There are a number of ways to lock parts of a model to the ground. One method is to use inverse kinematics. The goal object, which could be a null, automatically locks a foot or hand to the bottom surface. Another method is to manually keyframe the part that needs to be motionless in the same spot. The character or its limbs will have to be moved and rotated, so that foot or hand stays in the same place. If you are using forward kinematics, then this could mean keyframing practically every frame until it is time to unlock that foot or hand.

8. **A character should exhibit weight.** One of the most challenging tasks in 3-D animation is to have a digital actor appear to have weight and mass. You can use several techniques to achieve this. Squash and stretch, or weight and recoil, one of the 12 principles of animation discussed in Chapter 12, is an excellent way to give your character weight.

By adding a little bounce to your human, he or she will appear to respond to the force of gravity. For example, if your character jumps up and lands, lift the body up a little after it makes contact. For a heavy character, you can do this several times and have it decrease over time. This will make it seem as if the force of the contact causes the body to vibrate a little.

Secondary actions, another one of the 12 principles of animation discussed in Chapter 12, are an important way to show the effects of gravity and mass. Using the previous example of a jumping character, when he or she lands, the belly could bounce up and down, the arms could have some spring to them, the head could tilt forward, and so on.

Moving or vibrating the object that comes in contact with the traveling entity is another method for showing the force of mass and gravity. A floor could vibrate or a chair that a person sits in respond to the weight by the seat going down and recovering back up a little. Sometimes an animator will shake the camera to indicate the effects of a force.

It is important to take into consideration the size and weight of a character. Heavy objects such as an elephant will spend more time on the ground, while a light character like a rabbit will spend more time in the air. The hopping rabbit hardly shows the effects of gravity and mass.

9. **Take the time to act out the action.** So often, it is too easy to just sit at the computer and try to solve all the problems of animating a human. Put some life into the performance by getting up and acting out the motions. This will make the character's actions more unique and also solve many timing and positioning problems. The best animators are also excellent actors. A mirror is an indispensable tool for the animator. Videotaping yourself can also be a great help.

10. **Decide whether to use IK, FK, or a blend of both.** Forward kinematics and inverse kinematics have their advantages and disadvantages. FK allows full control over the motions of different body parts. A bone can be rotated and moved to the exact degree and location one desires. The disadvantage to using FK is that when your person has to interact within an environment, simple movements become difficult. Anchoring a foot to the ground so it does not move is challenging because whenever you move the body, the feet slide. A hand resting on a desk has the same problem.

IK moves the skeleton with goal objects such as a null. Using IK, the task of anchoring feet and hands becomes very simple. The disadvantage to IK is that a great amount of control is packed together into the goal objects. Certain poses become very difficult to achieve.

If the upper body does not require any interaction with its environment, then consider a blend of both IK and FK. IK can be set up for the lower half of the body to anchor the feet to the ground, while FK on the upper body allows greater freedom and precision of movements.

Every situation involves a different approach. Use your judgment to decide which setup fits the animation most reliably.

11. **Add dialogue.** It has been said that more than 90% of student animations that are submitted to companies lack dialogue. The few that incorporate speech in their animations make their work highly noticeable. If the animation and dialogue are well done, then those few have a greater advantage than their competition. Companies understand that it takes extra effort and skill to create animation with dialogue.

When you plan your story, think about creating interaction between characters not only on a physical level but through dialogue as well. There are several techniques, discussed in this chapter, that can be used to make dialogue manageable.

12. **Use the graph editor to clean up your animations.** The graph editor is a useful tool that all 3-D animators should become familiar with. It is basically a representation of all the objects, lights, and cameras in your scene. It keeps track of all their activities and properties.

A good use of the graph editor is to clean up morph targets after animating facial expressions. If the default incoming curve in your graph editor is set to arcs rather than straight lines, you will most likely find that sometimes splines in the graph editor will curve below a value of zero. This can yield some unpredictable results. The facial morph targets begin to take on negative values that lead to undesirable facial expressions. Whenever you see a curve bend below a value of zero, select the first keyframe point to the right of the arc and set its curve to linear. A more detailed discussion of the graph editor will be found in a later part of this chapter.

ANIMATING IN STAGES

All the various components that can be moved on a human model often become confusing if you try to change them at the same time. The performance quickly deteriorates into a mechanical routine if you try to alter all these parts at the same keyframes. Remember, you are trying to create human qualities, not robotic ones.

Isolating areas to be moved means that you can look for the parts of the body that have motion over time and concentrate on just a few of those. For example, the first thing you can move is the body and legs. When you are done moving them around over the entire timeline, then try rotating the spine. You might do this by moving individual spine bones or using an inverse kinematics chain. Now that you have the body moving around and bending, concentrate on the arms. If you are not using an IK chain to move the arms, hands, and fingers, then rotate the bones for the upper and lower arm. Do not forget the wrist. Finger movements can be animated as one of the last parts. Facial expressions can also be animated last.

Example movies showing the same character animated in stages can be viewed on the CD-ROM as CD11-1AnimationStagesMovies. Some sample images from the animations can also be seen in Figure 11-1. The first movie shows movement only in the body and legs. During the second stage, the spine and head were animated. The third time, the arms were moved. Finally, in the fourth and final stage, facial expressions and finger movements were added.

Animating in successive passes should simplify the process. Some final stages would be used to clean up or edit the animation.

Sometimes the animation switches from one part of the body leading to another. For example, somewhere during the middle of an animation the upper body begins to lead the lower one. In a case like this, you would then switch from animating the lower body first to moving the upper part before the lower one.

The order in which one animates can be a matter of personal choice. Some people may prefer to do facial animation first or perhaps they like to move the arms before anything else. Following is a summary of how someone might animate a human.

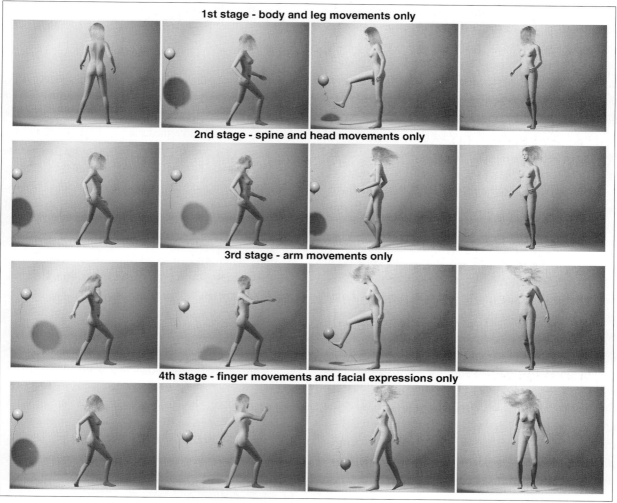

Fig. 11-1 Images from the example animations in which the female was moved in stages.

1. First pass: Move the body and legs.
2. Second pass: Move or rotate the spinal bones, neck, and head.
3. Third pass: Move or rotate the arms and hands.
4. Fourth pass: Animate the fingers.
5. Fifth pass: Animate the eyes blinking.
6. Sixth pass: Animate eye movements.
7. Seventh pass: Animate the mouth, eyebrows, nose, jaw, and cheeks (you can break these up into separate passes).

247

Most movement starts at the hips. Athletes often begin with a windup action in the pelvic area that works its way outward to the extreme parts of the body. This whiplike activity can even be observed in just about any mundane act. It is interesting to note that people who study martial arts learn that most of their power comes from the lower torso.

Students are often too lazy to make finger movements a part of their animation. There are several methods that can make the process less time consuming.

One way is to create morph targets of the finger positions and then use shape shifting to move the various digits. Each finger is positioned in an open and fistlike closed posture. For example, the sections of the index finger are closed, while the others are left in an open, relaxed position for one morph target. The next morph target would have only the ring finger closed while keeping the others open. During the animation, sliders are then used to open and close the fingers and/or thumbs.

Another method to create finger movements is to animate them in both closed and open positions and then save the motion files for each digit. Anytime you animate the same character, you can load the motions into your new scene file. It then becomes a simple process of selecting either the closed or the open position for each finger and thumb and keyframing them wherever you desire.

DIALOGUE

Knowing how to make your humans talk is a crucial part of character animation. Once you add dialogue, you should notice a livelier performance and a greater personality in your character. At first, dialogue may seem too great a challenge to attempt. Actually, if you follow some simple rules, you will find that adding speech to your animations is not as daunting a task as one would think. The following suggestions should help.

DIALOGUE ESSENTIALS

1. **Look in the mirror.** Before animating, use a mirror or a reflective surface such as that on a CD to follow lip movements and facial expressions.

2. **The eyes, mouth, and brows change the most.** The parts of the face that contain the greatest amount of muscle groups are the eyes, brows, and mouth. Therefore, these are the areas that change the most when creating expressions.

3. **The head constantly moves during dialogue.** Animate random head movements, no matter how small, during the entire animation. Involuntary motions of the head make a point without having to state it outright. For example, nodding and shaking the head communicate, respectively, positive and negative responses. Leaning the head forward can show anger, while a downward movement communicates sadness. Move the head to accentuate and emphasize certain statements. Listen to the words that are stressed and add extra head movements to them.

4. **Communicate emotions.** There are six recognizable universal emotions: sadness, anger, joy, fear, disgust, and surprise. Other, more ambiguous states are pain, sleepiness, passion, physical exertion, shyness, embarrassment, worry, disdain, sternness, skepticism, laughter, yelling, vanity, impatience, and awe.

5. **Use phonemes and visemes.** Phonemes are the individual sounds we hear in speech. Rather than trying to spell out a word, recreate the word as a phoneme. For example, the word *computer* is phonetically spelled "cumpewtrr." Visemes are the mouth shapes and tongue positions employed

during speech. It helps tremendously to draw a chart that recreates speech as phonemes combined with mouth shapes (visemes) above or below a timeline with the frames marked and the sound and volume indicated.

6. **Never animate behind the dialogue.** It is better to make the mouth shapes one or two frames before the dialogue.

7. **Don't overstate.** Realistic facial movements are fairly limited. The mouth does not open that much when talking.

8. **Blinking is always a part of facial animation.** It occurs about every two seconds. Different emotional states affect the rate of blinking. Nervousness increases the rate of blinking, while anger decreases it.

9. **Move the eyes.** To make the character appear to be alive, be sure to add eye motions. About 80% of the time is spent watching the eyes and mouth, while about 20% is focused on the hands and body.

10. **Breathing should be a part of facial animation.** Opening the mouth and moving the head back slightly will show an intake of air, while flaring the nostrils and having the head nod forward a little can show exhalation. Breathing movements should be very subtle and hardly noticeable.

11. **It takes at least two frames to read an expression.** In order to be noticed, consonants require a minimum of two frames. The mouth has to be closed for at least two frames when keying P, B, M, F, and T. If there are not enough frames to do this, then swipe some frames from the previous phoneme.

12. **Move the body.** Unless it is dead, no body can be motionless. Even though the movement is very small, it should be discernible. Body movement is a result of breathing, shifting weight, experiencing emotional states, and emphasizing certain words. The attitude of the body should echo the facial expression.

13. **Show the motivation.** Show what is driving your character to say certain things. Keep in mind the circumstance and thoughts that might be running through the person's mind while he or she is talking.

14. **Use simplified phrasing.** Simplify the dialogue into expressions of the dominant vowel and consonant sounds, especially in fast dialogue. A sound graph of the dialogue is a useful tool for picking out the vowels and consonants with the most emphasis. These will show up on the graph as the highest peaks and also as the lowest on the wave. Try not to close the mouth for every consonant. For example, when articulating the word *robot,* there is no need to close the mouth again at the *b* consonant. You can skip the *b* enunciation and go directly to the *t* to close the mouth.

15. **Reflect dialogue modulation.** Lift the body up four frames before major highs and lows on the sound graph.

16. **Hold the pose after a major change.** When there is a major dialogue sound or modification in the facial expression, hold the pose for a little while so that it can be perceived. When the head moves too much, it is difficult to see changes on the face.

17. **The first six to eight frames are hard to read.** Try not to do anything major during the first eight frames. The audience will have a hard time figuring it out.

18. **Never "in-between" the tongue.** In speech the tongue moves too fast to be seen in motion. Use only two frames to move it up and down or down and up.

WAYS OF MAKING THEM TALK

Three-dimensional animation always offers many solutions for the same challenge. There are several popular approaches to creating dialogue. No matter which one you choose, you will now have the opportunity to use all those morph targets that you set up when working through Chapter 9.

One method is to make an exposure sheet. This is a timing chart that maps out the sound wave, along with the frame rate and the phonemes. Once you have converted the sound into numbered animation frames along with the phonemes, you will not even need to listen to the audio file as you animate the mouth movements. If you have never animated dialogue, you definitely owe it to yourself to create an exposure sheet. It will teach you how to translate an audio track into frame numbers and work with phonemes. It is the classical method for creating speech that every animator should experience.

Another solution for animating dialogue is to import the audio file into the animation program itself. You can then move the frame slider back and forth to listen to the sounds to determine at which keyframes they occur. While looking in a mirror, you can animate the mouth movements according to the sounds along the timeline.

A third way of animating speech is to import a video clip along with the sound track into the animation program. This makes it possible to watch the actor's lips and other facial expressions while listening to the audio. While moving the frame slider along the timeline, you can determine when to change the character's expressions.

Using an Exposure Sheet

Figure 11-2 illustrates an exposure sheet with the audio wave, frames, and phonemes. To create a chart like this, start by opening the audio file in a video editing program. Enlarge the audio window until you can see the audio wave. Try to make the display large enough that you can see all the ridges of the wave.

If you are animating at 30 frames per second, then set the audio window properties to 30 frames per second non-drop-frame timecode. This will make it possible to see what frame you are at along the audio track.

When you click on the different parts of the track you should see the frame number listed below. In some programs, the frame number changes to 1:00 at frame 30.

Copy the screen window showing the audio track. You now have the choice of printing out the audio

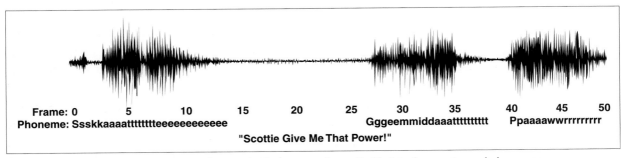

Frame: 0   5   10   15   20   25   30   35   40   45   50
Phoneme: Sssskkaaaattttttteeeeeeeeeeeee   Gggeemmiddaaatttttttttt   Ppaaaawwrrrrrrrrr

"Scottie Give Me That Power!"

Fig. 11-2 The exposure sheet, or timing chart, is used to convert the audio file into frame rates and phonemes.

wave or you can paste the screen copy into your favorite image editing program. If you print the audio track, then write the frame numbers and phonemes on the print while playing through them in the video editing program.

If you decide to paste the screen shot of the audio into an image editing program, then do the following. Work back and forth between the video and the image editing programs to label the frames on the audio track. When you are in the video editing program, click on the audio wave to determine where every fifth frame occurs. Go to the image editing program and use the Type tool to type the number under the audio wave. The sine wave of the audio track should help you determine the location of each frame.

After you finish naming the frames on the audio track, work back and forth between the two programs to type the phonetic pronunciation of the audio underneath the frame numbers. In your video editing program, you can scrub back and forth using the time slider or mark the in and out parts on sections of the track to find each specific sound.

After you finish labeling the audio track in your image editing program, print your exposure sheet. Refer to this timing chart when you work in the 3-D program to set the mouth shapes. Use a mirror to mimic the mouth movements. You should notice that animating the mouth is a fairly fast process once you have an exposure sheet. Be sure to refer to the "Dialogue Essentials" subsection earlier in this chapter. One of the biggest mistakes you can make is to try to animate every phoneme on the audio track.

When you are finished animating the mouth, make a test animation and add the audio to it in your video editing program. You might even decide to move the audio track a few frames past the beginning part of the animation. It is always better to animate a few frames before the audio.

When you run your test animation, you will most likely find that some of the mouth movements should be toned down. It is a common mistake to move the mouth too much or too often. Try to blur the distinction between various mouth expressions. Turning on motion blur also helps.

Once you are satisfied with the mouth movements, then concentrate on adding other facial expressions such as blinking, raising and lowering eyebrows, moving the eyes, and so on. You will also need to add body movements such as tilting the head and breathing. The worst thing you can do is to leave a visible part of the body rigid like a statue.

Since this is an exercise for creating dialogue, the mouth was the first part to be animated. Normally when working on an animation, the order is reversed. Animate the body first, then the eyes, and finally the mouth. Figure 11-3 depicts a talking head with the previously illustrated exposure sheet. The color image can be viewed on the CD-ROM in the Chapter 11 folder as CD11-3DialogueFaces.

Importing Audio into the Animation Program

Most high-end 3-D programs have the option of importing sound tracks so that animators can listen to the audio while changing their characters' facial expressions. This is a useful feature, but animators will still need a mirror for imitating facial expressions (Figure 11-4).

After importing the audio track into your 3-D program, isolate the number of frames that you will work on. You can do this by setting the start and end frames. For example, you can set your start frame at 10 and the ending frame at 20. This allows you the option of listening to the sound track for only those 10 frames. If you have to, make a preview animation of only the 10 frames. Listen to the sound and watch the frame counter to see when they occur. Mimic the mouth

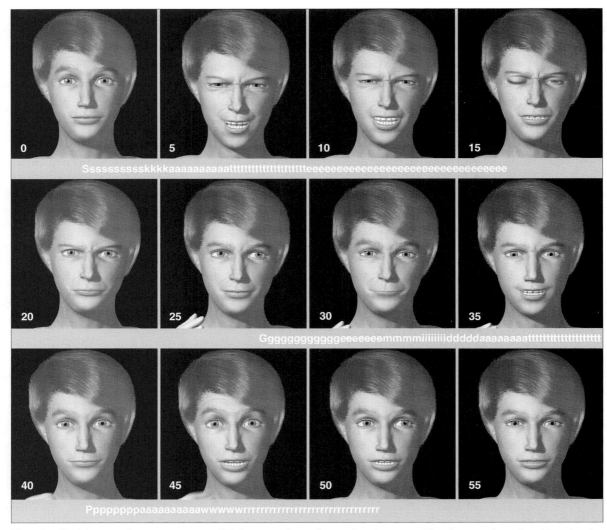

Fig. 11-3 Facial expressions seen at every fifth frame as they relate to the phonemes. The character is saying, "Scottie, give me that power."

movements and watch yourself in a mirror. Set the facial expressions accordingly.

Importing Video into the Animation Program

Animating to video or film is often referred to as *roto-scoping*. This works very well for animating facial expressions. Since you can watch the actor's mouth movements on your computer monitor, you most likely will not even have to use a mirror (Figure 11-5).

Make sure your software supports the video format that you want to import. You may have to separate the audio from the video and then import it as another

Fig. 11-4 Importing the sound track into the 3-D program and using a mirror. Notice the shape-shifting controls for morphing the face.

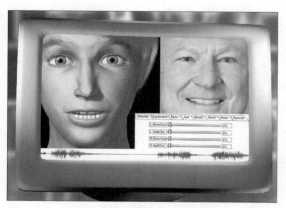

Fig. 11-5 Video, along with the sound track, is imported into the 3-D program.

file. Once both the audio and the video portions are in your program, you can move the time slider while listening to the sound and watching the actor's face on the video. The video can be displayed in the background or mapped onto a 2-D rectangle. Changes in the actor's expressions and speech can be seen along the timeline as you move the frame slider.

Isolate the animation by setting limited ranges for the beginning and ending frames. You might want to show only 10 to 15 frames at a time. Making previews

that play the sound along with the images will help you determine where to change expressions.

Completing the Dialogue

When you finish your animation, import it into your video editing program. Bring in the audio file. Place the animation and audio on separate tracks. Preview the dialogue animation. As mentioned before, you may have to shift the audio over a few frames so that it starts a little later than the video portion. Finally, make a movie, and you are done. The Chapter 11 folder on the CD-ROM has a short dialogue animation example.

STORYBOARDING

Storyboards are used to outline the actions of a video or film animation (Figure 11-6). These usually comprise a number of frames indicating key actions. Each scene has a frame for a sketch and a smaller box for describing the action, dialogue, camera angle, and lighting. They can also be a series of individual drawings that are pinned up on a board. Verbal descriptions are sometimes attached underneath. For the sake of clarity the sketches are usually drawn with a marker or pencil and the verbal descriptions are typed or written underneath. Storyboards have been used in the advertising and film industries for ages—long before the advent of the computer.

Use storyboards to refine the quality of your animation. It is a lot less painful to work out problems in the storyboard stage rather than losing days of work spent on parts of an animation because it does not fit the story, the characters' actions are wrong, the dialogue is weak, or the like.

The storyboard stage is also the one in which the characters' activities are often acted out. This is the time to make faces and strike poses in front of a mir-

Fig. 11-6 A storyboard without a promising future.

ror. The expressions and mannerisms are then recorded on paper. A character's attitude, the manner in which it is viewed through the camera, composition, light and dark patterning, as well as dialogue, can all be indicated in the storyboard.

Although one often starts with a written script, it is important to note that since animation is a visual medium, the storyboard sketches are much more important. These drawings should also be perceived as an adjustable vehicle, subject to many changes. This is especially true when the animation is a group effort.

The primary goal of a story is to be entertaining. Without that, you have already lost the audience. The best way to make a work entertaining is to present the story through the personalities of your characters. If you can make the audience see the event through the characters' eyes, then you have successfully met that goal.

Most people think that a story is about what happens next. It is better to think in terms of how people act and react in certain situations. Relationships between characters are more fascinating than a series of events.

If you are working alone on an animation, consider bringing in a writer. Try working together on the storyboard. Two or more people can energize each other's thought processes and emotions. Even if they do not work together well, the tension that results from trying to outdo each other could lead to some interesting ideas.

Present your storyboard to others. If it has any feeling in it, then it should excite them. Be sure to show the characters' personalities through their facial expressions and postures. The drawings should display what happens by describing the action visually.

If you work as a storyboard artist in a studio, then you will most likely learn to become detached from your drawings. Since the nature of storyboarding is change, be prepared to have your work rejected, ignored, and mistreated.

ROTOSCOPING

This is a process in which an animator follows the movements of a performer on videotape or film. Traditional cell animators sometimes rotoscoped by tracing images from film frames. Animators in 3-D usually rotoscope by following the actions of a movie projected on the background or a flat plane.

The technique dates back to 1917 when the animator Max Fleischer patented the Rotoscope machine, a device that projected live-action footage onto the animator's drawing board. Lifelike drawings were then produced by simply tracing the projected images. Max Fleischer's studio is known for characters such as Betty Boop, Popeye, Koko the Clown, and Superman. His studio also produced the full-feature animations *Gulliver's Travels* and *Mr. Bug Goes to Town*.

Besides technical innovations such as the Rotoscope, Fleischer's studio was the first to use sound, back in 1924. Max Fleischer was also the first to interact with a cartoon character. The live-action actor Fleischer interacted with the cartoon character Koko the Clown and his dog Fitz. He accomplished this by using another one of his inventions: the Rotograph.

Before the invention of the Rotoscope, early animated films were primitive and unsteady. People watched them mainly out of curiosity. By using rotoscoping and studying an actor's movements frame by frame, animators learned a great deal about the activity of the human form. As a result, animators began to create characters whose movements were more graceful and realistic. Audiences responded to the new animations in a much more positive way.

This was an important step for the art of animation. Even if the animator did not follow the exact motions of a filmed actor, it proved that imagination alone was not enough to record the perspective and realism of the figure in action.

After a while, animators realized that if they followed the movements of a figure too closely, the character lacked its own identity. The moves appeared realistic enough, but there was an absence of emotional involvement with the cartoon persona. By not infusing one's own personality into the performance, the animator was unable to create characters that audiences could feel empathy with.

It is easy to make analogies in the art world. The paintings that evoke the most deeply felt emotions are not superrealistic. Compare the works of the Impressionists and Postimpressionists to those of the superrealist artists whose paintings date mostly from the 1960s and 1970s. The superrealists often projected slides onto their canvases and painted over these. Their work may look technically sound, but it leaves the viewer cold. On the other hand, more than 100 years later, the works of the Impressionists and Postimpressionists still evoke strong feelings in viewers.

Apart from the previously mentioned deficiencies, rotoscoping is a great aid in determining correct timing and learning the subtle nuances of human and animal locomotion. The following paragraphs discuss some inadequacies that can be overcome with proper discrimination.

When moving back and forth on the timeline, you are watching the movie in close-up mode. Each motion is displayed in minute detail. It is similar to being too close to a painting and admiring the brush strokes and various details but failing to see the overall composition. To really understand the painting you also have to step back and observe the entire work. The same holds true for rotoscoping. Although moving the time slider one frame at a time may reveal subtle movements, you often fail to grasp a series of motions as one entire action.

To remedy this weakness, open the movie that you are using for rotoscoping in a video or media player. This will play the movie in real time. Work back and forth between observing the videotaped motions in close-up mode within the animation program and watching it play in real time in your video player window. Use one to study the overall action and the other to see how it breaks down into various subtle movements.

Rotoscoping has another flaw. If you slavishly follow the movie and keyframe every single motion according to what you see, you will have too many keyframes. Movements will look unsteady and stilted. They will lack the natural flow and rhythm characteristic of good animation. This problem is similar to one found with motion capture, which records every single frame. Artists then have to clean up the motion capture data by eliminating unnecessary keyframes.

To avoid this problem of excess, look for key movements and extract these. Observe the overall look and feel of a motion and try not to copy everything you see too precisely. Whenever you think it will improve the performance, improvise with your own made-up movements. Condense or eliminate extraneous motions that do not add to the quality of the animation. Develop an ability to make sound judgments as to what should be included and what parts to leave out.

Another problem that results from rotoscoping too closely is that the actions can often be boring. This is especially true if you are rotoscoping to a bad actor or actress. So the first consideration is to use source material that is entertaining. To make your movements more noticeable, exaggerate them. Broader motions will enliven the animation. Another approach is to videotape yourself or others performing in an exaggerated manner. Mimes, circus clowns, and vaudeville and stage actors have always used the principle of exaggeration to make their performances more noticeable.

Another predicament that can prove troublesome to animators is the matter of matching the form of the digital character to that of the filmed actor. If you are animating a dancing elephant while trying to match the movements of a recorded skinny actor, the perfor-

mance will ring false as a cracked bell. The body type and sex of the actor should generally correspond to the one you are trying to animate. If they do not, then you will have to change a lot of the movements and the timing. Otherwise, your digital actor's performance will look contrived.

Figure 11-7 illustrates some scenes from a rotoscoped animation found in the Chapter 11 folder of the CD-ROM as CD11-7RotoscopeMovies.

Fig. 11-7 Rotoscoping to a video clip.

THE GRAPH EDITOR

The graph editor displays all keyframable editing capabilities on a two-dimensional chart. It provides an overall view of all items in a scene along a timeline. Envelopes that control the characteristics of various items such as lights over time can also be observed and controlled through the graph editor. By observing the slope of a curve in relation to the timeline, one can identify when an item turns, moves a certain amount, speeds up, and slows down. One can also see when something changes color, dissolves, appears, becomes brighter or dimmer, and so on.

The graph editor is a device that at first appears antithetical to all artistic sensibilities. It is no wonder that many animation students wish to avoid using it. Although accountants and businesspeople may love them, graphs have never been an inspiration to artists.

If you can overcome your initial aversion to the graph editor, you will find that it can be an invaluable device for editing and creating new motions. The following paragraphs discuss some examples of how the graph editor can be used as a tool to enhance and edit your animations. Obviously there are many more ways to use a graph editor. One could write an entire book about animation and the graph editor.

CLEANING UP AN ANIMATION WITH THE GRAPH EDITOR

A previous section mentioned using the graph editor to clean up parts of an animation such as dialogue. The following exercise shows how you can use the graph editor to eliminate unwanted movements between keyframes. This is useful for holds, in which a character or its parts are held still for a number of frames before moving.

Holds are used quite often in animation to add drama, create accents, and build tension. When the hold is released, it can show a discharge of energy, creating a climax. Most of the time you do not want a part of or all of the person to hold perfectly still, but sometimes extraneous motions have to be controlled. This is one case in which the graph editor becomes useful.

Start in a scene that has your character all set up for animation. Go to frame 14 and rotate it about 71 degrees on the heading, or y, axis so it looks as if the character is turning around. As an alternative motion

you can just rotate a leg or arm instead of the entire body. If you are using inverse kinematics, you will most likely have to rotate the goal objects as well as the body or the object that controls all of them.

Open the graph editor, select the character's channel at the heading, or y, axis rotation. The line between 0 and 14 should show an unvarying incline or descent.

Figure 11-8 shows a person that is rotated 71 degrees. The three images depict the female's position at frames 0, 6, and 14. The motion is distributed evenly across the 14 frames. The graph editor in Figure 11-9 illustrates a straight and steady line, indicating the motion.

The next step is to change the animation so that the person does not begin to turn around until after frame 6. Go to frame 0 and select the character. Create a keyframe and type in 6. Open the graph editor and select the person turning on the heading, or y, axis. Select frames 0 and 6 in the graph and make sure both values are the same. Now the character does not start turning until the time slider moves past frame 6.

Figure 11-10 shows the body in the same position at frames 0 and 6. The turning motion is now between 6 and 14. The graph editor in Figure 11-11 illustrates the curve, showing keyframes at 0, 6, and 14. Notice the upward curve that is present between frames 0 and 6.

If your software defaults to a spline for every incoming curve, then your graph editor will most likely show a curve between frames 0 and 6. When you move the time slider back and forth between these two frames you will most likely detect some extraneous movements. The body may slide around a little or vibrate.

In your graph editor, select the keyframe at 6 and set its incoming curve to linear. This should straighten the curve, eliminating any excess motions between frames 0 and 6. Test it by moving the time slider back

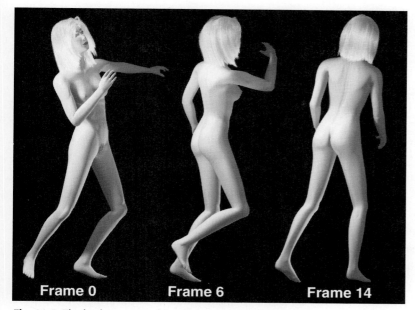

Frame 0   Frame 6   Frame 14

Fig. 11-8 The body turns 71 degrees, starting at frame 0 and ending at frame 14. This motion is evenly continuous throughout the 14 frames.

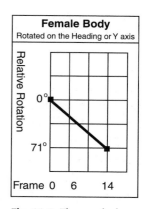

Female Body
Rotated on the Heading or Y axis

Relative Rotation

0°

71°

Frame 0   6   14

Fig. 11-9 The graph showing the body turning 71 degrees on the heading, or y, axis. Notice the evenness of the line, depicting a steady turn.

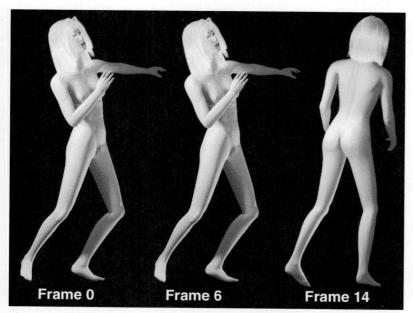

Frame 0   Frame 6   Frame 14

Fig. 11-10 At frame 0 the body is keyframed for frame 6. This duplicates the position of the body so that it is in the same placement at frames 0 and 6.

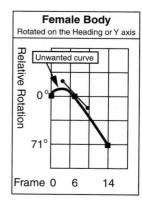

Female Body
Rotated on the Heading or Y axis

Relative Rotation

Unwanted curve

0°

71°

Frame 0   6   14

Fig. 11-11 The motion graph shows the two matching frames at 0 and 6. Adding an extra frame at 6 results in an undesirable curve between the two frames. This curve can cause unwanted extra motions between frame 0 and frame 6.

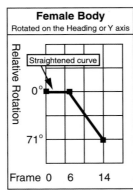

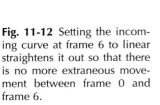

Fig. 11-12 Setting the incoming curve at frame 6 to linear straightens it out so that there is no more extraneous movement between frame 0 and frame 6.

and forth between those first six frames. You should not see any movement over the course of those frames. Figure 11-12 illustrates the straightened curve in the graph editor.

This is just one of many examples showing how the graph editor can be used to edit animations. A few additional functions are as follows:

1. Motions can be dampened or magnified in the graph editor by selecting a keyframe(s) and moving it up or down.
2. Keyframes in the graph editor can also be shifted in time by moving them left or right on the timeline, thus increasing or decreasing the in-between frames.
3. Duplicating keyframes can be as easy as selecting and pasting them.
4. You can add or delete keyframes in the graph editor.
5. The quality of curves can also be edited by manipulating the keyframes' control vertices, making the curve bend more.
6. Pre and post behavior can be set for effects such as cycling motions.
7. Modifiers can be added to motions for effects such as an oscillator for vibrating an object.

Your software manual will most likely list many other methods of altering movements in the graph editor.

ANIMATING WITHIN THE GRAPH EDITOR

Animating repeating motions can sometimes become a tedious task. Once you have the basic movement, you can then work in the graph editor to create a duplicate cycle of the same gestures.

For some reason, audiences enjoy watching recurring movements in animation. Perhaps it has to do with the eye finding patterns pleasing to look at. The next set of instructions explains how to create repeating motions in the graph editor.

Figure 11-13 depicts some repeating actions from an animation. The rotations of the arms and spine are recurrent events that take place over a set number of frames. These duplicate motions were made in the graph editor. To keep the person's movements from appearing too mechanical, the curves in the graph editor were made with some variations.

You can start by opening a scene file with your character. Select a bone or an IK goal object to rotate or move. In this case, the upper arm bone was selected.

Open the graph editor and pick the rotate on the pitch, or x, axis for the item that you will move or turn. Select the tool that allows you to add keys. Click or draw on the graph until you have a wavy line like the one in Figure 11-14. The graph in Figure 11-14 has pairs of keyframes on each up and down curve. These create a hold for a few frames in which the arm remains in its new position for brief period of time.

You can now check your view window to see the repeating action. By moving the time slider back and forth, you should see the part perform its motion over and over again.

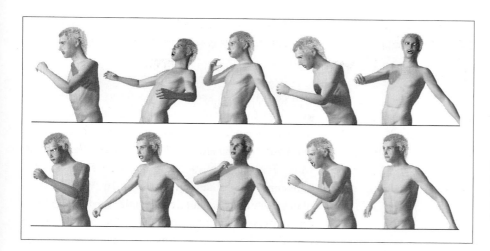

Fig. 11-13 Images from an animation in which body movements are repeated by manipulating the graph editor's curves.

Post behavior could have been set to Repeat or Offset Repeat. A modifier such as Cycle or Oscillate could also make a repeating motion. The trouble with using these is that the motion is too mechanical since it repeats the action too precisely.

In the graph editor edit the motion so it is even more inexact. Moving keyframe points higher and lower or left to right to change the spacing should make the action less machinelike.

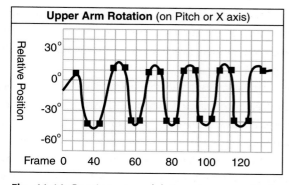

Fig. 11-14 Creating an undulating sine wave in the graph editor makes the arm rotate back and forth over a set number of frames.

USING THE GRAPH EDITOR FOR CYCLING ACTIONS

The graph editor is also a useful tool for simplifying cycling motions such as those found in walking and running. Both use repeating actions that do not have to be keyframed manually over the entire course of an animation. The walk can be set up over a course of 32 frames, while the run uses 24 frames. After that, the graph editor can be set up to take care of any of the subsequent frames. In essence, the character should then be able to walk or run indefinitely.

Walking

Although one would think the most common form of locomotion should be easy to animate, it is in fact one of the most complicated actions to put together. Walking includes some of the 12 principles of animation. It has follow-through, overlapping action, arcs, secondary actions, and timing. Walking can also show squash and stretch, exaggeration, and appeal. In this exercise, the principle of pose-to-pose animation will be used to establish the basic postures within a 32-cycle walk.

Once you understand the raw elements of a walk cycle, you can add your own refinements to give your

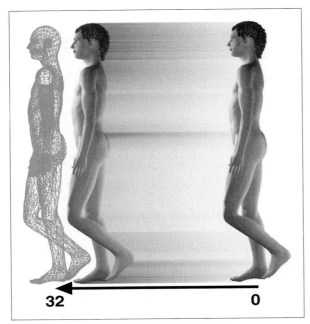

32 ← **0**

Fig. 11-15 A 3-D template of the figure in the same pose as the one at frame 0 is placed at frame 32 (wireframe). The body is then moved and positioned in the same way as the template.

character more appeal. Just like all the rest of the exercises in this book, creating a walk cycle can be done in many different ways. This is just one method that might work for you.

Using 32 frames to establish the basic motions makes it easier to break down the walk into even keyframes. These occur at frames 0, 8, 16, 24, and 32. A partial IK setup is used to anchor the feet. The upper body motions are made by rotating bones directly. Nulls are used as goal objects to move the IK chain. Whenever the instructions mention moving a null it refers to the goal object that is activating the IK chain. This pertains to moving the knees and feet.

Start by posing your figure in half stride at frame 0. The right toe null is on the ground. The left toe null

is up and back to position the left foot behind the right one. The left knee is in front of the right one. (See Figure 11.15.)

You can use the images in Figure 11-16 to pose your own person in the same way. As far as the true placement of the poses in relationship to each other, these images are not accurate. Instead, use Figure 11-17 for the actual placement of the feet during the 32-cycle walk. The Chapter 11 folder on the CD-ROM contains another folder titled CD11-16 WalkingTemplates, which has duplicate male models in their appropriate poses at frames 0, 8, 16, 24, and 32. These simplified models can be brought into your software program to act as a sort of 3-D template for positioning your own character.

Figures 11-18 and 11-19 consist of walking charts that show the relative positions of the nulls, and body, for 32 frames. They also illustrate the relative rotations of the upper body bones. You can compare this chart to your own graph editor as you work through the walking exercise.

If you would rather pose your person in a different manner at frame 0, that will work fine also, but be sure to start with the right foot on the ground and pose the model in *exactly* the same posture at frame 32. One way to do this is to save the character as a transformed object. You can then load the transformed object into the scene, move it forward at frame 32, and position your person the same way as the transformed object (Figure 11-15).

After arranging the model at frame 0, move the time slider to frame 32 and position your person forward. For average strides, measure the distance of the person from the bottom of the feet to the middle of the thoracic arch (chest area). At frame 32, move the character forward this amount. The nulls on the legs will keep the lower half back distorting the person,

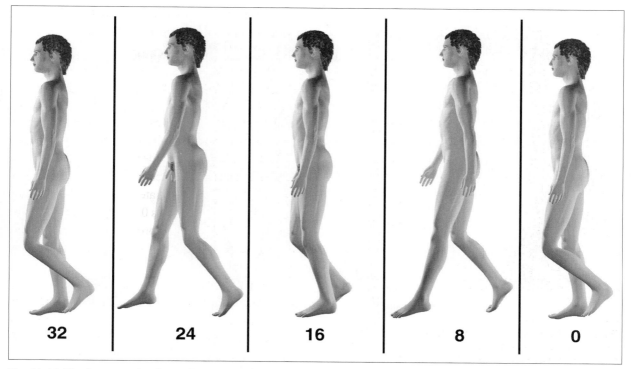

Fig. 11-16 The five poses for the 32-frame walk cycle. Frames 0 and 32 have identical poses. Frame 16 has the same pose as frames 0 and 32, except the limbs are in opposite positions. Frames 8 and 24 are similar but opposite poses.

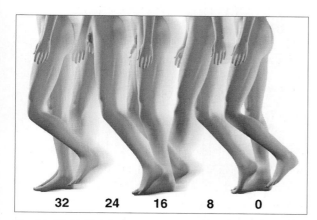

Fig. 11-17 Unlike the poses in Figure 11-16, these show the actual placements of the legs in relationship to each other.

but do not worry about that now. Just try to position the upper half of the model the same distance that you measured from the feet to the thoracic arch. Keyframe the person at frame 32.

You can now fix the legs at frame 32 by moving the toe and knee nulls until the model has the exact same posture as it had at frame 0. The 3-D template can be a useful device for the placement of the legs and feet. Keyframe all the toe and knee nulls at frame 32.

The posture at frame 16 is exactly the same as the ones at frames 0 and 32, except the opposite limbs are positioned forward and back. For example, if the right

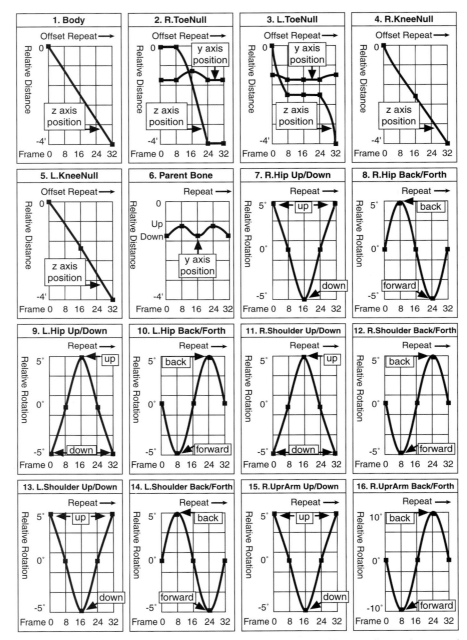

Fig. 11-18 The 32-frame walk cycle motion graphs. The toe and knee nulls are the IK goal objects that move the legs. This graph is continued in Figure 11-19.

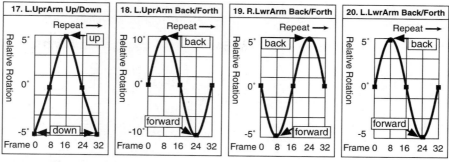

Fig. 11-19 The walk cycle graph continued. The lower arm is keyframed forward a few frames after the upper arm motions to show follow-through.

foot was in the up and back position at frame 0, it is now on the ground at frame 16 and the left foot is in the up and back position. Use the template provided for frame 16 or take the transformed object you made at frame 0 and mirror it. Use this mirror-duplicate object as your template at frame 16. Move the toe and knee nulls until they match the template. Keyframe all the toe and knee nulls at frame 16.

Assuming that you posed your model the same at frame 0 as the one in Figure 11-16 and the 3-D template, the right toe null is on the ground. At frame 0, keyframe the right toe null in the same position for frame 8. To prevent the feet from sliding, go into your graph editor and, for the right toe null, set the incoming curves at frames 0 and 32 to linear. You can do this for just the x, y, or z direction that your character is walking toward or simply make all three axes' positions linear.

Move your time slider to frame 32 and keyframe the right toe null in the same position for frame 24. This takes care of all the right foot movements.

Go to frame 16, select the left toe null, and keyframe it in the same position for frames 8 and 24. In your graph editor, make the incoming curve for the

left toe null linear at frames 16 and 24. Again, you can do this to just the axis that the person is walking along or to all three axes' positions.

The body moves the person forward, while the parent bone is used for up-and-down motions. Setting the parent bone to move up and down will add some bounce to the walk. At frame 0, keyframe the parent bone in the same position for frames 16 and 32. At frame 8 move the parent bone up slightly and keyframe it in the up position at frames 8 and 24.

Play the 32-frame animation. You should see an up-and-down motion while the body moves forward. If everything checks out fine, then you are ready to work in the graph editor to make all the nulls (IK goal objects), body, and parent bone repeat indefinitely.

Select your character and in the graph editor, select the x, y, and z positions, and set their post behavior to Offset Repeat. This repeats the motions between frames 0 and 32 but offsets the difference between these first and last values. For example, setting post behavior to only Repeat would make the body go back to its original position at frame 0. Offset Repeat continues the forward motion by calculating how much the body was moved between frames 0 and

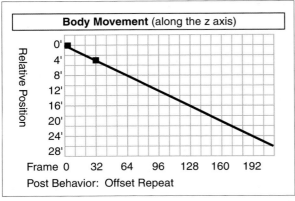
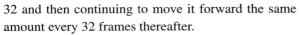

Fig. 11-20 Turning on Offset Repeat for the advancing body movement continues the forward motion indefinitely.

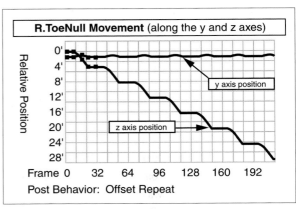

Fig. 11-21 After turning on its Offset Repeat, the right toe null moves the foot up and forward indefinitely.

32 and then continuing to move it forward the same amount every 32 frames thereafter.

Of course, you could just specify Offset Repeat for the axis position along which you are moving the body. Figure 11-20 shows the offset repeat graph for the body moving along the z axis.

Select the right toe null and in the graph editor select Offset Repeat for its post behavior. You can set it for just the axes that have motion curves or for all three x, y, and z axes. Figure 11-21 illustrates the offset repeat for the right toe null.

In the graph editor, turn on Offset Repeat for the post behaviors of the left toe, right knee, and left knee nulls. Select the parent bone and set its post behavior to Repeat for the axis that shows a curve.

Test your animation by setting the end frame to whatever number you want. If you positioned everything correctly within the first 32 frames, the person should walk forever in the same manner by repeating the cycling motions of the nulls, body, and parent bone. Although the charts do not show motions for the

ankle null, you might decide to move these in order to bend the foot more at the end of the toes. This would occur just before the foot is about to lift off. If you move the ankle nulls, then you will most likely have to make adjustments to the toe nulls. In order for Repeat to work on the ankle null, be sure to use the same settings at frames 0 and 32.

If the walk checks out all right, then you are ready to set up the bone positions for the upper body. Refer to Figures 11-18 and 11-19 to set the motions correctly. The actions of the right and left hipbones are the opposites of each other. They move up and down like a teeter-totter. The hips also travel forward and back. Like the hips, the shoulder bones also go up and down as well as forward and back. The big difference is that they always go in the opposite direction of the hips (Figure 11-22). Try to rotate the bones of the hips and shoulders only a little. Larger motions will make the walk look unnatural. After setting the rotations for the hips and shoulders, turn on Repeat for their post behavior.

When you rotate the shoulders up and down it will affect the position of the arms. Therefore, you will need to rotate the upper arm bone to bring the arm in line with the torso. As long as you are working with the upper arm bone, have it swing forward and back. This cycle is the opposite of the forward and backward movements of the legs. When the right leg advances, the right arm is in the back position.

To get some follow-through, rotate the lower part of the arm forward and back at the keyframes indicated in Figure 11-19. Make sure the keyframes for the arms are the same at 0 and at 32. Turn on Repeat

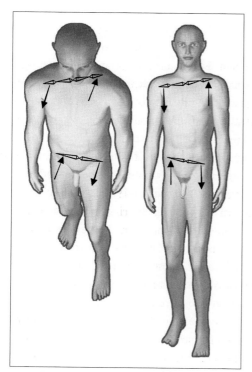

Fig. 11-22 The hips and shoulders rotate in opposite directions during a walk cycle.

for their post behavior. An example movie of this walk can be viewed in the Chapter 11 folder on the CD-ROM.

Even though all the movements so far cycle in a mechanical manner, you should add some random actions such as motions in the head and neck, spine, fingers, facial expressions, and so on. At the very least, move the head somewhat and have the person blink once in a while.

Everyone walks differently, so consider personalizing the walk to your character. The feet might shuffle, drag, step gingerly, or step heavily. All of this depends on the appearance and persona of the character as well as the intent of the animation.

Running

Animating a running sequence can be as simple as setting up rotation values for bones, moving the parent bone up and down, turning on Repeat for each of these bones in the graph editor, pointing the character in the right direction, and moving it there. In the following exercise a 12-frame running cycle is established. Frames 0 and 12 have identical body poses so that the movements can be repeated indefinitely.

Figure 11-23 illustrates the key poses that occur over the course of 12 frames. You can use these as a guide or utilize the 2-D and 3-D templates in the Chapter 11 folder of the CD-ROM. Figure 11-24 shows the graphs outlining each bone rotation and movement. Be sure to use these when you set up your model. Each diagram should resemble the graph editor of the various bones.

Unlike the walking animation, there is no need to use an IK setup, so be sure to turn it off if your character has it. When people run they move too fast to show the feet sticking to the ground; hence, FK works

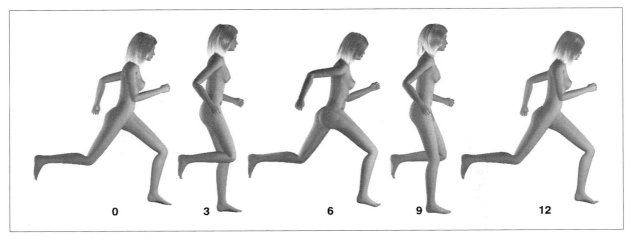

Fig. 11-23 A 12-frame repeating run cycle.

fine for this. Once you establish the rotation values for the bones and the up-and-down movement of the parent bone, turn on Repeat in the graph editor. You can then move the person to a specific location from point A to point B. The up-and-down parent bone movements take care of the wave motion for the path of action. The body then only needs to be propelled forward to complete the run cycle.

Referring to the graph editor chart in Figure 11-24, rotate the right upper leg back at frame 0 and keyframe it that way for both frame 0 and frame 12. The illustration in Figure 11-23 can serve as a guide for the leg placement. At frame 3 pose the leg forward a little and keyframe it there and also in the same manner at frame 9. The leg is rotated forward even more at frame 6.

Continue to use Figures 11-23 and 11-24 as well as the 2-D and 3-D templates on the CD-ROM, if necessary, to complete all the rotations indicated in the chart. When animating the female figure, the breast-

bone can be rotated for secondary motions. The parent bone is moved up at frames 3 and 4 as well as at frames 9 and 10. This brings each foot onto the running surface so that the figure lands and stays on the ground for a count of two frames. The rest of the time the person is in the air. If you are animating a heavier character, then keep the feet on the ground for several more frames. You may also want to apply squash and stretch to add to the illusion of weight and mass.

If you want to make the figure appear to run fast and cover a lot of ground, then move it a longer length and with fewer frames. A character running the same distance over a course of 30 frames will appear to run faster than one lasting 60 frames. Moving the body a longer length also makes your character look as if it is taking longer strides.

Another method for varying the speed of a run is to use a different lens. A long lens, such as 100 mm, shows less of the scene, so the person appears to speed

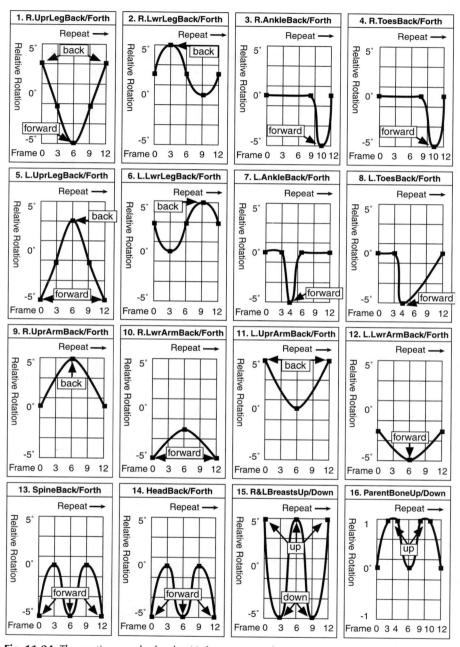

Fig. 11-24 The motion graphs for the 12-frame run cycle.

by faster. A wide-angle lens, such as 15 mm, shows a greater amount of the environment and thus the figure appears to run more slowly because it seems to be covering a greater distance. A stationary camera also adds to the illusion of speed. A camera that follows and tracks a character makes the action appear slower.

A figure that turns while running will appear to lean toward the outside of a curve. Tilting the body at the turn will add character and make it look less rigid than just keeping it upright the entire time. Be sure to add other refinements to the figure so that it has its own running style. Some sample running animations can be found in the Chapter 11 folder of the CD-ROM.

THE 12 PRINCIPLES OF ANIMATION

Although 3-D character animation often resembles live-action movie making, it still has more in common with traditional 2-D cell animation. In order for animation to communicate clearly, the fundamental knowledge of traditional animation principles needs to be understood. This system was developed by Disney animators in the early and mid-1930s.

Just like most art forms, animation is based on previously discovered fundamentals. Many of these came from theater and vaudeville. Unlike movie or television actors, Broadway performers had to make their actions more discernible not only by exaggerating their movements but also by speaking louder. Intentions had to be signaled first or the audience could easily miss them. The early movie and television comedies also show the influence of vaudeville.

The mid-1930s were the most exciting times for Disney animators. It was during this period that many discoveries that are still utilized today were first used. Walt Disney encouraged his animators to see the great vaudeville acts whenever they came to town.

The animation principles developed during the 1930s still serve as the basis for creating successful 2-D and 3-D animation. These are:

1. Squash and stretch
2. Anticipation
3. Staging
4. Straight-ahead versus pose-to-pose action
5. Follow-through and overlapping action
6. Slow in and slow out
7. Arcs
8. Secondary actions
9. Timing
10. Exaggeration
11. Solid drawing
12. Appeal

Example Avi and QuickTime movies can be found in the Chapter 12 folder on the CD-ROM. Their purpose is to illustrate the principles of animation.

When a character is created, it should have a specific personality. Whenever it is animated, this character then exhibits its own unique traits. Once viewers become familiar with the character, they expect it to behave in a certain way.

The two male characters that were created for this chapter assume the roles of wacky clowns. Their goofy personalities make it easier to illustrate specific principles because their actions can be exaggerated to make them more discernible.

The female was created as a counterpoint to the male characters. She plays a supportive role. Therefore, her actions are more conservative and not as noticeable as the ones performed by the males. When she is in the presence of other characters she acts shy and demure. This keeps the attention mostly on the males' actions.

1. SQUASH AND STRETCH (WEIGHT AND RECOIL)

Think of your character as a flexible mass. Humans are not rigid statues. Adding distortion to your human character gives it a more dynamic quality by punctuating movement. Squash and stretch is an essential principle for conveying weight to your character.

The compressed position can show the figure flattened out from the effects of gravity, mass, or an opposing object such as a wall. It can also depict the character squeezed together like an accordion. The stretched view of your character extends it beyond normal.

Squash and stretch can also be applied to facial animation. Eyes can pop open wide or be shown tightly squinted shut. The mouth can alternate between being stretched wide open and being firmly closed. The entire face can distort when alternating between certain actions such as showing anger and displaying forgiveness.

A simple example of squash and stretch can be demonstrated with a half-filled flour sack. Figures 12-1 and 12-2, as well as CD12-1NoSquash&Stretch-Sack and CD12-2Squash&StretchSack found in the Chapter 12 "Squash and Stretch" folder on the

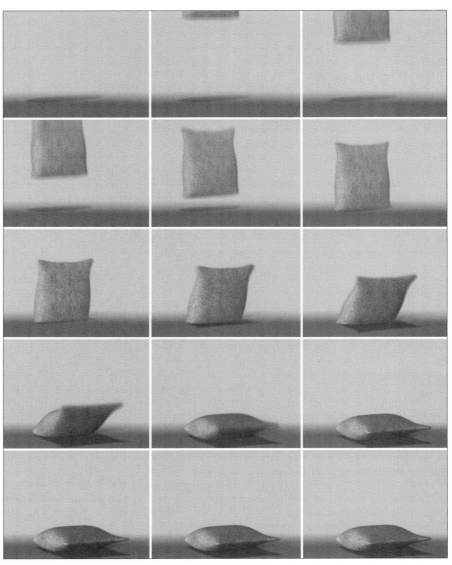

Fig. 12-1 Images from the sack of flour animation without squash and stretch applied.

Fig. 12-2 Images from the sack of flour animation with squash and stretch applied.

CD-ROM, demonstrate the effectiveness of squash and stretch. When the sack is dropped, it stretches. As it hits the ground, it compresses. When the sack rolls over from the force of the impact, it stretches a little.

The example of the sack without squash and stretch looks very stiff and lifeless, while the one with it appears more lively and realistic. The squash and stretch sack also gives the impression of having weight and mass, while the one without it seems insubstantial.

Methods for Creating Squash and Stretch

Method 1: Soft-Body Dynamics. If your software supports soft-body dynamics, you can create some interesting examples of squash and stretch. The sack of flour uses soft-body dynamics. A cloth sack was created first as the target object (the elastic-body model that is influenced by other target or collision objects). An object was placed inside the sack to serve as the flour and had its properties adjusted as the fixed object (the body that remains intact). The fixed object also functions as a collision object. Its geometry was set as invisible to the camera. The floor was added as an extra collision object (Figure 12-3).

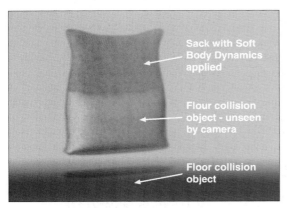

Fig. 12-3 The soft-body dynamics setup for the flour sack.

The sack was parented to the invisible flour object. The flour was keyframed manually at the top, hitting the ground and rolling over. The flexible sack followed its motions and the soft-body dynamics took into account the actions and collision settings of the flour as well as the floor.

Method 2: Manual Adjustments. You can show weight and recoil by using morph targets, which can make the character both long and squatty or stretch the bones of its skeleton during the animation. An easy method is to simply stretch and shrink the entire body during certain movements.

Figure 12-4 and the animation CD12-4Squash&Stretch found in the Chapter 12 "Squash and Stretch" folder on the CD-ROM illustrate the principle of squash and stretch as applied to a human character. When the fat man jumps up, the body elongates, and when he hits the ground, he compresses. Secondary motions such as the jiggle of the belly help reinforce the principle of weight and recoil.

2. Anticipation

Previous to naming the principle *anticipation,* Walt Disney called it *aiming.* He understood that the audience needed some kind of alert to an upcoming action. Earlier animation movements were too abrupt and unexpected. People often missed the gag because they did not expect it. Anticipation prepares the audience for the next major movement.

Before any action occurs, signal your intent first. Communicating an anticipated outcome guides your planned actions and makes it easier to understand the event that is to follow. A simple rule is that whenever a character goes from one place to another, always go in the opposite direction first. The reverse movement accents the forward motion. Imagine a boxer pulling back his fist before striking forward against an opponent. He aims himself toward the object first.

In life, many movements involve anticipation. Sports analogies are the most obvious. A quarterback draws his arm back before throwing the football; a hockey player twists his body back, moving his stick backward before swinging forward to hit the puck; a tennis player swings her arm back before hitting the

Fig. 12-4 Images from the character animation with squash and stretch applied.

ball in a forward motion. All these movements are necessary or the athlete will not have enough power in his or her delivery.

You can demonstrate anticipation using simple objects. Figures 12-5 and 12-6 show images from the animations named CD12-5NoAnticipationSack, and

CD12-6AnticipationSack found in the Chapter 12 "Anticipation" folder of the CD-ROM. This time the flour sack is utilized to demonstrate the effects of anticipation. The images in Figure 12-5 and the animation CD12-5NoAnticipationSack depict the sack without any anticipation added. Needless to say, the

Fig. 12-5 Images from the sack animation without anticipation applied.

animation looks lifeless. The Figure 12-6 images and the animation CD12-6AnticipationSack have anticipation. In the beginning the sack winds up by rotating in the opposite direction before jumping forward. After landing it revolves in a reverse direction before unwinding and jumping back. One should be able to

tell that the sack with anticipation has more life and personality.

Anticipation applied to a human character can be viewed in the Chapter 12 "Anticipation" folder on the CD-ROM as CD12-7Anticipation. Figure 12-7 depicts some illustrations from the animation. The

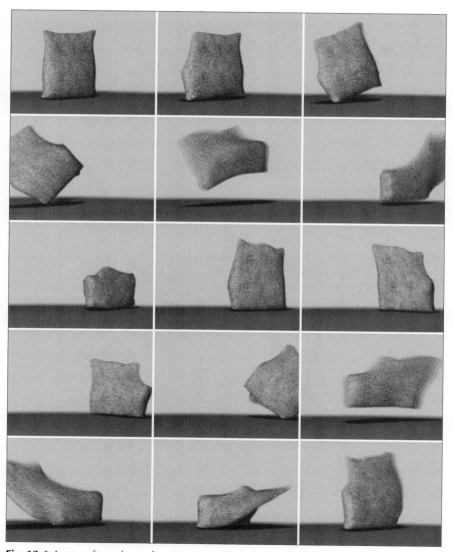

Fig. 12-6 Images from the sack animation with anticipation applied.

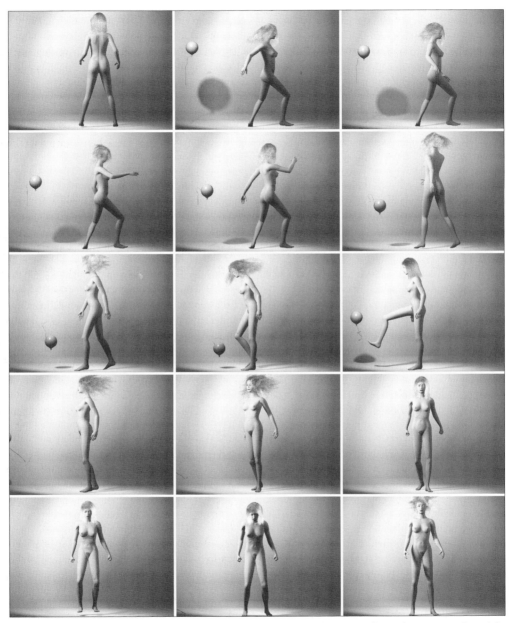

Fig. 12-7 Some images from the female anticipation animation. Notice how she turns to her right before spinning around to kick the balloon. A move in the opposite direction is a sign of anticipation.

windup action, similar to that of a spring, is a typical way of showing anticipation. In this case, the female turns to her right before unwinding to her left to kick the balloon.

Anticipation is a good example of how the 12 principles of animation overlap each other. Often it becomes very difficult to separate them. A squash and stretch movement can be part of anticipation. Follow-through and overlapping action are also an important aspect of anticipation. Anticipation itself can also be used as an example of exaggeration. Similarities to other principles could easily be pointed out here. Perhaps more important is the ability to identify the use of each principle in the total presentation. This is why students should learn to consciously concentrate on one at a time until they can subconsciously incorporate them in all their animations.

3. STAGING

An idea needs to be presented in the clearest manner possible. Composition is the key element that directs the viewer's eye to the featured event. A scene can be set up using various devices. The position of the camera and its focal length can add mental and emotional impact to the action. The pose of the actor(s) communicates its intent and directs the attention to the primary object. Drawing or rendering the character(s) in silhouette illuminates the action since it shows which pose has the most clarity. Objects in a scene can be set up to create circular, curved, or straight vertical and/or horizontal lines. Each configuration has a different psychological impact.

Staging an animation means to present it in such a way that the event is understandable and that the character's personality is easily perceived. When these are properly staged the viewer should have no problem understanding the animation.

When you are trying to make a point, think about how you will position the camera, pose the actor, light the scene, place props, and move the camera.

Staging an idea means presenting only one action at a time. An audience can easily lose track of what you are showing if something else is going on, some artifact gets in the way, the camera is too far away, or the lighting is too dim. Always show exactly what you want to be seen.

Figure 12-8 illustrates some images from an animation demonstrating the principle of Staging. You can view the animation in the Chapter 12 "Staging" folder on the CD-ROM as CD12-8Staging. Even though there is no sound, it is clear from the man's actions that he is giving an impassioned speech. The podium acts as a prop that reinforces the idea of a speaker on stage. It also keeps things less distracting by hiding his nudity. A low camera angle that looks up at the speaker adds drama and makes him look more important. His grand gestures and facial expressions also communicate his fervent speech.

Animators in 2-D used a device to check whether a character's pose communicated clearly. They would shade the drawing so that it became a silhouette. This would let them see whether anything was obscuring the attitude of the character. If something important was held by a hand, it would not be sketched so that it was in front of the body. The silhouette drawing would show that this would hide the object.

The silhouette gimmick can be adapted to 3-D animation. One method is to place the light(s) behind the character with none in front. The background should be white. The resulting rendering should show the digital actor in silhouette. This technique is used in broadcasting when the person that is being interviewed desires to remain anonymous.

Another way of obtaining a silhouette is to render with an alpha channel. In your image editing program,

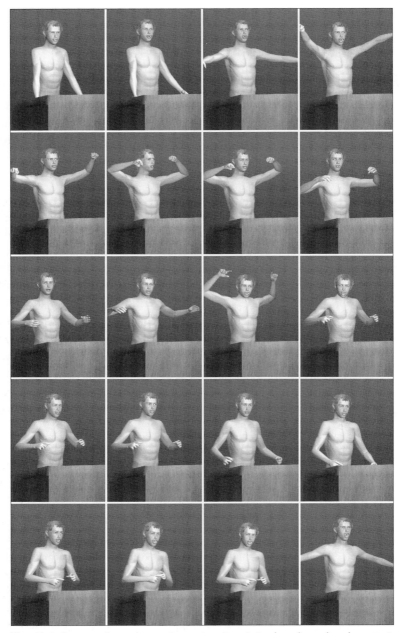

Fig. 12-8 Excerpts from the staging animation. It is clear from the character's actions and location behind a podium that he is giving a fiery speech.

the alpha image of the person can be selected and filled with black.

Figure 12-9 illustrates poor versus good staging. The top character is poorly staged. This becomes even more obvious from the silhouette. The frying pan and

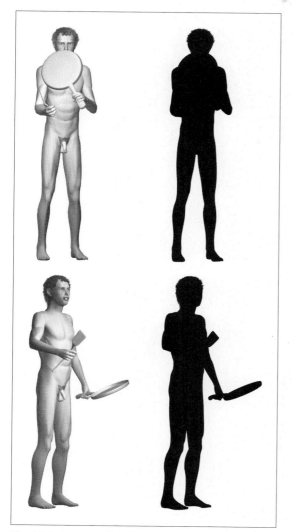

Fig. 12-9 An example of bad and good staging. The top character and camera position are poorly staged. The bottom image shows the improved version in which the meaning is clarified.

spatula that the man is holding blend right into his body so that it becomes difficult to discern the meaning of the image.

The bottom character shows improved staging because the objects he is holding are easier to pick out since they can be seen separately from the body. The picture's intent becomes clearer. One can also see this in the silhouette, which distinctly shows the frying pan and part of the spatula.

4. STRAIGHT-AHEAD VERSUS POSE-TO-POSE ACTION

These are two contrasting ways of animating. Sometimes they can be combined.

Straight-Ahead animation is for the most part improvised. Every action is a result of previous ones. Thus the animation grows until one reaches the end of the scene. Although this type of animation looks very spontaneous, it can sometimes be based on planned actions in the form of roughs and rhythm lines. The result of straight-ahead animation is often wacky and wild action with scrambling movements.

When doing straight-ahead animation, the animator derives new ideas from former actions. Acting out the performance during the animation process makes it easier to visualize and judge the activity. Usually there is not enough time to use previously sketched poses or filmed sequences as reference material. The person may know what the goal of the animation is, but there will be no plan of action outlining the manner in which it will be accomplished. All of this gives the animator a great amount of freedom to experiment and rely on intuition as a springboard for new ideas.

Figure 12-10 shows some excerpts from a straight-ahead animation found as CD12StraightAhead on the CD-ROM in the Chapter 12 "Straight Ahead" folder, in which a man is seen performing in an irrational manner. Most of the actions were acted out first

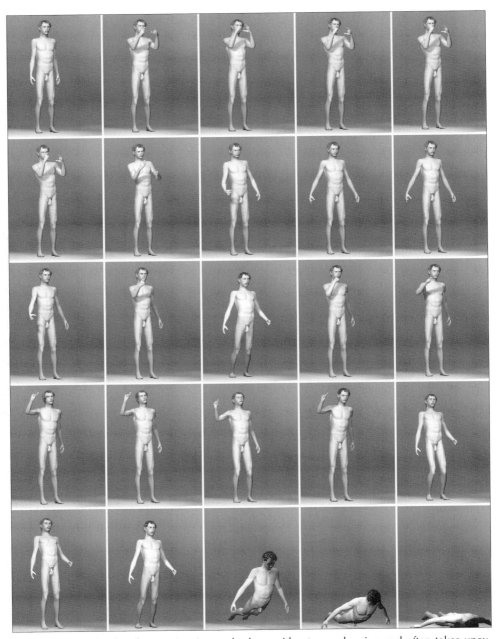

Fig. 12-10 Straight-ahead animation is mostly done without any planning and often takes unexpected turns.

before animating them. There was no pose planning in the form of drawings or other imagery involved.

Straight-ahead animation requires a flawless sense of timing. Without experience, it is difficult to accomplish successfully. This is why it is normally done by seasoned professionals.

The greatest advantage of straight-ahead animation is that it often leads to unexpected results. The animator is often just as surprised as anyone else at the way the performance turns out. When you want your animation to have a fresh and capricious look, try straight-ahead animation.

Pose-to-pose animation is carefully planned out with a series of poses. Sometimes it is referred to as *pose extremes*. Unlike straight-ahead animation, which is based mostly on action, pose extremes relies on the drama, gesture, and attitude of poses. In computer animation, pose planning might have to be set up on more than one plane. Since the character exists in 3-D space, what might look fine in one view could look problematic in another. A typical occurrence is when a character appears fine in the side view but shows hands, arms, legs, and so on intersecting the body when viewed from the camera view.

Since pose-to-pose animation involves more planning, the action is usually easier to understand. The imagery will also have a solid look because the poses have been calculated beforehand to convey strength of character.

When planning your poses beforehand, make sure they relate to each other well. The character's stance should be interesting and easy to comprehend, it should express emotion, and it should convey meaning to the scene.

Pose-to-pose action can be combined with straight-ahead action. Rough drawings are used as a guide for the overall performance while leaving enough room to improvise certain movements. Since the goal is more clear-cut, the straight-ahead animation is kept from going haywire.

Figures 12-11 and 12-12 illustrate the process of pose planning. The images in Figure 12-11 show the first stage, in which drawings depict various poses of the male and female characters. Figure 12-12 portrays images from the pose-to-pose animation found on the CD-ROM in the Chapter 12 "Pose to Pose" folder titled CD12-12PoseToPose.

When you decide to use straight-ahead action, pose-to-pose action, or a combination of both, keep in mind that actions without variation can quickly become too predictable and dull. Accents such as a motion hold or a wobble during a recoil action can change the pace or lead to a different activity. Contrasting quick and slow movements make the timing unpredictable. These snappy, fast actions combined with languid, slow ones create a more enjoyable performance.

Several other methods of animating in 3-D include rotoscoping and motion capture. Rotoscoping uses video of live action as a guide along which to animate, while motion capture uses data acquired from performers. Both methods require adding exaggeration and blending actions. One does not want to end up with too many keyframes close together since this will make the animation too choppy.

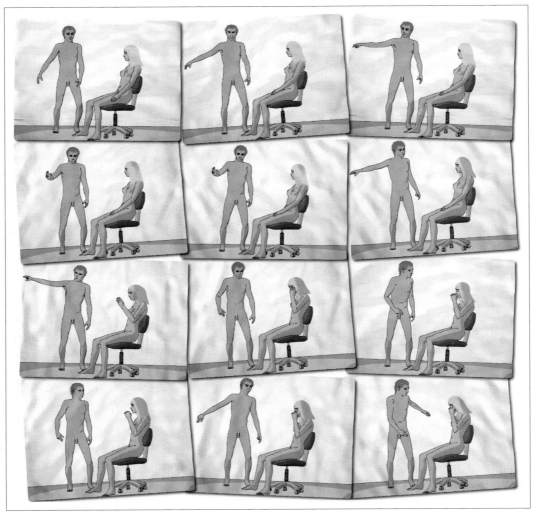

Fig. 12-11 The sketches used to plan the pose-to-pose animation.

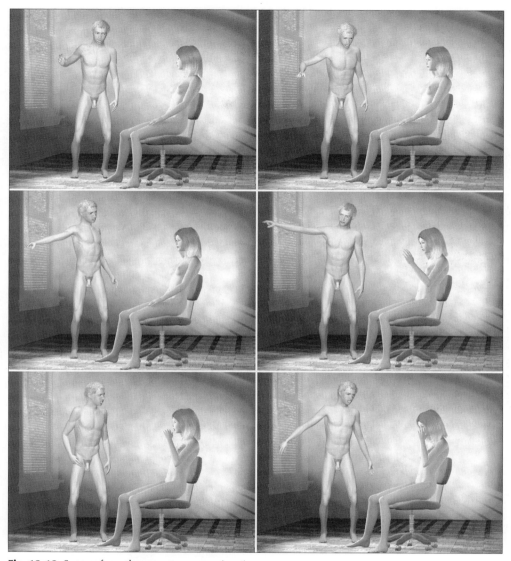

Fig. 12-12 Scenes from the pose-to-pose animation.

5. FOLLOW-THROUGH AND OVERLAPPING ACTION

Basically both of these principles mean that nothing stops abruptly. Every action is related to another one.

Follow-through occurs when an object affects another, causing it to have its own movement. A char-

acter waves a flag, which in turn follows its own curving path. There is usually a lag time between the motions of the primary object and those of the secondary object. Follow-through is most discernible in loose objects such as cloth, floppy ears, and hair.

285

Examples of follow-through and overlapping action can be viewed on the CD-ROM in the Chapter 12 "Follow Through" folder as CD12-13NoFollowThrough-Balloon, CD12-14FollowThroughBalloon, and CD12-15FollowThrough. Figures 12-13 through 12-15 show some images from the animations. Figure 12-14 illustrates a simple example of how an attached object such as a streamer, lacking any movement of its own, is

Fig. 12-13 A few images from the balloon animation without follow-through and overlapping action. The streamer attached to the balloon just hangs rigid and does not appear to be affected by the movement of the balloon.

Fig. 12-14 These images from the balloon animation with follow-through and overlapping action show how the attached streamer's movements are strictly the result of the balloon's motions.

affected by the motion of the balloon. The female's actions in Figure 12-15 make her hair wave around wildly. Soft-body dynamics should be applied to most follow-through actions since it is an involuntary response activated by dynamic physical forces.

Overlapping action means that a secondary action occurs before the first one is finished. This prevents dead time between actions and makes the animation more interesting. Never animate a character with all parts starting and ending at the same time. The main

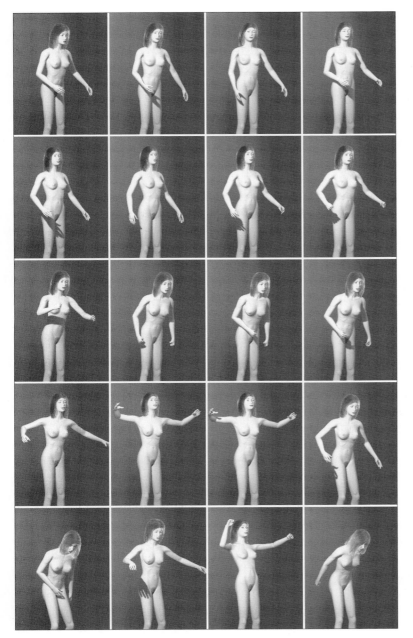

Fig. 12-15 Images from the character animation with follow-through and overlapping action applied.

action can be preceded and followed by lesser ones that are the result of or relate to the primary motion. A turn of the head can lead to a twist in the body, followed by the movement of the arms. The lag time may be just a few frames, but each motion starts before the other ends.

An important thing to keep in mind is to add accents to the ends of movements. Go slightly beyond the pose before settling into it. When reaching out to grab an object, the hand goes slightly past it before settling on it. One can create a natural curve at the end of actions by keyframing the last movement twice. The frame space could vary from 3 to 15. For example, when pointing a finger that stops at frame 10, keyframe the same action again at frame 14. The arc in the motion curve at the end will make the hand move a little instead of coming to a dead stop.

6. SLOW IN AND SLOW OUT

In the early Disney animation days, animators who had worked over their pose extremes naturally wanted the audience to notice them. So they timed these key drawings in such a way that most of the footage would show these extremes. They did this by placing most of the in-between drawings close to the pose extremes and only one in-between drawing halfway between. Thus, they were able to achieve a lively performance, showing the character rapidly moving from one posture to another. This method of timing in-betweens became known as *slow in and slow out.* Too much dependence on this kind of timing made the action too mechanical. Therefore, other timing methods such as fast in and fast out, slow in and fast out, and so on, were also utilized.

A variation in keyframe spacing allows for a change of speed during the animation. A metronome does not have slow in and slow out since every tick is evenly spaced. Cycling animations such as walks and runs have evenly spaced keyframes. A man lifting a heavy object slows in with closely spaced keyframes. When he overcomes mass and gravity, his movements speed up, resulting in more widely spaced keyframes. As he decelerates to balance the weight in his arms, he slows out with closely spaced keyframes.

Make your animations more interesting by varying the speed of your character's motions. When he or she goes into and out of a pose, slow down the action. You can also have fast in and slow out, slow in and fast out, fast in and fast out, and so on.

Figure 12-16 shows some excerpts from the animation titled CD12-16SlowInOut found in the Chapter 12 "Slow In Slow Out" folder of the CD-ROM. Observe the changing velocities in the male character's motions. At first he winds up by executing a gradual anticipation (slow in) in which he bends down and moves his arms back. This is also the squash part. His motions accelerate as he unwinds and reaches up to move into the stretch segment of the animation. The male then decelerates (slow out) as he moves into the next pose extreme. For a while he holds the pose and shakes a little. This is followed by another slow in and slow out when he moves his fist back into another anticipation. The action speeds up again as he punches the air and then slows down. One more slow in and slow out sequence ends the animation.

Figure 12-17 shows a close-up view of one part of the animation. One can see that most of the keyframes are at the beginning (slow in) and at the end (slow out).

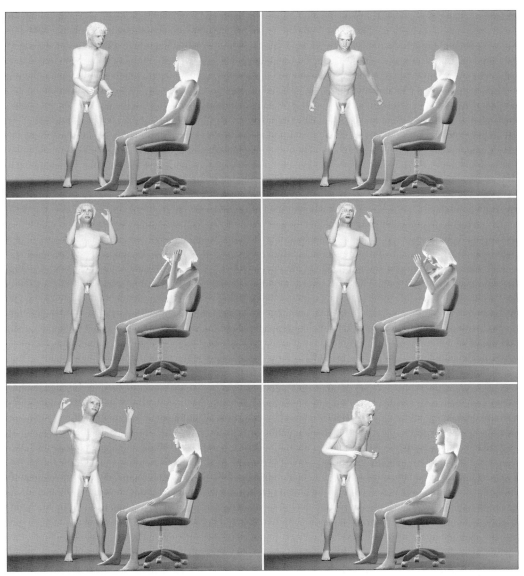

Fig. 12-16 A few rendered frames from the slow in and slow out animation. Most of the keyframes are at the pose extremes, while the transitional ones that are in between them are far fewer in number.

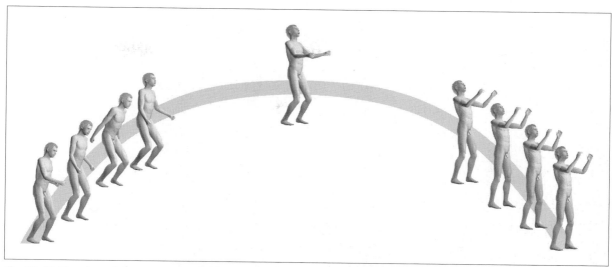

Fig. 12-17 Slow in and slow out on a timeline. A greater number of keyframes are located at the slow in (beginning) and slow out (end). The middle section moves quickly, with a minimum amount of keyframes to arrive at slow out. Also note anticipation with squash and stretch.

7. Arcs

These are the visual paths of action for natural movement. In nature almost all actions move in curves. The manner in which muscles and tendons exert force on the bones and the structure of joints makes all human movements arclike.

Your character should always have curving movements. Rather than going straight from point A to point C, keyframe also at point B. For example, when turning the head, add an extra keyframe in the middle that raises or lowers the head slightly. This will create an arc that looks more natural than a straight-line, mechanical movement.

When animating a walk, have the body and legs arc over at the top of a step and arc under at the bottom of a step. This will make the walk appear less mechanical. Figure 12-18 depicts some other human motions that illustrate arcs. When animating humans, it is important to keep the default graph editor's incoming curve on spline rather than linear. Straight-line or linear motions can be set when you have identical keyframes spaced apart for an object that you do not want to move or change over time.

Cycling motions such as walks and runs should always be animated with arcs. This means the character follows a wavy path that slopes up and down. One method for achieving this is to propel the body straight ahead while moving the parent bone up and down. These two motions combined will make the character run or walk in a curving path of action.

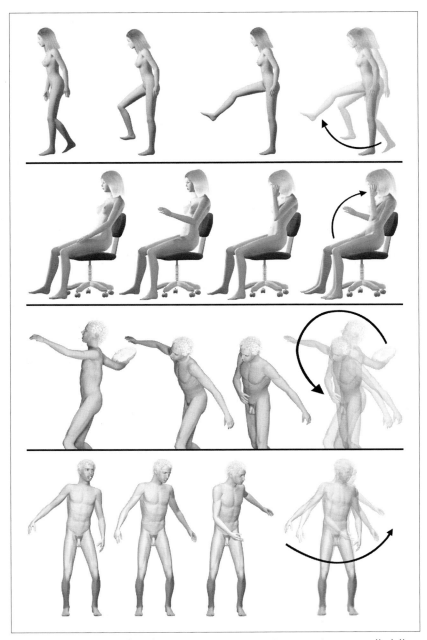

Fig. 12-18 Some examples of curving motions (arcs). Human actions naturally follow circular paths.

8. SECONDARY ACTIONS

Secondary actions supplement and reinforce the main action. A running person's primary action is the forward movement of the body, while the pumping of the arms, motion of the legs, and up-and-down bobbing of the head make for the secondary actions. Secondary action should support the main action but never overwhelm it. Facial expressions supported by subtle body movements such as shrugging the shoulders constitute another example of secondary actions.

Most movements are secondary actions and take on the form of follow-through and overlapping action. They often conform to a hierarchical order. For example, as the torso turns, the arm follows, but various parts of the arm arrive at different times. Starting at the top, the movement works its way down the arm to the fingertips. The motions of the upper and lower arm, the hand, and the fingers are keyframed several frames apart.

When animating a figure, pay attention to the secondary actions to see whether they support the main one. If they do not add anything to the primary movement or they become a distraction, then consider moderating them to lessen their intensity or strength.

Secondary actions can easily compete with the main ones, destroying the unity of the animation. Then again, if the secondary action is too subdued, it will appear to be too soft, unimportant, and too restrained. Right discrimination and an artistic sensibility will determine how well secondary actions are applied.

Sometimes the animator has to show a change in the character's mood. The modification in the person's facial expression has to be timed in a way that can be seen. If it occurs during a major move of the head, then it will most likely be missed. Even though it is a secondary action, the expression has to be timed to occur either before or after the head rotates.

Some people may find it useful to animate secondary actions in stages. This method was discussed earlier. The primary action is animated first for the entire scene. Various secondary actions are then animated in subsequent passes.

Figure 12-19 contains images from an animation with secondary actions. It can be viewed in the Chapter 12 "Secondary Action" folder of the CD-ROM as CD12-19SecondaryActions. In the animation, the male figure dances to a tune played on a trumpet by the female. A number of secondary actions support the main movement of the figure.

Fig. 12-19 Excerpts from the secondary action animation. Different parts of the body arrive after each other to support the main action of the body.

9. TIMING

Timing is the essence of the animator's art. It gives both physical and psychological meaning to an action. At its most basic, when keyframes are spaced wide apart, movements appear slower. They may look smooth, but if the timing is inappropriate, the actions will look too soft, like an underwater ballet. Keyframes that are close together on the timeline create quick and crisp movements. The timing from one pose to another is fast and snappy. Cartoon animation is often characterized by this kind of motion. A variety of sharp and soft actions within a scene adds texture and interest to the animation.

The way an object is perceived is affected by timing. Picking up a heavy object may take 10 frames, while lifting a lighter one takes only 5.

An example of how timing can change the meaning of an animation transpires when a character jumps up:

One in-between: He is very heavy.
Two in-betweens: His weight is average.
Three in-betweens: He is light and can jump high.
Four in-betweens: He is jumping underwater.
Six in-betweens: He is now on the moon.
Ten in-betweens: He can fly.

Another example of varying the timing in the same animation can be viewed on the CD-ROM in the Chapter 12 "Timing" folder. The three animations are named CD12-20TimingFast, CD12-20TimingMedium, and CD12-20TimingSlow. Images from these can also be seen in Figure 12-20.

The animation with fast timing can be interpreted as a frustrated male who is fed up with sitting still in a chair while being videotaped. The medium-speed animation's meaning might be that he is performing for the camera. The slow animation could be construed as a weary performer who lacks the motivation to do any more acting.

When you want to vary the speed of an animation, try scaling the keys. This can be done to an individual part or to everything in a scene. If you decide to change the speed of all items, then you can set the beginning and ending frames in order to alter just a section of the animation. Of course, you could change the entire animation by just setting your beginning frame at zero and the end frame as the last one. When you want the animation to move faster, scale the time by typing in a decimal number. Typing .5 for the scale time option will make the animation twice as fast. A 60-frame animation will now last only 30 frames. To slow down your animation, type a higher number than 1 for the scale time option. If you type in 2, a 60-frame animation will now last 120 frames and everything will move twice as slowly.

It is best to vary speed in an animation. Having a character hold a pose for a number of frames can make the action more dramatic and well defined. It also gives the audience a chance to absorb the significance of the action. Depending on the meaning you are trying to get across, the model can freeze-hold a pose or continue with other subtle movements while holding it. The timing of going into and out of a motion hold is also an important consideration when animating.

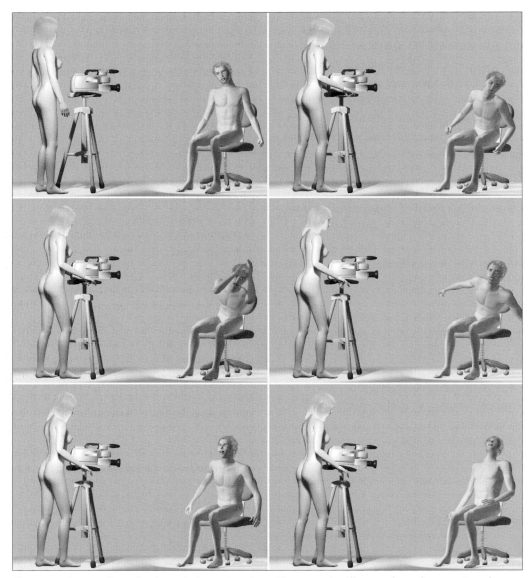

Fig. 12-20 Images from the three timing animations. These movies illustrate how the meaning changes when the characters move at fast, medium, and slow rates.

10. EXAGGERATION

This is perhaps one of the most important and, unfortunately, often overlooked principles. In animation, for actions to register with the viewer, they often have to be broad.

Characters animated with straight motion capture might be accurate but more often appear stiff and mechanical. They also lack personality. As actors, they are bland and uninspiring. The audience cares little about what happens to them.

A movie that will remain nameless in this book went to great lengths to advertise its use of true-to-life digital actors. Using motion capture, it sought to portray its human characters in a very realistic way. Despite having beautiful computer-generated characters, and costing millions of dollars to produce, the movie was a box office flop. It is my belief that a large part of the problem was that the animators did not exaggerate the movements and facial expressions of their characters. As actors, they lacked interest, and when they died, most people did not care.

Exploring the meaning behind an action will tell you how much to exaggerate. When you understand the intention, you will know what it takes to communicate it to the audience. If characters are happy, make them joyful. If they are sad, make them extremely depressed.

Animators have to persuade the audience that their characters' actions are real. A bad actor will look phony, and the same is true of animated characters that lack exaggeration. Their actions will appear contrived and unnatural. Do not be afraid to let digital actors ham it up in order to make each motion more noticeable.

If you ever have the chance to study the movements of a great vaudeville actor, notice that they often strike dramatic poses that would look artificial in real life. For some reason, when it takes place in front of an audience the performance looks normal and does not seem out of place.

A good animator knows when to move a character and when to have it hold a pose. Holding a pose is often just as important as the movement that precedes or follows it. You can show a motion hold by keyframing the same movement several times. The spacing depends on how long you want to hold the same pose.

Figure 12-21 illustrates an example of an animation with exaggeration. The movie can be viewed on the CD-ROM in the Chapter 12 "Exaggeration" folder as CD12-21Exaggeration. When you view the animation, notice the broad movements of the digital actor. The poses and facial expressions are extreme and at times appear ludicrous. Instead of portraying the actor in a normal way, he is shown in an absurd and nonsensical manner. This makes it easier to see each action.

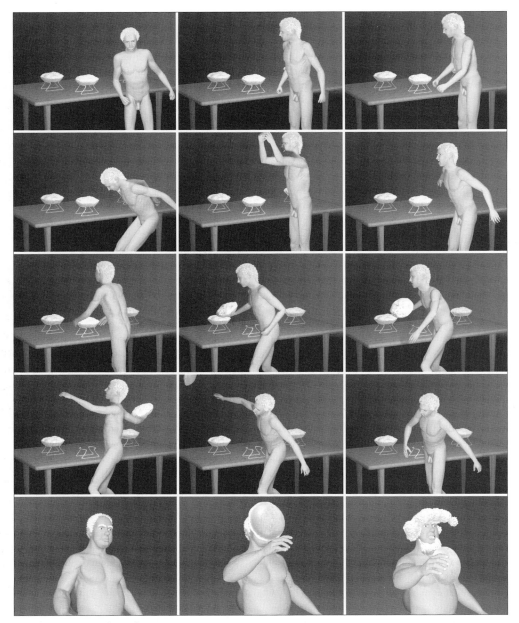

Fig. 12-21 Scenes from the exaggeration animation.

11. SOLID DRAWING

In traditional cel animation this means learning to draw well. In computer animation it signifies that you need to have good models before you can create good animations.

The ability to draw well is directly related to good 3-D modeling. Drawing requires an understanding of proportion, form, construction, detail, and human anatomy. Aside from these acquired skills, artists must develop an innate sensibility in order to judge what is right and wrong about their own work. This is a level of maturity they attain only after years of diligent work. Artists may be born with talent and an interest in art, but if they lack the discipline to work hard at perfecting their skills, their work will never become fully developed.

These underlying values are also an essential part of 3-D modeling and animation. Although knowing how to use specific software is important, it is not the most significant consideration in 3-D design. The animation field is not about learning gimmicks to fool the eye and impress viewers. Its focus is to communicate liveliness, balance, weight, and structure—the same considerations found in traditional art.

There are several ways to approach 3-D modeling. One method is to just build a character with as much detail as possible without worrying about how well it deforms during animation. This type of model might be well suited for still images but will most likely create many problems when trying to animate it.

A second way is to plan for animation by building a character that will change form in the best way possible. This often means omitting certain details that might impede its actions. Particular attention is paid around the joints, where most deformations occur. A model made for animation should be both pliable and interesting to look at.

In traditional cel animation, artists were warned about "twins." This referred to drawings in which the character was portrayed in a totally symmetrical pose. Varying each part of the body made the subject look more natural. Twins can also occur in 3-D animation. If the animator is not careful, the model could be shown with its arms and legs parallel and performing the exact same actions. Figure 12-22 shows an example of twins.

12. APPEAL

Appeal does not refer to cute and cuddly characters. It can mean the quality of the animation itself. A good story, interesting characters, quality models, lighting, surfacing, and animation make a pleasing presentation.

Characters have appeal because the animator understands good acting and is able to instill it into the animation. Animators should be able to convey emotion through their characters. Digital actors can express feelings, have their own personalities, and sway the audience with humor, fear, anger, and so on. The greatest compliment you can give an animator is to say that his or her character affected you emotionally.

In essence, appeal means something the viewer wants to see. If the animation lacks appeal, then all is lost, since viewers will not be interested in seeing it. One can think of appeal as the sum total of all 12 animation principles. If the animator has the awareness and skill to combine them into an interesting presentation, then the animation will have appeal.

Figure 12-23 illustrates a few selections from an animation found in the Chapter 12 "Appeal" folder of the CD-ROM, titled CD12-23Appeal.

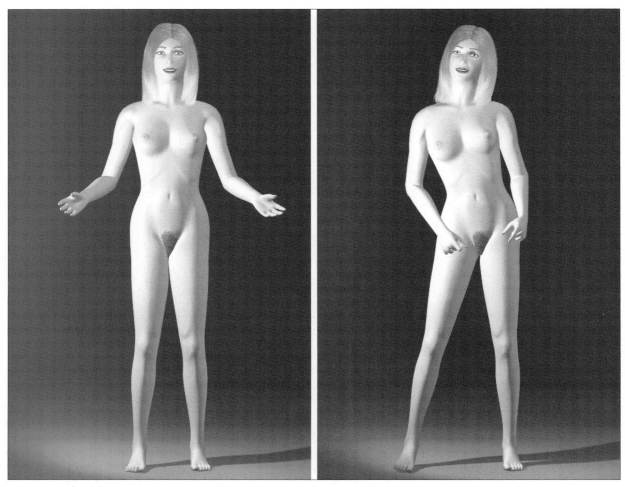

Fig. 12-22 The symmetrical pose on the left looks unnatural compared to the one on the right.

Fig. 12-23 A few sequences from the appeal animation.

THE ELEMENTS OF ANIMATION

The 12 principles of animation establish a basis for a number of animation elements. These are offshoots that build upon the foundation set up by the 12 principles. The most important ones are:

1. Pacing and impact
2. Action reaction
3. Rhythm and lines of action
4. Paths of action
5. Spatial relationships
6. Accents
7. Cycles
8. Postures
9. The take
10. Emotions
11. Balance/imbalance
12. Weight, mass, and gravity

1. PACING AND IMPACT

Imagine listening to a symphony. Sometimes the music is soft and slow. At other times it builds up to a crescendo. As the music reaches its apex, it appears to collide into a cacophony of jarring sounds, followed by a calm, peaceful state of exhaustion or resignation.

Because animation, like music, is time based, it often shares the same qualities. A veteran animator knows when it is time to change the tempo. Slowing it down or speeding it up makes the performance more interesting. The crescendo is often displayed with some kind of collision. In order for the impact to have a dramatic effect, there has to be a gradual buildup to give it meaning and make it easy to understand.

When there is an impact between two or more objects, it should be followed immediately by consequences. The camera may vibrate from the effects of the shock waves, smoke may appear, and/or objects may jump up and fall back down. Double images and speed lines resulting from motion blur also enhance the shock effect.

An impact should always be followed by some kind of resolution. In music a dissonant chord is followed by a consonant chord. Settling down into a more serene state would be the sensible event to conclude the animation. Pacing and impact rely on all 12 principles of animation.

2. ACTION REACTION

Anticipation is the basis of this animation effect. When a character acts, it first winds up, points toward its goal, or moves in the opposite direction. This is the anticipation part of the action. The second component is the main action, followed by a movement past the goal object. The conclusion of the motion is a return to a more natural stance. An example of this can be seen when a tennis player winds up by turning his or her body and moving the racket back before striking the ball (opposite direction of the goal). After making contact with the tennis ball, the player continues the forward motion past the point of impact. Once the action is completed, the tennis player returns to a ready stance for the next set of actions. All of this also relates to the previous method of pacing and impact. All 12 principles of animation play a role here to make action reaction effective.

3. RHYTHM AND LINES OF ACTION

A character exhibits certain lines of action. Professional animators can spot these very easily because they are the understructure of all motions. They can see that clumsy and ill-timed motions often ring false, lacking rhythm and appearing out of sync.

Training the eye to see an imaginary line extending through the character helps one see the main line of action. You can start by looking at the foot that establishes the center of balance. Tracing an imaginary spline from there up through the spinal column will delineate the main line of action. Secondary actions in the arms and legs can also be visualized as lines of motion.

Establishing the lines of action is only the beginning. Their movements and interaction with other lines and objects determine the success or failure of an animation. Rhythm and counterpoint are composed of repetitive and opposing lines that tense and relax during key moments. This combination of contrasting and pulsating lines running through the body, legs, and arms creates a tapestry of motion that is very interesting to watch.

4. PATHS OF ACTION

Unlike the lines of action that can be found within a character, the paths of action trace the direction that an entire movement makes. When someone runs, there is an up-and-down motion that appears as an undulating wave. This natural flow of events occurs as a result of gravity, mass, and the opposing actions of muscles. The body is composed of a pressure system of flexor and extensor muscles. Whenever one pulls, another contracts in the opposite direction. This gives the body a springiness that varies according to the weight of a character. A light and sprightly character will exhibit more bounciness than a heavier one. The principles of squash and stretch and arcs are key components for showing paths of action.

5. SPATIAL RELATIONSHIPS

Spatial relationships are closely allied with timing. Evenly spaced keyframes may work fine for cycling actions, which repeat the same motions over and over again, but can be monotonous for other movements. The principle of slow in and slow out can add variation but when used too often can also yield animations lacking in variety. Changing the spacing to fast in and fast out, slow in and fast out, fast out and slow in, and so on, will add variety and interest to your scenes. Follow-through and overlapping action add another layer of spatial relationships that contribute to the flow of an animation.

6. ACCENTS

To punctuate actions, one should utilize certain movements and facial expressions. When an actor shrugs, he or she will usually throw up the hands in an open gesture and change the facial expression to one of puzzlement or resignation. These extra flourishes are accents. They clarify and impart meaning to actions. They also make it easier to see what a character is thinking. They usually occur quickly so as to transcend and accentuate the main action.

Accents can also signal a radical change in the timing of the action. They can be the beginning of a pause or hold, a jump to another action, a reverse motion, a slower activity, or a faster series of behavior.

Squash and stretch accents in an animation, describe the effects of weight and recoil. A motion hold also acts as an accent. An accent can be shown on one level while other parts are performing at another. For example, while a person turns, he or she can do a thumbs-up as the accent to showing approval. Accents should never be shown within the first six frames because most people will not notice them. This also applies to important parts of dialogue.

7. CYCLES

Cycles are usually the result of planned actions. They form patterns of behavior. Even though they are basically repeating actions, they can contain a variety of movements within each cycle. Various walks and runs are examples of cycling actions. One does not always have to move the character forward. Moving the background in the direction opposite that in which the character is pointing will make it appear as if the actor is moving forward. Camera movement can also make it seem as if a cycling character is moving forward.

8. POSTURES

Mannerisms and attitudes reveal the personality of a character. The various gestures and postures that a character strikes are what give it appeal. A digital actor should exhibit a specific personality that elicits definite emotional responses in the viewer. A wacky and hyperactive actor will most likely display zany, open postures and move quickly from one pose to another. A depressed one will in all likelihood move slowly and show closely held attitudes.

When placing your digital actor in a motion hold, be sure to pause it long enough to register. Pose-to-pose animation forms the basis of postures. By planning your poses, you can clearly identify the ones that communicate effectively.

9. THE TAKE

Closely allied with anticipation, the take is a familiar animation tool. Surprise is the most recognizable form of the take. A familiar scenario might be a terrified person prowling around a haunted mansion. Something taps him on the shoulder, he goes into anticipation by cringing, and then he does a take by quickly flying into an attitude of frozen terror as he confronts a ghost.

Most takes should be held for a number of frames. They are, in effect, accents and motion holds. Takes can vary. Some might be subtle, while others could be intense. A variety of acts can occur during a take. The person may tremble, stagger backward, jump up, fall back, soar through the air, and so on. Secondary motions such as eyes popping out and hair, clothes, hats, and glasses lifting off enhance the take. A typical take will have the character sink into a crouch (anticipation). This is held briefly before the character leaps into a stretch (take). The take is also held for a short time before the character struggles back to normal size to look at the object that provoked him in the first place. The struggle to regain composure lasts longest and can involve another crouch before returning to normal size to gaze toward the object of incitement.

10. EMOTIONS

When animating a character, be aware of its personality. By getting in touch with its temperamental characteristics you can have it act in a more emotional manner. Certain parts of a human express emotions to a greater degree than others. Facial expressions communicate emotions more clearly than anything else. Hand gestures come second. The attitude of the body comes third. Rather than isolating parts, one should use everything to support the essence of a person's attitude.

No matter what, take time to act out the action. Even when rotoscoping or using motion capture, it is important to go through the gestures to get a full understanding of them. This will make the entire performance more genuine.

11. BALANCE/IMBALANCE

From the core of the earth, gravity exerts its force on every object. The human figure's center of gravity is its center of weight. From this center, a line can be drawn to indicate the line of gravity or balance.

Symmetrical balance is an equal distribution of weight between both legs. The line of gravity or balance would start between the feet and end at the head.

Asymmetrical balance refers to an unequal distribution of weight. Instead of having the same amount of mass resting on both feet, only the sole of one foot supports the body. The line of gravity or balance would start at the supporting foot and proceed straight up.

The line of gravity or balance shifts continually, so it is important to be aware of its position if the goal is to show weight and mass. Beginning animators typically ignore the center of balance and as a result their characters appear to be weightless. Their figures will often be posed in attitudes that would make any human fall over. Distributing the various body parts equally over and around the base of support will correct this problem. Inverse kinematics plays an important role here. Since IK anchors the feet to the ground, it establishes an artificial form of gravity. When the weight of the body shifts, it can be distributed evenly over one of the grounded feet.

12. WEIGHT, MASS, AND GRAVITY

The depiction of weight is one of the most challenging and important qualities of an animation. It is a characteristic that has to be consciously planned through the wise use of select principles and elements of animation. One has to be aware of not only the weight of the character itself but also the weight of objects and the manner in which they affect the person.

Squash and stretch is the primary principle employed for depicting weight, mass, and gravity. By deforming the character according to specific actions, it will appear to be affected by the forces of weight and gravity.

Timing is another important principle for showing weight, mass, and gravity. During the squash phase, the recoil action takes longer with a heavyweight than it does with a lightweight character. The heavy character spends more time on the ground than the lighter one. Therefore, extra keyframes are set when a big character is on the ground and fewer when it is in the stretch phase. The opposite happens with a smaller character. Timing is also an important consideration when showing someone lifting an object. The heavier it is, the longer it should take to move it.

Slow in and slow out is another key principle to keep in mind when depicting weight. When you have someone lifting a massive object, then the movement should start slowly to show the person's effort to overcome the pull of gravity. The action then picks up speed as inertia is surmounted. The slow out part occurs in the end when the task is nearly complete and the actor is trying to balance the weight.

The element of balance/imbalance also plays a role in showing weight, mass, and gravity. Anytime someone tries to lift an object, there has to be a rearrangement of the body. When there is extra weight to be supported, then the center of gravity or balance becomes the center of all the weight. In order to preserve equilibrium, counterbalance for the added burden has to be made.

Facial expressions are an excellent way of communicating the struggle of exertion. The stress and strain of moving a heavy burden can easily be communicated by the look on a person's face.

The depiction of weight, mass, and gravity is another one of those elements that relies on an understanding of all 12 principles of animation. Most of the time the rules of physics do not apply in a computer graphics environment. It is up to the animator to make use of the discoveries made by Disney animators in the 1930s. The Chapter 12 folder on the CD-ROM contains some example animations showing weight, mass, and gravity.

CONCLUSION

Three-dimensional modeling and animation is an exciting and thought-provoking art form. Its marriage to technology will ensure that it will continually evolve to meet new challenges. This is what makes it so unique compared to the other fine arts. While the tools may change, the methods for achieving compelling animations will continue to rely on basic elements and principles established many years ago by artists working with traditional media.

Conventional art materials such as charcoal, paint, clay, fiber, and so on, are tactile. The artist who works with these has an emotional link that is often lacking when compared to the one who relies on hardware and software. The computer artist is forced to instill the quality of emotion into a medium that is for the most part cerebral. This is one of the greatest challenges. Without emotional content, the work will appear cold and removed from the human experience. Unlike other artists, computer animators work mostly in the mental realm to put feeling into their work.

Lesson Plans

The following lesson plans can be used as a guide when preparing for courses with this book. They are set up for three levels of animation: beginning, intermediate, and advanced. It is understandable that each class will have its own characteristics. Students come from a variety of backgrounds, experiences, and abilities. Class size, meeting times, and length of each class, as well as the number of weeks in a semester, can vary greatly. Therefore, to make these plans more flexible I have included the Microsoft Word documents. They can be found on the CD-ROM in the "Lesson Plans" folder. This will allow professors to alter them according to their own circumstances.

SEMESTER #1	ANIMATION 1	CALENDAR	
1ST MONTH		**3RD MONTH**	
Introduction to class. Hand out syllabus. Assignment: Purchase textbook and materials.	Examine software. In class model a knife with splines/ NURBS (Chapter 1). Assignment: Study software.	Human head due. Begin work on torso (Chapter 5). Assignment: Continue work on torso.	Continue work on torso (Chapter 5). Assignment: Continue work on torso.
Spline/NURBS knife due. Model a spoon and spatula (Chapter 1). Assignment: Continue to study software.	Spoon and spatula due. Model a frying pan and palette knife (Chapter 1). Assignment: Continue to study software.	Continue work on torso (Chapter 5). Assignment: Continue work on torso—due next class.	Torso due today. Assignment: Work on arm outside of class (Chapter 6). Begin learning simple character animation using a preexisting model.
Frying pan and palette knife due. Model a subdivision hammer and armchair (Chapter 1). Assignment: Continue to study software.	Subdivision hammer and armchair due. Model a subdivision cow (Chapter 2). Assignment: Continue to . study software.	Continue learning character animation with the preexisting model. Assignment: Continue working on the arm outside of class (Chapter 6).	Continue learning character animation with the preexisting model. Assignment: Continue working on the arm outside of class (Chapter 6).
Continue modeling a subdivision cow (Chapter 2). Assignment: Continue to study software.	Continue modeling a subdivision cow (Chapter 2). Assignment: Continue to study software.	Continue learning character animation with the preexisting model. Assignment: Continue working on the arm outside of class—due next class.	Arm due today. Work on leg outside of class (Chapter 7). In class continue learning character animation—study surfacing and lighting a character (Chapter 10).
2ND MONTH		**4TH MONTH**	
Subdivision cow due. Model a subdivision chicken (Chapter 2). Assignment: Continue to study software.	Finish modeling a subdivision chicken (Chapter 2). Assignment: Continue to study software.	Assignment: Continue work on leg outside of class (Chapter 7). In class continue learning character animation—study surfacing and lighting a character (Chapter 10).	Assignment: Continue work on leg outside of class (Chapter 7). In class continue learning character animation—study surfacing and lighting a character (Chapter 10).
Begin modeling a spline/ NURBS chicken using the subdivision one as a template (Chapter 2). Assignment: Continue to study software.	Continue modeling spline/ NURBS chicken (Chapter 2)— due next class.	Assignment: Continue work on leg outside of class (Chapter 7)—due next class. In class continue learning character animation—study surfacing and lighting a character (Chapter 10).	Complete figure due with legs, arms, torso, and head. In class learn how to set up a skeleton and weight maps for the human. Assignment: Model eyes, eyelashes, eyebrows, and mouth parts (Chapter 8).
Spline/NURBS chicken due. Lecture on anatomy (Chapter 3). Assignment: Read Chapter 3 on anatomy.	Begin modeling a human head using either spline/NURBS or subdivision modeling (Chapter 4). Assignment: Work on human head.	In class finish skeleton and weight maps. Continue modeling eyes, eyelashes, eyebrows, and mouth parts— due next class.	Complete human due with skeleton, weight maps, eyes, eyelashes, eyebrows, and mouth parts. Using the completed human, animate a running sequence (Chapter 11).
Continue work on human head. Assignment: Work on human head.	Continue work on human head. Assignment: Work on human head—due next class.	Continue animating running sequence—animation due next class.	Last day of class—running animation due.

SEMESTER #1	ANIMATION 2	CALENDAR	
1ST MONTH		**3RD MONTH**	
Introduction to class. Hand out syllabus. Assignment: Purchase textbook and materials.	In class study UV mapping. Assignment: Map face textures on the human character (Chapter 10).	Continue working on dialogue animation—due next class.	Dialogue animation due today. Study inverse and forward kinematics (Chapter 9). Set up the human with IK.
Textured human due. Learn how to model hair or hair guides (Chapter 8). Assignment: Model hair.	Continue modeling hair—due next class.	IK setup due today. Learn about walking animations (Chapter 11). Assignment: create a 32-frame IK walking animation.	Continue work on 32-frame IK walk animation—due next class.
Person with hair due today. Learn how to use a hair generator on the hair guides. Alternative assignment: Model clothes.	Continue working on hair using a hair generator. Learn how to apply weight maps or section hair for soft-body dynamics. Collision head and shoulders will have to be modeled (Chapter 8). Alternative assignment: Continue modeling clothes.	32-frame IK walking animation due today. Learn how to repeat the walk cycle in the graph editor (Chapter 11). Assignment: Create an extended walk cycle animation—due next class.	Final walk animation due today. Study rotoscoping for animation (Chapter 11). Videotape students and convert to digital format for rotoscoping. Assignment: Create an animation using rotoscoping.
Learn how to use soft-body dynamics to move the hair (Chapter 8). Assignment: Create a simple animation in which the hair is moved by the motion of the character. Alternative assignment: Finish modeling clothes.	Animation due showing soft-body dynamics on the hair. Alternative: Clothes due. Begin modeling all the morph targets for facial animation (Chapter 9).	Continue work on rotoscoping.	Continue work on rotoscoping. Animation due next class.
2ND MONTH		**4TH MONTH**	
Continue modeling face morph targets. In class learn more about lighting (Chapter 10).	Continue modeling face morph targets. In class continue lighting lessons.	Rotoscoping animation due. Study squash and stretch (Chapter 12). Create a squash and stretch animation.	Continue work on squash and stretch animation—due next class.
Continue modeling face morph targets. In class learn more about surfacing (Chapter 10).	Continue modeling face morph targets. In class continue surfacing lessons.	Squash and stretch animation due. Study and work on anticipation animation (Chapter 12).	Continue anticipation animation—due next class.
Continue modeling face morph targets. In class study the graph editor (Chapter 11).	Continue modeling face morph targets—due next class. In class learn more about the graph editor.	Anticipation animation due. Study and work on staging animation (Chapter 12).	Continue staging animation.
Human with all the facial morph targets due. In class learn about animating with dialogue (Chapter 11). Assignment: Using the newly made morph targets, create a dialogue animation.	Continue working on dialogue animation.	Continue staging animation—due next class.	Last day of class—staging animation due.

SEMESTER #1	ANIMATION 3	CALENDAR	
1ST MONTH		**3RD MONTH**	
Introduction to class. Hand out syllabus. Assignment: Purchase textbook and materials.	Study straight-ahead vs. pose-to-pose animation (Chapter 12). Assignment: Sketch storyboard drawings (Chapter 11) for pose-to-pose animation—due next class.	Slow in and slow out animation due. Study arcs and secondary actions (Chapter 12). Assignment: Create an animation illustrating these.	Continue secondary action animation.
Storyboard drawings due for pose-to-pose animation. Begin pose-to-pose animation using storyboard drawings.	Continue pose-to-pose animation.	Continue secondary action animation—due next class.	Secondary action animation due. Study the principle of timing (Chapter 12). Create three versions of the same animation, showing how timing changes the meaning. The speeds should be slow, medium, and fast.
Continue pose-to-pose animation—due next class.	Pose-to-pose animation due. Assignment: Create a straight-ahead unplanned animation (Chapter 12).	Continue the three timing animations.	Continue the three timing animations.
Continue straight-ahead animation.	Continue straight-ahead animation—due next class.	Continue the three timing animations—due next class.	Timing animations due. Study exaggeration principle. Create an animation illustrating exaggeration.
2ND MONTH		**4TH MONTH**	
Straight-ahead animation due. Study soft-body dynamics (Chapter 8) and the principles of follow-through and overlapping action (Chapter 12). Create an animation illustrating this principle with clothes and/or hair moved by soft-body dynamics.	Continue follow-through and overlapping action animation.	Continue the exaggeration animation.	Continue the exaggeration animation—due next class.
Continue follow-through and overlapping action animation.	Continue follow-through and overlapping action animation.	Exaggeration animation due. Discussion about solid drawing and appeal (Chapter 12). Create an animation showing appeal.	Continue the appeal animation.
Continue follow-through and overlapping action animation—due next class.	Follow-through and overlapping action animation due. Study slow in and slow out (Chapter 12). Create an animation illustrating this principle.	Continue the appeal animation.	Continue the appeal animation.
Continue slow in and slow out animation.	Continue slow in and slow out animation—due next class.	Continue the appeal animation—due next class.	Last day of class—appeal animation due.

BIBLIOGRAPHY

ON ANIMATION

Blair, Preston. *Cartoon Animation.* Laguna Hills, CA: Walter Foster Publishing, 1980.

Blair, Preston. *Film Cartoons.* Laguna Hills, CA: Walter Foster Publishing, 1980.

Muybridge, Eadweard. *Muybridge's Complete Human and Animal Locomotion.* Mineola, NY: Dover Publications, Inc., 1979.

Thomas, Frank, and Ollie Johnston. *The Illusion of Life: Disney Animation.* New York: Disney Editions, 1981.

ON ANATOMY

Bridgman, George. *Constructive Anatomy.* New York: Dover Publications, Inc., 1920.

Goldstein, Nathan. *Figure Drawing.* Englewood Cliffs, NJ: Prentice Hall, Inc., 1976.

Peck, Stephen. *Atlas of Human Anatomy for the Artist.* Oxford, NY: Oxford University Press, 1951.

Reed, Walt. *The Figure.* Cincinnati, OH: North Light Books, 1976.

Rubins, David. *The Human Figure: An Anatomy for Artists.* New York: Penguin Books, 1953.

INDEX

ABOUT THE AUTHOR

Peter Ratner is a Professor of 3-D Computer Animation in the School of Art and Art History at James Madison University. He is the founder of the computer animation program at the university and the first to create an animation concentration in the state of Virginia. Professor Ratner has written two other books about 3-D modeling and animation, *3-D Human Modeling and Animation* and *Mastering 3-D Animation*. Besides teaching and writing books, he has exhibited his oil paintings, animations, and computer graphics in numerous national and international juried exhibitions.